SWEETHEART

SWEETHEART

CHELSEA CAIN

THORNDIKE
WINDSOR
PARAGON

This Large Print edition is published by Thorndike Press, Waterville, Maine USA and by BBC Audiobooks Ltd, Bath, England

Copyright © 2008 by Verite, Inc.

The moral right of the author has been asserted.

Thorndike Press, a part of Gale, Cengage Learning.

Thorndike Press® Large Print Crime Scene.

The text of this Large Print edition is unabridged.

Other aspects of the book may vary from the original edition.

Set in 16 pt. Plantin.

Printed on permanent paper.

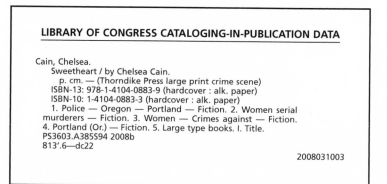

LIBRARY OF CONGRESS CATALOGING-IN-PUBLICATION DATA

Cain, Chelsea.
  Sweetheart / by Chelsea Cain.
    p. cm. — (Thorndike Press large print crime scene)
  ISBN-13: 978-1-4104-0883-9 (hardcover : alk. paper)
  ISBN-10: 1-4104-0883-3 (hardcover : alk. paper)
    1. Police — Oregon — Portland — Fiction. 2. Women serial
murderers — Fiction. 3. Women — Crimes against — Fiction.
4. Portland (Or.) — Fiction. 5. Large type books. I. Title.
PS3603.A385S94 2008b
813'.6—dc22

                                                    2008031003

BRITISH LIBRARY CATALOGUING-IN-PUBLICATION DATA AVAILABLE
Published in the U.S. 2008 in arrangement with St. Martin's Press, LLC.
Published in the U.K. in 2009 in arrangement with Pan Macmillan Ltd.

U.K. Hardcover: 978 1 408 41375 3 (Windsor Large Print)
U.K. Softcover: 978 1 408 41376 0 (Paragon Large Print)

Printed in the United States of America
1 2 3 4 5 6 7 12 11 10 09 08

*For Village Books in Bellingham, Washington,
for taking me in as a kid,
and letting me sit for hours reading books
on all those cold winter evenings.
You are to blame for this.*

CHAPTER
1

Forest Park was pretty in the summer. Portland's ash sky was barely visible behind a canopy of aspens, hemlock, cedars, and maples that filtered the light to a shimmering pale green. A light breeze tickled the leaves. Morning glories and ivy crept up the mossy tree trunks and strangled the blackberry bushes and ferns, a mass of crawling vines that piled up waist-high on either side of the packed dirt path. The creek hummed and churned, birds chirped. It was all very lovely, very Walden, except for the corpse.

The woman had been dead awhile. Her skull was exposed; her scalp had been pulled back, a tangle of red hair separated from the hairline by several inches. Animals had eaten her face, exposing her eyes and brain to the forces of putrefaction. Her nose was gone, revealing the triangular bony notch beneath it; her eye sockets were concave bowls of greasy, soaplike fat. The flesh of her neck and ears was blistered and curdled, peeled back in strips to frame that horrible skull face, mouth open like a Halloween skeleton.

"Are you there?"

Archie turned his attention back to the cell phone he held against his ear. "Yeah."

"Want me to wait on dinner?"

He glanced down at the dead woman, his mind already working the case. Could be an OD. Could be murder. Could be she fell from the wheel well of a 747. Archie had seen that last one on an episode of *Law & Order.* "I'm thinking no," he said into the phone.

He could hear the familiar concern in Debbie's voice. He'd been doing well. He'd cut back on the pain pills, gained a little weight. But he and Debbie both knew it was all too tenuous. Mostly, he pretended. He pretended to live, to breathe, to work; he pretended he was going to be okay. It seemed to help the people he loved. And that was something. He could do that, at least, for them. "Be sure you eat something," she said with a sigh.

"I'll grab something with Henry." Archie flipped the phone shut and dropped it into his coat pocket. His fingers touched the brass pillbox that was also in his pocket, and lingered there for a moment. It had been more than two and a half years since his ordeal. He'd only been off medical leave a few months. Long enough to catch his second serial killer. He was thinking of getting some business cards made up: SERIAL KILLER APPREHENSION SPECIALIST. Maybe something embossed. His head hurt and he reflexively moved to open the lid of the pillbox, then let his fingers drop and lifted his hand from his pocket and ran it through his hair. No. Not now.

He squatted next to Lorenzo Robbins, who sat on his heels inches from the body, his dreadlocks hidden under the hood of his white Tyvek suit. The smooth stones of the creek bed were slick with moss.

"That your wife?" Robbins asked.

Archie pulled a small notebook and a pen out of his other pocket. A flashbulb went off as a crime photographer took a picture behind them. "My ex-wife."

"You guys still close?"

Archie drew an outline of the woman in his notebook. Marked where the surrounding trees were, the creek below. "We live together."

"Oh."

The flashbulb went off again. "It's a long

story," Archie said, rubbing his eyes with one hand.

Robbins used a pair of forceps to lift the woman's loose scalp, so he could peer under it. When he did, dozens of black ants scurried out over her skull and into the decomposing tissue inside her nasal aperture. "Dogs have been here."

"Wild?" Archie asked, twisting around to look up at the thick surrounding forest. Forest Park was five thousand acres, the largest urban wilderness park in the country. Parts of it were remote; parts of it were crowded. The area where the body had been found was in the lower part of the park, which was frequented by a steady stream of joggers, hikers, and mountain bikers. Several houses were even visible up the hillside.

"Domestic probably," Robbins said. He turned and jabbed a latex-gloved thumb up the hillside. "Way the body's down here behind the scrub, can't see it from the path. People come running through with their dogs off leash. Sparky scrambles down here, tears a hunk of cheek off the corpse." He looked down at the corpse and shrugged. "They think he's found a dead bird or whatever. Owner lets him sniff around a little. Then they run on."

"You're saying she was eaten by pugs?"

"Over time. A few weeks."

Archie shook his head. "Nice."

Robbins raised an eyebrow as he glanced back up at the path. "Funny no one smelled anything."

"There was a sewer leak," Archie said. "One of the houses at the top of the hill."

The eyebrow shot up another few millimeters. "For two weeks?"

Archie drew the hiking path across the page of his notebook. It was maybe forty feet above, at its closest point. Then it curved and headed farther up the hillside, deeper into the woods. "People rationalize."

"You thinking she was a prostitute?"

"Based on the shoes?" She was still wearing one — an amber Lucite pump. The other they had found nestled in moss underneath a fern a few yards away. "Maybe. Maybe she was a stylish thirteen-year-old. Hard to tell." Archie looked at the grinning mouth, the teeth straight and white against all the surrounding blood and gristle. "She's got nice teeth."

"Yeah," Robbins agreed softly. "She's got nice teeth."

Archie watched as his partner, Henry Sobol, came slowly, tentatively, down the hillside. He was wearing black jeans, a black T-shirt,

11

and a black leather jacket, despite the heat. Henry kept his eyes down, lips pursed in concentration, arms outstretched for balance. With his arms extended and his shaved head, he looked like a circus strongman. He walked sideways, trying to step in Archie's footprints, but his feet were bigger than Archie's and each step sent a spit of dirt and small rocks rattling down the embankment. Above them, on the hillside, Archie could see that everyone had stopped to watch, their faces anxious. A homeless man looking for a place to set up camp had found the body and called the police from a convenience store a few blocks outside the park. He had met the first officer to respond and taken him to the site, where the officer had promptly lost his footing in the loose dirt and slid down the hillside into the creek, polluting the crime scene and nearly breaking his leg. They would have to wait for the autopsy results to even know if they had a homicide.

Henry reached the bottom, winked at Archie, and then turned and waved merrily up above. The cops at the top of the hill all turned back to their work taping the crime scene off, and keeping the growing group of sportily dressed hikers and joggers at bay.

Henry smoothed his salt-and-pepper

mustache thoughtfully with a thumb and forefinger and rocked forward to examine the body, allowing himself a reflexive grimace. Then business. "What killed her?" he asked.

Robbins placed a bag over one of her bloated, mottled hands and secured it with a twist-tie. He did it gingerly, as if she had nodded off and he didn't want to wake her. The fingers curled, blistered and swollen, and the nail beds were black, but the hand was still recognizable, though probably not printable. The other, which lay half buried in the earth and moss, was crawling with beetles. "Search me," Robbins said.

"She die here?" Henry asked.

"Hard to say until we know what killed her," Robbins answered. He gazed up at Henry. "Do you wax your head or is it naturally that shiny?"

Archie smiled. Henry had called Robbins out at the police softball game that spring. It had been like this ever since.

"I was just asking," Henry said to Robbins.

"Ask me after the autopsy," Robbins muttered. He produced another bag and gave it a snap in the air, and then gently lifted her other hand so he could slide it into the bag. The beetles scattered, and Henry took a small step back.

Archie wrote something in his notebook. It had been thirteen years since they had stood over another dead girl in that park. That had set them on the trail of the Beauty Killer. They didn't know back then it would become a career. Or that Archie would become one of her victims.

A voice from up the hillside hollered, "Hey."

Henry looked up at the path, where Claire Masland was waving for them to come back up the hill. He put his hands on his hips. "You've got to be kidding me," he said to Archie.

Claire motioned again. This time she put her whole arm into it.

"I'll go first," Archie said. He glanced back at Henry and added, "So when you fall you won't take us both down."

"Ha, ha," said Henry.

"What do you have?" Archie asked Claire when they reached the path. Claire was small and angular with a very short haircut. She was wearing a striped T-shirt and jeans. Her gold shield was clipped to her waistband, along with a phone, a gun in a leather holster, and a pair of red plastic sunglasses jauntily hooked through a belt loop. She tilted her head at a young

14

uniformed cop who was covered in dirt.

"This is Officer Bennett," she said. "The first responder."

Bennett looked like a kid, tall with a baby face and a slight double chin that pressed fretfully against a skinny neck. He hunched his shoulders miserably. "I'm so sorry," he said.

"Show them," Claire told Bennett. He sighed glumly and turned around. He had taken a header down the ravine and his uniform was stained with muck, and tiny bits of vegetation still clung to his shirt.

Both Henry and Archie leaned forward to get a better look. Clinging to Bennett's shoulder blade, among the fern seeds, the moss particulate, and the dirt, was, unmistakably, a clue.

Henry looked at Archie. "That would be a human hair," he said.

"When you, uh, fell," Archie asked Bennett. "Did you actually make contact with the body?"

Bennett's spine stiffened. "Jesus no, sir. I swear."

"Must have picked it up on the way down," said Henry.

Archie pulled a slim black flashlight out of his pocket and shone it along the length of the red hair. He held it for Henry to look.

There was a tiny clump of tissue at the base of the hair. "It's got a scalp fragment on it," Archie said.

Bennett whipped his head around, eyes wide. "Get it off me," he pleaded. "Get it off me, okay?"

"Easy, son," Henry said.

Claire, who was a good foot shorter than Bennett, reached up and plucked the hair off and dropped it in an evidence bag.

Archie called a crime scene tech over. "Bag all his clothes. Socks, everything."

"But what will I wear?" Bennett asked as the crime scene tech led him off.

Claire turned to Archie and Henry. The path they were on was about three feet wide, carved worryingly out of the hillside. The back foot of it had been taped off to let the fifty-year-old women by, so they didn't have to backtrack a mile into the woods and miss afternoon spa appointments. A chocolate Lab bounded through the foliage on the hillside as its owner, in cargo shorts, hiking books, and reflective sunglasses, walked past without even a second glance at the activity at the bottom of the glen. "So?" Claire said.

"Head injury," said Archie.

"Yep," said Henry.

"Maybe she fell," Claire theorized. "Like T. J. Hooker, there. Hit her head on a rock."

"Or maybe the rock hit her," Henry said.

"Or," Archie said, "maybe Sparky scrambled down there and stuck his snout in our corpse, and the hair dropped off his tongue on his way back up the embankment."

Claire and Henry both looked at Archie.

"Sparky?" Henry said.

"That is so gross," said Claire.

CHAPTER
2

Susan Ward felt sick to her stomach. Maybe it was nerves. Maybe it was the heat. Maybe it was the bar's toxic smog of cigarette smoke.

"You want another drink?" Quentin Parker asked. Parker had been the crime-beat reporter for the *Herald* for as long as anyone could remember. Susan didn't know if he'd started out an alcoholic, or if it had something to do with the job.

"Something with an umbrella this time?" he said.

Parker drank Wild Turkey. No ice. The waitress had poured him one before they'd even sat down.

Susan ignored the crack about the umbrella and slid a cigarette from the pack she had set on the table. "I'll just smoke," she said, surveying the bar. Parker had suggested it. It was downtown, and easy to get to from the paper. Susan had never heard of it, but Parker seemed to know everyone in the place. He knew a lot of people in a lot of bars.

The bar was small, so Susan was able to keep an eye on the door, to watch for the man they were supposed to meet. Parker had set it up. Susan usually worked with the features editor, but this story was crime, and that meant Parker. She'd been trying to get this meeting for two months. Parker set it up with one phone call. But the whole story had been like that. She was about to single-handedly decimate the career of an esteemed politician. Most of the staff at the *Herald* had voted for the guy. Susan had voted for him. She'd take that vote back now if she could.

"I could have come by myself," Susan said.

"He doesn't know you," Parker said. "And I like to help." He was kidding, of course. Generosity was not the word that came to mind when you thought of Quentin Parker. Belligerent? Yes. Sexist? Yes. Great fucking writer? Yes. Drunk? Absolutely.

Almost everyone thought he was an asshole.

But for some reason, from that first day at the paper two years ago, Parker had looked out for Susan. She didn't know why. Maybe he'd liked her smart-ass mouth. Or her

19

inappropriate clothes. Or whatever color her hair had been at the time. It didn't matter. She'd take a bullet for him, and she was pretty sure that, barring the distraction of a drink or a hot lead, he'd do the same for her.

Susan looked around the bar again. Parker had chosen it well. There was little chance anyone would see them all together. There was a vague maritime theme: a steering wheel from an old boat on the wall, an anchor nailed above the bar. The bartender looked about a hundred and ten, and the waitress not much younger. The only food in the place was popcorn. The bar stank of it. But it was dark and cool, which was more than could be said about outside. Susan pulled at her black tank top. It said I SMELL BULLSHIT in cursive across the chest, and the letters tended to stick to her skin when she sweated.

The door to the bar opened and a blinding rectangle of light streamed into the darkness, transforming the bar's smoke-choked atmosphere into pretty swirls of carcinogenic mist. Susan's stomach clenched. A middle-aged man walked in wearing a suit and fiddling with a BlackBerry. He was heavy, though not nearly as heavy as Parker, and he wore rectangular glasses that seemed too fashionable for him. She turned to Parker.

"Hide your valuables," Parker whispered, taking a handful of popcorn from the bowl in front of them.

"You're sure it's him?" Susan asked, pulling at her tank top.

Parker guffawed, a quick laugh that sounded like a wheeze. He lifted the fistful of popcorn into his mouth and chewed. "Thirty years on the crime beat," he said, mouth full. "You get to know a lot of lawyers."

"Here," Parker said, gesturing the lawyer over with a popcorn-greasy hand.

The lawyer sat. He looked ten years older up close. "Parker," he said with a nod. Then he looked at Susan. His glasses said PRADA in big letters on each side. "This her?" he asked.

"Our Brenda Starr," Parker said, still chewing. He grinned, his yellow teeth small and shiny in the bar's low light. "Kid does my heart good, the way she went after your boy."

"My 'boy,'" the lawyer said, "is a sitting U.S. senator."

Parker picked up another handful of popcorn. "Not for long," he said through the grin.

Susan took a drag off her cigarette and felt for the small digital recorder she had hidden on her lap to make sure it was on. It whirred under her fingertips and she felt immediately calmer. Beyond the lawyer, a young man wearing a red baseball cap came into the bar and sat down alone.

The lawyer wiped the sheen of sweat from his forehead. "So the *Herald*'s running the story?"

"Senator Castle want to comment?" Parker asked. He brought his fist up and dropped a few kernels of popcorn into his open mouth.

"He denies it," the lawyer said.

Susan laughed.

The lawyer pushed his Prada glasses up on his nose. "You're lucky to get any comment at all," he said, his face coloring.

Susan pledged right then and there that she was going to take down John Castle and the motherfuckers who'd protected him over the years. People idolized Castle for what he'd done for the state. But after Thursday, they would see him for what he was, a rapist, a manipulator, a blackmailer, and a fraud. She ground the rest of her cigarette out in the black plastic ashtray on the table. "He denies it?" she said. "He fucked his kids' babysitter and he went to enormous lengths to cover it up, including paying her off." She pulled another cigarette out of the pack and lit it with a plastic lighter. Susan smoked only when she was nervous. But the lawyer didn't know that. "I've spent two months on this story," she said. "I've got Molly Palmer on record. I've got interviews with Molly's friends at the time that match Molly's version of events. I've got bank records showing money passing from your law firm to her account."

"Ms. Palmer was an intern," the lawyer said, spreading his hands innocently.

"For one summer," Susan said. She took a drag off the cigarette, leaned her head back, and exhaled. She took her time, because she knew she had him. "Your firm continued paying her for five years."

The corner of the lawyer's mouth twitched. "There may have been a clerical error," he said.

Susan wanted to wipe the smirk off his face with her elbow. Why had he even bothered to show? A denial could have been delivered over the phone. "This is such bullshit," she said.

The lawyer stood up and looked Susan up and down. When you looked like she did, you got used to that, but coming from this guy, it made her a little furious. "How old are you?" he asked Susan. "Twenty-five?" He flipped a hand at her head. "You think the people of this state are going to let some girl with blue hair and some sort of political agenda take down a beloved five-term senator?" He put his face right in front of hers, so close she could smell his aftershave. "Even if you publish the story, it will go away. And you won't publish it. Because if the *Herald* goes near it, I will sue you." He jabbed a finger at Parker. "And you." He pushed his glasses up his nose one last time and stepped back from the table. "The senator denies all allegations," he said. "Other than that, he has no comment." He turned around and started for the door.

"I'm twenty-eight," Susan called after him. "And my hair is Atomic Turquoise."

Parker lifted his glass of whiskey to his mouth. "I thought that went well," he said.

"Right," Susan said. "They're quaking in their boots."

"Trust me," Parker said. He picked up a toothpick from a dish on the table and dug at a piece of popcorn kernel stuck between his teeth, his jowls swinging.

Susan had never loved him more.

He looked at her and winked. "They're scared shitless," he said.

Susan thought his face flushed with pride.

But it might have just been the whiskey.

CHAPTER
3

Archie stood at his front door, his keys in his hands. In the year and a half he and Debbie had been separated she'd never asked for the house key, and he'd never offered it. It had stayed on his key ring the whole time, a constant reminder of what he'd lost. He had been a mess when she had asked him to leave. He had only been out of the hospital a couple of months, and he was still in the blackest dregs of his recovery. He didn't blame her. He had forced her into it. It was easier to be alone.

He pulled the brass pillbox out of his pocket, opened it, and extracted three white oval pills. He held them for a moment before he put them in his mouth, enjoying the familiar bitter taste before swallowing them. Then he pushed the key into the lock and pushed open the big door. The house was a low-slung, mid-century ranch that had been restored by the previous owners. Debbie had been pregnant with Sara when they bought it. It was far above his pay rate, but Debbie had just been hired as a designer at Nike, so they had splurged.

Debbie had left a lamp on, and it threw a warm half-circle of light across the dark hallway. Archie slipped his muddy shoes off at the door and walked over to the hall table and dropped his keys next to the lamp. A photograph of him and Debbie and the kids sat propped on the table in a silver frame. He looked happy, but he couldn't remember when or where it had been taken.

He felt Debbie behind him a moment before her arms moved around his waist.

"Hi," he said.

She leaned her cheek against his shoulder blade and held him. "Was it bad?"

"I've seen worse." That hung in the air for a minute. Then Archie turned around and wrapped his arms around her. Debbie's short brown hair was tousled and she was wearing a black tank top and red cotton underpants. Her body was toned and strong in his arms. It was a body he knew as well as his own. "Kids okay?" he asked.

She leaned in and kissed him lightly on the neck below his jawbone. "They've been asleep for hours," she said.

Archie lifted a hand to Debbie's cheek and

looked at her face, kind and open, strong cheekbones, a long fine nose, a blush of freckles. And then, a flash of blond, the smell of lilacs, and there she was: Gretchen Lowell. Always at the periphery of his consciousness. Archie winced.

He could feel Debbie's body tense under his hands.

"Is it her?" she asked.

He cleared his throat and shook the image from his head. His hand fell away from her cheek. "I should get some sleep." He wanted to get the pills out of his pocket again, to take just one more, but he didn't want to do it in front of Debbie. It hurt her too much.

"Is it hard not seeing her?" Debbie asked.

Archie wondered sometimes how much Debbie knew about his relationship with Gretchen. Debbie knew that Gretchen haunted him. She might have even used the word "obsessed." But he didn't think Debbie knew how far he had crossed the line.

"We said we wouldn't talk about this," Archie said gently.

Debbie turned Archie around to face the mirror that hung on the wall behind the table. "Look," she said, and she slipped her hands under his shirttails and lifted his shirt up above his nipples and held it there. Archie hesitated and then looked at their reflection.

27

His ex-wife was pressed beside him, her head resting against his shoulder, dark eyes shining. His face looked creased, half cast in the shadow thrown by the lamp, his long nose and lopsided mouth, thick hair and sad eyes, each a physical remnant of an ancestor, black Irish, Croatian, Jewish. He allowed himself a wry smile. Christ. Even his genotype was tragic.

Debbie moved a hand down to his abdomen and touched the long scar over his diaphragm where his spleen had been removed. It was his thickest scar, an ugly six-inch slash, the raised white scars from the stitches still visible around it, giving it a particularly Frankensteinian appearance. The scar tissue was tough, and he could barely feel Debbie's fingertips brush over it. She moved then to the smaller scars that scattered his chest. These were finer, the scalpel pressed firmly into his flesh more to pass the time than to inflict pain. They looked like silver blades of grass, each laid out even with the one before it, like hash marks on a grotesque score card. Debbie traced her fingers over the slightly puckered lump of flesh that marked the stab wound below his left ribs.

"We had a deal," Archie said. "Life, in exchange for the locations of her victims.

She kept her part of the bargain. I was the one who couldn't handle it. She won't talk to anyone else, Debbie. Think of the two hundred people she killed. Think about their families." It was a speech he had given often to himself over the two years he had gone every week to meet with Gretchen Lowell. It was all part of his effort to convince himself that he was just doing his job. He didn't believe it anymore. He wondered if Debbie did.

"One hundred and ninety-nine," Debbie said. "You were number two hundred, Archie. And you're still alive."

She moved her hand up to the other scar, the scar that began below his left nipple, arced through his chest hair, and traveled down to its original point, in the shape of a heart. Gretchen Lowell carved a heart on all her victims. It was her signature. But her other victims had been corpses, the hearts bloody wounds obscured by decomposition and a litany of torture. As head of the Beauty Killer Task Force, Archie had stood over their bodies, stared at their morgue photographs, been one step behind for ten years. Until he walked into the trap that Gretchen had set for him.

She had infiltrated the task force six weeks before she revealed herself to him the night she drugged him. They had thought she was a psychiatrist, offering her expertise. He wondered now if he would have been so quick to trust her if she hadn't been so beautiful.

The heart scar was delicate, the new flesh a dainty thread of pale skin. His prettiest scar. For months he couldn't bring himself to look at it. Now it felt as much a part of his body as the beating heart beneath. Debbie's fingers grazed it and Archie felt an electrical jolt run through his nervous system.

He reached up and took her hand by the wrist. "Don't," he said.

Debbie pressed her face into his shoulder. "She's killing you," she said, the words small and muffled in the cloth. "She's killing us."

Archie's voice was barely above a whisper. "I love you," he said. He meant it. He loved her and their children more than anything. He loved them completely, and it wasn't enough. "But I can't just forget about her."

Debbie looked up at Archie's reflection. "I won't let her win."

It broke his heart. Not because she was worried that he was in danger, but because she thought she had a chance of saving him. Whatever fucked-up game he and Gretchen played, it was between them. Gretchen didn't care about Debbie because she knew that Debbie wasn't a threat. "It's not a contest." What he didn't say was, she's already won.

Debbie looked at him for a minute, not saying anything. And then, slowly, sweetly, she kissed him on the cheek. "Let's sit up for a while," she said. "Watch TV or something."

Archie was grateful for the shift in topic. "Like married people," he said.

Debbie smiled. "Yeah."

Pretending to be normal. That was something that Archie was good at. "I'll be the husband," he said. He followed her into the living room, just as the pills kicked in and the codeine rushed through his system. Like a kiss, it was soft and warm and full of promise.

CHAPTER 4

Susan sat naked on the floor in front of the oscillating fan, goose bumps rising on her flesh every time the fan's warm air hit her. She'd taken a cool bath and her turquoise hair was wet, her bob combed flat against her head. She had just changed her hair from pink to turquoise two days before, and her scalp still stung from the bleach. That, and the fact that it was ninety-five degrees on the second story of the cramped Victorian, made sleep elusive. The bath had helped. She'd gotten the cigarette smoke smell out of her hair. Though not, somehow, the smell of Parker's buttered popcorn.

She stared at the white laptop that sat on the floor next to her. The final draft of the Molly Palmer story was due the next day. The fucker was finally going to get what was coming to him.

The door to the room flew open.

"Mom!" Susan cried.

Susan's mother, Bliss, looked startled. Her long bleached dreads were wrapped up on top of her head; her cotton caftan floated loosely around her wiry, yoga-toned body. She was carrying a Japanese teapot on a wicker tray. "I'm just bringing you mint tea," she said.

Susan ran her hands through her wet hair and brought her knees up to her chest to hide her naked body. Whereas her mother was fifty and had the body of a thirty-year-old, Susan was twenty-eight and had the body of a fifteen-year-old. "Knock. Okay? I don't want tea. It's like a hundred degrees."

"I'll just set it here," Bliss said, bending over to place the tray on the floor. She looked up at Susan. "Have you been eating popcorn?" she asked.

Susan had moved back in with her mother. This is not how Susan described it to anyone who would listen. To anyone who would listen, she explained that she was merely staying with her mother. "Staying" being the operative word, implying an impermanence to the condition.

In fact she was "staying" in her old room.

It had been Susan's room, ten years ago. But Bliss had transformed it into a meditation room two minutes after Susan

33

was out the door to college. The walls were painted tangerine, silver beaded Indian curtains hung over the windows, and tatami mats covered the floor. There wasn't a bed, or any other furniture, but Bliss had had the foresight to hang a hammock, should a guest room ever be required. When Susan suggested that she might purchase an air mattress, say, or a futon, Bliss had explained how a quarter of the world slept in hammocks and how this hammock was an authentic triple-weave hammock from the Yucatán, not like the single-weave crap hammocks that people hung in their backyards. Susan knew better than to argue with Bliss. But she hadn't been able to twist around without a fiery pain in her shoulder blade since her first night in that fucking hammock, triple weave or no.

The room smelled like the sweet, stale smoke of a hundred Chinese incense sticks. It was worse in the heat, and even with the windows open, the air in the cramped Victorian's second story was oppressive, like too-tight clothes. At least the hammock offered ventilation.

Susan told herself that she would get an apartment when she finished the story about the senator's relationship with Molly Palmer. Right now, the story had to come first. Time could not be wasted browsing rental sites and viewing apartments. The story must have priority.

She turned to her laptop and opened it. The story glowed white on the pale blue screen. The cursor blinked. She started typing.

She would have died before she told anyone the truth: that she was scared to be alone. That she still felt the pressure of the belt around her neck. That she still had dreams about the After School Strangler.

She entered Castle's "no comment" into the second paragraph of the story, and smiled. It hadn't been that long ago that she'd written personal essays and cute features about salmon festivals and logging shows.

A lot had changed in the past nine weeks, since she'd been assigned the story of profiling Detective Archie Sheridan as he worked to hunt down the Strangler. She had changed.

She had thought about calling Archie a dozen times over the past two months. But she never had. There was no reason to. Her profile series had run. He'd sent a nice note about her last story on the Strangler, and wished her all the best in the world. No invitation to get coffee. No "let's keep in touch." She supposed he had bigger things on his mind.

It was for the best. Don't fall for older, involved men. This was her new rule. And Archie Sheridan? Twelve years older than she was, and in love with his ex-wife. Just her type, and therefore totally off-limits. Plus, she had a job to do.

She refocused her attention on the screen in front of her.

Her current priority: unmasking Senator Castle for the jackass he was. The paper had fought her at every turn, dismissing the whole story as an old rumor. Until Susan found Molly. There had been talk about the senator's so-called affair for years. And several reporters had even tried to track Molly down. Molly had refused to talk to any of them. But she and Susan had something in common. They had both had shit happen to them as kids that made them stupid about men.

For Susan that had led to bad boyfriends, drugs, if you counted marijuana, which no one in Portland, Oregon, did, and the worst sort of exhibitionism, confessional journalism. Molly was worse off than Susan in all departments.

Maybe, Susan thought, they could help each other find their ways out of the woods.

Or at least be less clichéd about it.

Susan reached over and picked up the mug of tea her mother had left her and touched the earthenware to her lips. But it was still too hot to drink.

Susan was aware, in the early morning, of the landline ringing. Her mother had the same phone she'd had when Susan was little, a red rotary phone that hung on the kitchen wall and had a cord so tangled you could pull the receiver only a few inches off the base. It had a loud bell ring that Bliss liked because she could hear it when she was in the backyard turning the compost pile or milking the goat. Why Bliss cared if she heard it, Susan didn't know, because her mother almost never answered the phone. So Susan was surprised when the phone stopped ringing after a few rings.

She rolled over — a complicated maneuver that caused the hammock to swing perilously — and in a few minutes she was rocked back to sleep.

She wasn't sure how much time had passed, but she felt her mother at her side. She squirmed and tried to pull a blanket over her head. She could hear the recycling truck out front so knew it was about seven A.M. The plastic bin of glass bottles and jars shattered against the thick metal bed of the truck. It was an awful, violent sound, like someone smashing the windshield of a car. Susan never got used to it. "Knock," she said to her mother. "Remember?"

Her mother pressed her hand gently into her upper arm. The hammock rocked. It was something about the touch that made her know something was wrong. It was too firm, too precise. She pulled herself up on her elbows, threading her fingers into the hammock weave for leverage. Bliss's face was pinched. Someone had died.

Susan's heart banged in her chest. Who? Susan thought of the city beat reporter she'd gone on a few dates with two months ago. "Derek?" she asked.

Bliss smoothed a piece of Susan's hair. "It's Parker, sweetie," she said. "And Senator Castle. They were in a car. It swerved off the Fremont Bridge this morning."

Susan clambered out of the hammock and huddled naked on the tatami mat below. "What?"

Bliss sat on her bare heels facing Susan, her face full of sadness. "They're both dead, sweetie."

"What?" Susan said again, the word barely more than a whisper.

"Ian called from the paper," Bliss said

softly. "They're dead."

Parker. Susan started to fold in on herself. In a flash she was fourteen and in the hospital room with her father, helpless, alone, furious. She pushed the helplessness and loneliness aside and let the fury take her.

"He fucking died?" she said. "The senator fucking died before my story could run? Two months I've spent on it." She could feel her face flush, a prickly sensation rising in her chest. *Not Parker,* she thought. *Please, not Parker.* "Two months."

Bliss just sat on her heels on the tatami mat, waiting.

Susan snorted in a flood of snot. "Parker's dead?" she asked, her voice tiny.

Her mother nodded.

It didn't make sense. What was Parker doing in a car with Castle? It was a mistake. She looked up at Bliss.

It wasn't a mistake.

Her face wrinkled. "Crap." She squeezed her eyes shut for a minute, trying to absorb the hot tears that threatened to spill, and then stood and began sorting through the cardboard box of clothes that sat in the corner.

"What are you doing?" Bliss asked.

Susan found a long black cotton dress and wiggled into it. "I'm going down there."

"To the paper?" Bliss asked.

"To the bridge. I'm going to find out what happened." She dug her phone out of her purse and began to punch in a number.

Bliss stood up, her cotton caftan fluttering in the breeze of the fan. "Who are you calling?"

Susan wiped a tear off her cheek with the back of her wrist and lifted the phone to her ear. "Archie Sheridan," she said.

She touched her hair, bringing a lock of turquoise to her nose. The smell of popcorn was gone.

CHAPTER
5

Archie stood on the Fremont Bridge. It was the newest of Portland's ten bridges, a two-layer, four-lane, seventies concrete highway that arced high above the Willamette, connecting the east and west sides of the city. Most Portlanders would admit to a favorite bridge: the Hawthorne, the Steel Bridge, the St. Johns. Few would have cited the Fremont. It was inelegant, functional; the pale blue paint peeling from the gray concrete, like skin sloughing off a sunburn. But Archie had always liked it. If you were driving west, it was the best view of the city, a wide-open vista north, south, and ahead of you, the glittering downtown skyline, the lush west hills, Forest Park, the river snaking lazily north, all of it dusted in a pink glow. Portland could be so beautiful sometimes Archie thought his heart might stop just looking at it.

"Ugly, isn't it?" a voice said behind him.

Archie turned a quarter step to see Raul Sanchez. He was a compact man with a neat gray beard and strong arms and a face that looked like it had been whittled out of driftwood. He was wearing a dark blue baseball cap that read FBI in big white letters, and a windbreaker that read FBI in small white letters on the chest and in big white letters on the back.

"Excuse me," said Archie. "Are you with the FBI?"

Sanchez smiled. "They like us to identify ourselves," he said, his Mexican accent wrapping delicately around the consonants. "So the citizens don't mistake us for the assholes at the CIA." He stepped up beside Archie. Behind them, a parking lot's worth of emergency vehicles sat on the now-closed bridge, their lights flashing red, white, blue, and orange.

"Look at that," Sanchez said, pushing his chin out toward the blinking red lights on the cell phone towers that looked like birthday candles rising out of the west hills, and the tall construction cranes that marked the current boom of condo projects and mixed-use developments. "It'll look like L.A. in ten years." He gave Archie a wicked grin. "Californians streaming over our borders. You know they're lazy. Don't even mow their own lawns."

"I've heard that," said Archie.

Sanchez stuffed his hands into his pockets and rocked back on the heels of his cowboy boots. "Been a while since we had a car go over a bridge," he said. The colored light from the emergency vehicles refracted on the cement behind him, so it looked like he was standing on a disco floor.

"Two in ten years," Archie said. "One suicide off the Marquam. One hydroplane off the Morrison."

Sanchez looked up at the clear morning sky. "Well, it wasn't hydroplaning," he said.

Archie looked up, too. A swarm of news helicopters hovered overhead, like ravens circling something dying in the woods. "Yeah," he said. He knew what Sanchez was thinking. It was harder than it looked to drive a car off a bridge. You had to defeat the efforts of several dozen engineering safety gaps: a three-foot cement bumper, a chain-link fence. You had to be profoundly unlucky. Or trying.

Claire appeared beside him. She was wearing jeans and a T-shirt with a picture of a bulldog on the chest. Her short hair was tucked into a Greek fisherman's cap. "Susan Ward's here," she said. "She said she called you."

Archie turned and squinted over at the east side of the bridge where the growing legion of press was kept at bay with crime tape and a phalanx of motorcycle cops.

"They pull the car up yet?" Archie asked Claire.

"Soon," she said. "There's like a hundred years of shit down there the divers have to clear it from first."

"Ah, the pristine Willamette," Sanchez said.

It was a zoo. Susan hadn't seen anything like it, except maybe the Oregon Country Fair outside Eugene. The fair was two hundred eighty acres of hippies and fire dancers and falafel stands, and this was a crush of cops, media, and onlookers. But people had the same excited looks on their faces. Like they were somewhere special.

Susan had parked seven blocks from the Kerby Street exit off the bridge and walked. She wore her *Herald* badge on a lanyard around her neck and talked her way through three separate police checkpoints. It was disconcerting to be on foot on the bridge. Unlike most of the other bridges in Portland, the Fremont was closed to pedestrians except for once a year when the city let a few thousand Portlanders pedal over it on bicycles. Susan, who inevitably forgot when the Bridge Pedal was coming and always found herself stuck in traffic, now saw the appeal. There was something otherworldly about being that far up above the city. And then she thought of the long seconds that the senator's car was in freefall and her fists tightened. Parker was dead. Now she had to step up. She had to do something that countered every reporter instinct she had: risk her exclusive.

She had to tell Archie Sheridan what she knew.

She had elbowed her way past the TV crews, each wanting a live shot with the impressive fleet of emergency vehicles in the background. Claire had spotted her and said she'd track down Archie for her. But there were so many people that once Claire had disappeared into the crowd of uniforms, Susan immediately lost track of her. So she waited, watching the cops, eavesdropping on the other reporters, gathering as much information as she could. She couldn't hear much. There was too much going on. And then it hit her: no skid marks. There were too many people, too many cars; if there had been skid marks, they would have taped them off. They'd have the crime scene unit all over them. No skid marks. No brakes.

She saw Archie then, and straightened up. He appeared from behind a police van, hands in the pockets of his sport coat, shoulders hunched against the vague morning chill. His hair was a thick mop of brown, but as he got close Susan could see a few strands of gray that had not been there the last time she'd seen him, two months before.

"I'm sorry," Archie said when he reached her. "I know that you and Parker were close."

Susan felt a black wave of tears in her throat and swallowed them. "What happened?" she said. Archie lifted the tape and Susan ducked under it and followed Archie as he spoke.

"It happened at about five this morning," he explained. "The car was going fast and swerved off the bridge at the crest." He motioned to where a large segment of the bridge's cement bumper was clearly missing, the rebar frame exposed like a bone in a compound fracture. A ten-foot segment of chain-link fence was broken and hanging perilously off the side. "Two drivers stopped and called nine-one-one. Search and Rescue were down there in seven minutes." The two stopped at the edge and stared down at the police barge and Search and Rescue boats

46

that floated on the river below; a rainbow of gasoline shimmered on the water's surface, marking where the car had gone under. "But both of them were dead," Archie continued. "The senator and Parker. They pulled the bodies out about an hour ago." He turned and looked at Susan, and raised an eyebrow. "It was Parker's car, Susan. You know what the *Herald*'s crime-beat reporter was doing driving our state's senior senator around at the crack of dawn?"

Susan's stomach ached. Why hadn't Parker told her he was going to meet with Castle? No skid marks. Christ.

"Susan?" Archie said, a slight warning in his voice. "You need to tell me now."

Susan glanced around at the cops and press corps, none of whom seemed to actually be doing anything. "Somewhere private," she said to Archie.

Archie raised his eyebrows and then motioned for her to follow him and he led her past two patrol cars and two police vans to a midnight-blue Crown Victoria, where Archie's partner, Henry Sobol, sat in the driver's seat scribbling in a notebook. The driver's door was open, and Archie leaned in and said, "I need the car."

Henry glanced up, smiling as he saw Susan. "Ms. Ward," he said. "You've changed your hair."

"It's called Atomic Turquoise," Susan said. "I considered Enchanted Forest but it seemed a little too punk."

"You're right," Henry said, climbing out of the car. He hooked a thumb behind his large silver-and-turquoise belt buckle. "Turquoise is more professional."

He didn't ask why they needed the car.

Archie opened the rear door and held it for Susan as she slid onto the warm navy blue vinyl backseat of the Crown Vic. Then Archie got in next to her and closed the door.

"Did he drown?" Susan asked.

"It looks like it," Archie said gently. "The car sank fast. Electric locks. They couldn't get out."

Susan twisted a piece of aqua hair into a tight rope. "I need this to be between us."

Archie looked at her for a moment. "I can't promise that. It's not my case. It's FBI. It's not even local FBI. If you tell me something that I think is relevant to the case, I'm going to be compelled to share it."

Susan let it all go in one breath. "Senator Castle had an affair with his children's babysitter. Ten years ago. She was fourteen. He then conspired to cover it up."

"Fourteen?" Archie said. "I thought she was older than that."

48

Susan was dumbfounded. "You know about Molly Palmer?"

Archie shrugged. "I didn't know her name. But there have been rumors."

Susan knew that there had been rumors. There had been rumors for years. But either no one had believed them, or no one had wanted to believe them, because the rumors had never appeared in print. But she didn't know that the police knew. "And the cops never investigated?" she asked.

"I was always assured that there was nothing to it," Archie said.

Susan fidgeted out of her sandals and twisted her legs up under her, careful to modestly arrange her dress. "Well, there was something to it. I've got a mountain of evidence, including Molly Palmer. They paid her off. They paid off a teenager to keep quiet." She pulled at her *Herald* lanyard. "The story was scheduled to run in two days. Parker and I met with Castle's lawyer yesterday to see if he had a comment. He didn't."

"You think Parker met with the senator again?" Archie asked.

"I don't know," Susan said. "Maybe. Maybe the senator decided to comment after all. But there is no way that the two of them being in that car isn't connected to the

Molly Palmer story."

Archie nodded to himself for a minute and then returned his attention to her. "Thank you," he said. "This is helpful."

Susan felt her face grow hot. "You're welcome."

Henry knocked on the car window, nearly causing Susan to jump out of her skin. Henry waved his fingers at her and then pointed at Archie and then at his watch. Archie saw him and nodded, a tiny, almost imperceptible gesture. Susan glanced at her own watch. It was almost eight-thirty.

"Salem?" she asked. She had watched Archie and Gretchen at one of their weekly sessions. It still haunted her.

Archie rubbed the back of his neck and squinted, like he had a sudden pain. "I don't go down there anymore," he said.

Susan was startled. "Really?"

Archie's face didn't register any emotion. "We're taking a break," he explained. It was the kind of thing you'd say about a trial separation, not a continuing homicide investigation. *We're taking a break. Seeing other people. Exploring our options.*

Gretchen Lowell. The Beauty Killer. The Queen of Evil. Susan had met her only once. Blond. Porcelain skin. She was even more beautiful in person than she was in all the pictures.

Susan had been sixteen when they discovered the Beauty Killer's first victim, and that's about how old Gretchen Lowell still made her feel.

There were newspaper stories almost every day back then, most of them written by Quentin Parker. That was how Susan first knew Archie Sheridan, as a photograph in the paper, standing behind a podium at a press conference or standing over some new corpse.

"I haven't seen her," Archie said. "Since the After School Strangler case."

An involuntary shiver raised the hairs on Susan's arms. She changed the subject. "I heard you got back together with your family," she said.

Archie smiled and picked at something on the leg of his pants. "We're working on it," he said, his voice softening.

Susan smiled. "That's good. That's really good."

They sat for a moment in completely awkward silence. Well, it was completely awkward for Susan. Archie seemed fine with it. But she didn't like silence. It made her feel as if she might blurt out something she would regret. Or start to cry. Which is exactly what happened.

"Oh, God," she said, wiping a tear from her cheek and examining it, as horrified as if it were blood.

Archie put his hand on hers. He didn't say anything. He just waited while she wept.

"I get scared sometimes, when I'm alone," she said, blubbering. She dug in her purse for an old tissue and blew her nose. "Isn't that pathetic?"

Archie was perfectly still. He squeezed her hand. "Not at all," he said quietly.

Susan closed her eyes. Sometimes she wished she could go back three months, before the case that had brought them together. And then she remembered Archie, and all he'd been through, and felt like a jerk.

"I'm sorry," she said. "Parker's making me feel sorry for myself."

"It's okay to be scared, Susan," Archie said. "You're going to be okay. There is nothing pathetic about you."

She smiled at him and nodded a few times. He always called her "Susan." Never "Sue," or "Suzy," or "Suze." She liked that about him.

"Do you really think the Atomic Turquoise is okay?" she asked.

She could see Archie eye her hair, considering his words carefully. "I like the fact that you have the guts to do it," he said.

She wiped her cheeks and nose with her palms and forearm and started to get out of the car.

Archie stopped her with a hand on her arm. "I might need your help with something else," he said. "I've got a body I need to identify. I might need to ask a favor. To get some coverage. I'm afraid the story will get lost in all this mess."

"The girl in the park?" Susan asked.

Archie raised an eyebrow in surprise. "Yeah."

"Let me know what you need," Susan said. "I'll do what I can."

Walking away, she wondered for a moment if Archie had been playing her a little, wanting her help getting coverage, and if she was being just a little bit manipulated. Then she pushed the thought out of her mind. Archie wasn't that calculating.

CHAPTER
6

Archie watched as Henry maneuvered his large frame into the driver's seat and started the car. "You get her to cover the park?" Henry asked, glancing in the rearview mirror as Susan made her way back to the assembled pen of reporters.

"Yeah," Archie said. It had been easy. He felt a little bit bad about that. But he felt worse for their Jane Doe. It was something that Debbie was always accusing him of — feeling more connection to the dead than the living.

Archie pulled his seat belt over his chest and fastened it.

"No questions?" Henry asked. "She just agreed?" He twisted around in his seat to get another look at Susan, who was easy to spot, her turquoise hair like the head of a match. "What did you do? Hypnotize her?"

It was hot in the car and Archie fiddled with the air conditioner. "You ever hear anything about the senator screwing his kids' babysitter?" he asked.

"Heard something like that," Henry said. "Didn't know she was his babysitter."

Archie winced. The air conditioner choked to life and some small bit of crud caught in the vent rattled and snapped. "Ever think about looking into it?" Archie asked. He slammed the heel of his palm into the dash near the vent and the rattling stopped.

"Thought she was sixteen," Henry said. The light was on the hood and Henry flipped it on, put one arm behind Archie's seat, and began to back up.

That was the cutoff for statutory rape. Sixteen and over, you could consent; under sixteen, you couldn't. It was one of those laws that depended a lot on context.

"Fourteen," Archie said. The context on this one wasn't very forgiving. "Castle was fifty-two at the time. Susan told me the *Herald*'s got a tell-all," he added. "An exclusive interview with the woman."

"No crime in it," Henry said. His eyes were still focused behind them as he slowly directed the car in a perfectly executed Y-turn. Henry had driver's licenses from seventeen states. He'd moved every year before he became a cop. Just to see more, he'd told Archie once when they were drunk.

Archie had never lived anywhere but Oregon. But then, he had only one ex-wife. Henry had five.

"The statute of limitations back then was three years," Henry continued. "You could stretch it to six if your vic was especially adorable." A bored-looking uniformed cop lifted a piece of crime tape to let them drive out of the cordoned area on the bridge. "Now you get six years after the kid tells someone or turns eighteen. Whichever comes first."

There was a steel travel cup of coffee on the dash, and it started to slide forward as Henry sped up. Archie reached for it and took a sip of the lukewarm coffee. Castle had a law degree. He'd probably popped a bottle of champagne the day he hit the three-year mark. "Lady Justice appears to not be Castle's primary fear," Archie said. The AC started rattling again and Archie hit the dash with the heel of his hand again. The rattling stopped.

"Yeah," Henry said with a wry chuckle. "Back when I worked in D.C., they used to call it the 'Three Dees': disgraced, disbarred, and divorced. Bad press. That's what really scares these motherfuckers."

"By 'motherfuckers' you mean politicians?" Archie asked, taking another sip of the lukewarm coffee.

"Yep," Henry said.

"And what were you doing in D.C.?" Archie asked.

"I was working for a motherfucker," Henry said. "Shaved my muttonchops and everything. Then I saw the invoices the public housing contractors were turning in. Ten thousand bucks per urinal." He shook his head slowly at the thought of it. "That was after I stopped teaching inner-city high school kids and before I became a bush pilot."

"When was the motorcycle trip across South America?" Archie asked.

"After I left Alaska," Henry said. "Char and I had just broken up. You know, I spent a month with a native tribe when my bike broke down in the mountains. They had this leaf there — if you chewed it, you saw an image of your future."

"What did you see?" Archie asked.

"A white horse, a kid holding a bird, and a big-titted woman with a sword."

Archie blinked silently at Henry for a moment. "So obviously you thought, 'I'll become a cop.'"

Henry smiled broadly, his mustache turning up at the corners. "It seemed like a clear omen."

Archie just shook his head. Closing the Fremont Bridge had fucked rush hour. I-5 north, 405, even the surface streets had come to a halt. Once they got through the roadblock at the end of the bridge, Henry put the siren on so they could ride the shoulder of the freeway. Technically, they weren't supposed to use the sirens in nonemergency situations. Henry considered traffic jams an emergency.

"So you think Castle decided to take the plunge?" Henry said. "Grabbed the wheel. Murder-suicide?"

"Maybe," Archie said.

"You gonna tell the Feds?" Henry asked.

Archie considered it. "We'll wait and see what the crime scene techs come up with," he said. "If it wasn't intentional, no point stepping on Susan's story."

Henry grinned, and slipped on his aviator sunglasses.

"What?" Archie asked.

"You're nice to her because she likes you," he said.

"I'm nice to her because I'm nice," Archie said. "And she likes me because I'm old —"

"A geriatric forty," objected Henry, who was ten years older than that.

"Old," repeated Archie. He added: "Powerful."

"Bossy," countered Henry.

Archie tried, "Commanding?"

Henry nodded in compromise. They were through downtown now, on the Marquim Bridge, headed back to the eastside. Traffic was better. The sun was out. And Mount Hood and Mount St. Helens loomed on the horizon. Archie always thought they looked strange in the summer, their massive rocky structures oddly naked.

"Not to mention," Archie said, "fucked up and unavailable." He rolled down the window and dumped the rest of the coffee out the window.

"Well," said Henry. "How could she resist?"

CHAPTER
7

Archie stood inside his front door. He'd
spent the rest of his Sunday morning at the
office filling out reports. Castle wasn't his
case, but he'd been on the scene, and that
meant paperwork. Henry had finally insisted
on driving him home.

He could hear Buddy Holly blasting
through the house. The air was heavy with
the smell of a freshly baked cake, and he
heard his son giggling in the kitchen. A
lifetime ago, that sound would have made
him smile; now it only made him stop, his
hand wrapped tight around the pillbox in his
pocket.

Two and a half years ago he had stood
outside of Gretchen Lowell's house. He
often thought about that night, reimagining
the sequence of events, telling himself to
turn around, to walk away, to get back in his
car and drive straight home to his family. If
he hadn't gone inside that night, everything

would be different.

But he had gone inside. And Gretchen had been waiting.

He stood just inside the door for another minute and then finally called: "I'm home."

Debbie's voice called back: "We're in the kitchen."

Archie took his briefcase into his office, still stalling. He didn't like to leave it out where the kids might get into it. No one should have to look at photographs like the ones he had to look at. His office was one of the extra bedrooms on the far end of the hall. A square, carpeted room with a desk, a fake Eames chair, and a sofa that folded out for the overflow visitors who never seemed to come. On the surface, the office looked innocuous enough. Shelves of forensic pathology books and crime references, a few commendations framed on the wall, a computer, three file cabinets teeming with reports and notes. There was a large closet with an accordion-style birch door. Inside on the back wall was a collage of photographs of every Beauty Killer victim that Archie had closed. Sometimes he would open the door, turn on the closet light, and just sit and look at them. Forty-two faces. Men. Women. Children. He knew every detail of each photograph. They were burned into his consciousness.

He sat down at his desk and unclipped his holster from his waistband, pulled his weapon out, and emptied the bullets into his hand. They were never as heavy as he thought they should be. He unlocked his desk drawer with a key from his key ring, and set the bullets in a cubby. Then he unlocked another drawer, laid the gun and holster in it, and locked it. This was their agreement when Ben was born. No loaded guns in the house. Even Henry had to lock his gun up when he came for dinner.

Out of the corner of his eye he saw a small face in the doorway. When he looked, it was gone.

"Sara?" he said.

She poked her head around again. "They're making me a cake for my birthday. I'm not supposed to look." She grinned and clapped her hands together. "For tomorrow," she said. She spun around in a little circle, danced in place for a moment, and then ran over to Archie, her dark braids swinging. Sara ran everywhere. She set a chubby hand on Archie's. "Did you have fun today?" she asked.

Archie hesitated, trying not to let his face betray his mental state. "I was at work. Work isn't always fun."

She gazed up at him, eyes bright, cheeks glowing. "When I'm seven, will I get to meet her?"

"Who?" Archie asked.

"Gretchen Lowell."

It took the breath out of him. Like a fist to the chest. His hand went up to the scar reflexively, like you might cover an old injury in the path of a blow. He could barely speak. "Where did you hear that name, sweetie?" he asked finally.

Sara, sensing his uneasiness, took a tiny step back. "Jacob Firebaugh gave Ben a book about you."

Archie's heart pounded in his chest. "What book?" He knew what book. *The Last Victim*. It was a trashy tale of Gretchen's escapades and Archie's suffering at her hands. He knew that they'd see it eventually. But he thought he had time.

"I don't know," she said.

"Did it have a picture of a woman on the cover?" he asked.

She smiled up at him, two rows of tiny teeth. "I want to meet her. I like her."

It was the saddest thing Archie thought he'd ever heard anyone say in his whole life. "Don't say that," he said, his voice barely above a whisper.

"You like her, too, don't you, Daddy?"

Sara said. "You used to go and see her all the time. Ben heard Mom and Henry talking."

Archie ran a hand over his face and worked to keep breathing. "Do you know where Ben keeps the book?"

She looked back toward the hall and then whispered: "He hides it."

He sat still for a moment, gathering himself. Then he wrapped a hand behind her head and kissed her on the forehead. "Okay," he said. He held out his hand and she took it, wrapping her fingers around his index finger. "Let's go."

He led her out into the hall, toward the kitchen.

She stopped, her face concerned. "I can't go in there, Daddy. My surprise."

Archie glanced up at the kitchen. The music. The cake. "Of course," he said. "Go to your room, okay?"

She nodded and turned and ran to her room, turning once to peek back at him from behind her bedroom door.

Archie walked into the kitchen. They were frosting the cake. Ben on his knees on a stool at the island. Debbie standing. She wore a white chef's apron over her black T-shirt and jeans, but had managed to get frosting everywhere, even her hair. She looked up at Archie when he came into the room, and grinned. "You're just in time for the marzipan flowers," she said.

Archie walked over to the white stereo that fit under the cabinet by the fridge and turned it off.

"He has a copy of the book," he said flatly.

The cake was on a lazy Susan cake tray and Debbie rotated it, holding the frosting knife steady across the top. "What book?"

Archie took a step forward, his hands in his pockets. "The book. Jacob Firebaugh gave him a copy." Archie didn't even know who Jacob Firebaugh was.

Ben stuck his finger along the edge of the glass frosting bowl. "He says you're famous."

"I don't want you reading that shit," Archie snapped at him.

Debbie lifted the knife from the cake. "Archie," she warned in a low voice.

Archie pulled his hands out of his pockets and ran them through his hair. "It's full of violence. Crime scene photos." The thought of his eight-year-old son reading what she'd done to him made his stomach burn. "Graphic descriptions of torture."

"A glimpse into your world," Debbie said.

He walked up to her. She smelled like buttercream. "It's completely inappropriate," he said. He felt shaky; his body ached for the pills. "He showed it to Sara."

Ben rolled his eyes. "She's such a tattler."

"Go get it," Archie ordered him, pointing toward Ben's room. "Right now."

Ben looked at Debbie. It had been like that since Archie had come home. His son always looked to his mother before he did anything. She nodded and he hopped off the stool and disappeared down the hall, still licking his fingers.

Debbie laid the knife back on the cake and spun the lazy Susan. "If you don't talk about it," she said carefully, "they're going to try to find answers other places."

"Not in that book," Archie said.

Debbie's mouth tightened. "They know you were lost. That you were hurt. They were just babies, then." He could hear her throat constrict, fighting the tears. "But they're going to have to hear the whole story."

Not the whole story. "Why?" he asked.

"What about your scars?" She set the frosting knife across the bowl and turned to face him. "How exactly do we explain that to them? All those trips to the prison. They remember that. They know you went to see her."

"It was my job," Archie stressed.

Debbie reached up with a sticky hand and touched his face. "Don't bullshit me, Archie. I've known you too long." She looked him in

66

the eye. "You went there because you needed to, because you liked it."

Archie took a step back and turned away. "I'm exhausted. I don't want to do this now," he said, opening a cabinet to get a glass.

"I just want you to be honest with us. With me."

He turned on the faucet and filled the glass with water. "Please, don't," he said.

"I want you to be honest with yourself."

Archie slowly lifted the glass to his lips and took a sip and then poured the rest down the drain. Then he set the glass in the sink. Self-awareness wasn't his problem. He knew exactly how fucked up he was. He would have given anything for a little denial. "I *am* honest with myself," he told Debbie. God, he was so tired of this. He resented her for it. For making everything so hard. For making him feel so guilty.

She wanted the truth? Fine. Fuck it. "I went there," he said slowly, enunciating each word as if it were a grammar lesson. "Because. I. Liked. It." In the sink, a cake pan sat soaking next to the glass, the grit of the cake floating in soapy water. "It was the only time of the week I actually felt like I was still alive." He looked up at Debbie. "I would still go. If I thought that I could get away with it."

She stood hugging her arms, her freckles like dark stars. "You can't see her. If you want to stay with us."

Archie smiled. "There it is," he said.

"What?" Debbie said.

"The ultimatum," Archie said. "You know how I like those."

He heard Ben's voice say, "Here." Both Debbie and Archie turned to see Ben standing at the entrance to the kitchen, the thick paperback in his hands, Gretchen's lovely face smiling seductively on the cover.

Archie turned and walked over to him and took the book from his hands. He bent over and kissed him on the cheek. "Thank you," he said into his ear. "I'm sorry I yelled." He smoothed his son's hair and walked past him toward the hall.

"Where are you going?" Debbie asked.

Archie spun around. "It's Sunday afternoon," he said. "I thought I'd go to the park."

Debbie's eyes were full of tears. "You shouldn't drive."

Archie kept walking. "I shouldn't do a lot of things."

CHAPTER
8

There were flowers on Parker's desk. A pot of African violets, a bouquet of yellow tulips, and a bouquet of some fleshy pink flower that Parker would have hated. One of the HR ladies from the third floor had brought that one up.

Neither of the bouquets was in water. They would just sit there and wilt and die and rot. What good that was supposed to do anyone, Susan couldn't figure. Someone dies, so you kill something beautiful?

The *Herald* building was downtown. It had been built a hundred years ago and then fallen victim to an unfortunate renovation in the 1970s. The floors were gutted, cubed, and affixed with fluorescent lights and drop ceilings. Susan's desk was on the fifth floor. The view was impressive, which was about the only nice thing you could say about the place. It was too quiet for Susan's taste, too corporate, and, no matter what the temperature outside, too cold.

Sundays at the *Herald* were usually Siberia. Anyone important was at home. The Sunday paper was printed. Monday was light. Things were run by one senior editor who drew the short straw and usually spent the day at his desk playing solitaire or surfing the Internet for gossip sites and blogs. There was a lot of sitting around. No one knows more Internet gossip than newspaper people, whether they admit it or not.

This particular Sunday was an all-in day. A sitting senator was dead. Parker, one of their own, was dead. They had an evening edition to get out, and a Web site that required a breaking story every few minutes to compete with the TV news. Most of the news department had come in, copy editors, features. But there were also the übereditors, the assistant editors, interns, HR people, receptionists, and the TV critic who planned to write a story about how TV was covering the story. Everyone wanted to get in on the action. The worse the tragedy, the more you wanted a piece of it. That's what separated reporters from regular people.

Susan pulled a hooded sweatshirt she kept in her desk drawer on over her black dress and rested her head in her hands. Molly Palmer had flaked out and wasn't returning

70

Susan's calls. She dialed her cell again. Nothing. They were planning coverage of the senator for the next day's paper. It would be a huge pickup day. Castle's photo on the front page. A huge, bold headline announcing his death. That was the kind of newspaper that people still bought and Susan wanted her story to be featured.

Susan leaned back in her desk chair to see if Ian was out of his meeting yet. The door to the conference room was still closed. Ian had been in there for an hour with Howard Jenkins and an assembly of *Herald* bigwigs planning the Castle coverage and deciding the fate of her story. She had thought she'd earned some capital with her series on Archie Sheridan and the After School Strangler. But in the end, it was all newspaper politics. And without Molly to confirm her story to the paper's fact checkers, the *Herald* was waffling.

Susan punched in Molly's number again. Nothing.

Fuck. Molly was not exactly a willing subject. She'd only agreed to meet in person twice. And getting ahold of her was always a pain in the ass. Molly would turn off her phone and forget to turn it on for days.

Susan had already made a three-foot-long paper-clip chain and worked six tiny braids into her blue hair. Now she unhooked the paper clips and put them back in their cardboard box and pulled the braids out and then rebraided them.

She could smell the honey-sweet pollen drifting from the flowers on Parker's desk.

The bank of TVs that were bolted on the wall above the copy editors were all live with the senator and Parker's accident. Susan couldn't look. She wanted out of the office. She wanted to find Molly. She wanted to be doing something.

Susan heard a voice ask, "Are you okay?" She looked up to see Derek Rogers. His sandy eyebrows were knitted in concern. She'd mostly avoided him since she'd broken things off. She'd tried to explain how he wasn't her type. He was square and responsible. She was chaotic. He drank his coffee with milk and sugar. She drank hers black.

The truth was, he wanted a girlfriend. And she didn't want to be anyone's girlfriend right now.

"I can't believe he's gone," he said, the dimple in his chin deepening. Then he shook his head. "What a stupid thing to say," he said. "Everyone says that, don't they?" Both Susan and Derek had scrambled for Parker's attention. It was one of the few things they had in common.

"I know you really liked him, too," she said.

"If you want to talk," Derek said, "you have my number."

Why did he have to be so nice?

The door to the conference room opened and Susan scooted back in her chair. It rolled too quickly and she nearly buckled backward.

Ian looked over at her and jabbed a thumb for her to come.

"Duty calls," she said to Derek, and she got up and walked down the carpeted aisle between desk clusters to his office. It had a window, but it just looked out onto the news floor. There were bulletin boards covered with feature clips, so he could call writers in one by one and go over every word of their stories until you wanted to cry or stab him in the neck.

She'd already decided she was going to quit if they didn't run it. Or stab him. Whatever impulse took hold hardest. Probably the stabbing.

He motioned for her to sit and she flung herself down on a chair.

"We're running it," he said. "But we're going to have to make some changes."

Susan pulled at the sleeves of her

sweatshirt. "Changes?"

Ian grabbed at his little ponytail. "The senator was an institution in this state. He was beloved. We have to present the story within that context. He had an affair with a teenager. And that was very bad judgment."

Susan could feel the story slipping away from her. Bad judgment? Yesterday it had been the story of the century. "It wasn't an affair," she said. "She was fourteen."

"Whatever," Ian said. He clicked his computer mouse, and a Word document sprang to life on his monitor. "I'm going to take a stab at reframing it. I'll run the edits by you. We're planning on running the story. But not in Monday's tribute edition. It just doesn't seem appropriate."

Appropriate? "Parker was my editor," Susan said.

She watched as Ian highlighted a sentence in her story and hit delete. "I know this is hard for you," he said.

"Parker was my editor," Susan said again. Behind Ian, pinned on the bulletin board, were photographs of Castle through the years, looking puffy and self-important. Someone had scribbled headline ideas on pieces of paper and pinned them up next to the pictures. STATE MOURNS FAVORITE SON. SENATOR DIES IN CRASH.

CHAMPION OF POOR DIES IN BRIDGE CALAMITY.

None of them mentioned Parker. He would be lucky to make the lead.

Ian picked up the telephone on his desk and hit the nine for an outside line. Susan saw right through the gesture. He didn't really need to make a call; it was just his clumsy signal that the meeting was over. "We'll need contact info for your source," he said distractedly, "for Molly Palmer."

"No problem," Susan said.

She stomped back to her desk, sat down on her task chair, and spun around slowly. Someone had left another bouquet on Parker's desk, a bundle of purple carnations and baby's breath. They were wrapped in green tissue paper and tied together with a black ribbon. Emblazoned on the ribbon were the words REST IN PEACE.

Susan dug her cell phone out of her sweatshirt pocket and punched in a number.

"I have to get out of here," she said into the phone. "Do you still want some ink on your Jane Doe?"

"I'm at the park right now," Archie Sheridan answered. "Can you meet me?"

Archie sat on the damp ground, just yards from where a girl had been murdered. The weather had changed — the sunny day gone, replaced with a sad drizzle. The park smelled like death. Rotting logs, fallen branches, spoiled blackberries. Archie brushed some dirt off his pants and closed his eyes.

This is where it had all begun. Archie and Henry had responded to a call about a dead woman in the upper park. She was just a kid. Scalped. Burned. Badly mutilated. That was thirteen years ago. The Beauty Killer's first victim. Archie's first homicide.

Archie glanced down at the paperback next to him in the dirt. Gretchen looked back at him. He didn't know why he had brought it, why he hadn't left it in the car, why he hadn't thrown it in the nearest gas station Dumpster. He knew one thing: This Jacob Firebaugh kid was going to get an earful.

There was a sudden rustling behind him on the hillside. Ferns bending under feet, earth sliding, vines snapping. Archie jerked back to alertness, opened his eyes, and in an instant found the gun on his hip, resting his hand lightly on the leather holster. He turned around and found a kid standing a few feet above him on the hillside.

The kid was maybe twelve, still panting from his trip down the hill, the ferns vibrating behind him. He was delicate looking, with pale skin and dark hair and a mouth full of glittery braces. He wore an Oregon Ducks T-shirt and a pair of knee-length shorts heavy with pockets and snaps, and his calves were straight and tiny, birdlike. He was carrying an old Peanuts metal lunch box. "Are you a detective?" he asked.

"Yeah," Archie said, pulling his hand away from his gun.

The kid sat down next to Archie, folding his legs Indian style, the lunch box on his lap.

Archie picked up the copy of *The Last Victim* and moved it to his other side, away from the kid. "Can I help you?" Archie asked.

"I'm okay," the kid said.

Archie tilted his head at the crime tape that surrounded them. "This is sort of a crime scene."

"I know," the kid said.

The two sat in silence for a moment, watching the stream gurgle by down below.

"Do you have kids?" the kid asked finally.

"Two," Archie answered. "Six and eight."

The kid nodded, satisfied. "I want to show you something."

Archie looked at the boy. He was lonely. Looking for attention. Archie didn't have time to indulge him. But there was something in his eyes, a seriousness that was enough to make Archie agree. What the hell. He'd look at the fort or whatever the hell the kid had, and then he'd go home to his family.

Archie stood.

"Don't forget your book," the kid said, pointing at *The Last Victim*.

Archie looked down at Gretchen's face, the pink background, the gold embossed lettering. "Right," he said, stooping over and picking it up.

The boy scrambled a few feet up the hill. Archie took a few careful steps up the muddy embankment after him, remembering the patrol cop who'd lost his footing. But the kid grew anxious and extended an impatient arm. Archie tucked the book into his waistband and took the kid's hand, and the kid led him up the hill, back to the main path, and started walking west, farther into the woods. The rain had picked up and was an insistent patter on the canopy of leaves overhead. The cuffs of Archie's pants were black with mud and his palms were covered with dirt from trying to leverage himself up the hillside. The light was fading quickly. The kid walked at a forty-degree angle, driven with purpose, his feet moving double time. Archie had to work to keep up with him. Then the kid came to a stop and looked at Archie and then up another hillside.

"Seriously?" said Archie.

The kid took a few steps up the hill and reached back for Archie. Archie took his hand again and the kid led him up the hillside. They were about halfway up when Archie felt a dull ache pound below his right rib cage. He winced, and his foot slipped in the mud, and he slid to his knees, grinding dirt into the calves of his pants. It took him a minute to catch a breath before he let the kid help pull him upright and they started climbing again. Archie tried to breathe into the pain. It wasn't a cramp. It wasn't that sharp. It was a flatter pain, more diffuse. At first Archie thought it was the book, tucked into his waistband, digging into his gut, but when he slid the book to the left, the pain stayed on the right. Still, he took the book out of his waistband and pinched it under his armpit, and focused on the kid, his mud-soaked green sneakers always a few feet up ahead, and in a few minutes the strange ache subsided. At the top the hillside leveled off. It was crowded with trees. The kid looked up at Archie. "I collect nests," he said.

Archie stopped to try to brush some slimy vegetation off his increasingly damp pants. "Great," he said.

"I found one here a few weeks ago." The kid tapped the ground with the tip of his sneaker. "Right here."

"Neat," said Archie.

"There's something wrong with it," the kid said.

"With the nest?" Archie said.

The kid gave Archie a grave look and then sat down cross-legged again, set the lunch box on his lap and opened it. Inside was a bird's nest. The kid lifted it carefully out of the lunch box and handed it up to Archie.

Archie took it. The sun set a little further and it felt suddenly very cold in the park. "You found this right here," he said quietly. "This spot."

The kid nodded gravely. "There's something wrong with it, right?"

"Yeah," said Archie. He got his cell phone out and called Henry, his arm still tight around the book.

"It's me," he said. "I'm at Forest Park. Get Search and Rescue out here. And a cadaver dog. I think we've got another corpse."

Woven into the nest, among the twigs and vines that had been gathered off the forest floor, were several hundred strands of long blond hair.

When Archie looked up again, the kid was gone.

CHAPTER
9

Susan thought about going home and changing into park clothes: hiking boots, a slicker, maybe a pair of lederhosen. But she didn't want to look like she was trying too hard. So she just wore her hooded sweatshirt over her black dress. She was wearing flip-flops, but she had a pair of sneakers in the trunk she kept for just such occasions. She only had to ruin one pair of expensive boots at a crime scene to learn that lesson. Now her trunk was full of reporter supplies: a change of shoes, a waterproof jacket, notebooks, water, a sun hat, batteries for her recorder, emergency tampons. You never knew where you might end up and for how long.

Traffic was bad. It had started to rain and the storm drains were overflowing and water pooled at every corner. Traffic was always bad when it rained during the summer. Even though it rained nine months out of the year,

Portlanders were always unsettled when it rained out of season.

Bliss found it charming, but then Bliss didn't drive. It made Susan want to murder someone.

It took forty minutes to get across the river and up to Northwest. Susan listened to people call in on a talk radio show to share their fond memories of the senator. But it just made her livid, so she switched the station to alternative rock. She'd given up on that, too, by the time she pulled her old Saab into the parking lot next to an undercover cop car and three patrol units. She pulled the hood of her sweatshirt over her turquoise hair and got out of the car.

There was a uniformed cop sitting in one of the patrol cars. He was wearing a rain slicker, sitting in the driver's seat with the dome light on and writing on a clipboard. Susan knocked on his window.

He looked up. His slicker was wet and he looked unhappy to be there. He rolled down the window half an inch.

"Archie Sheridan?" she asked.

He pointed at the trailhead, and beyond it, the dark woods. And then rolled the window back up.

"Thanks," Susan said. She thought about asking to borrow his flashlight, but he didn't seem to be in that great a mood.

She changed into her sneakers, put her hands into the pockets of her sweatshirt, and started walking. The ground on either side of the cement path to the trailhead was already a field of mud. It glistened under the park lights. When she reached the edge of the dark woods, she thought about going back to her car, going home, going to bed, but then she thought of Parker and how far he would go to get a story, and she hunched her shoulders and headed into the darkness.

The overcast sky held enough light that the trees were shadowed and every branch looked like a bent, angry arm. Susan couldn't help but think of Gretchen Lowell as she walked down the gravel path, the mud sucking at her feet. Gretchen had dumped at least two bodies in these woods. Is that what this was about? Another Beauty Killer victim? Susan dug her hands deeper into her pockets and picked up the pace.

She'd walked about a quarter mile when she found them. She could see the flashlights up ahead, the long white beams refracting off the cedar trunks. Cops, bless their hearts, were always easy to spot.

They were also hard to sneak up on, and she was still thirty feet away when one of the flashlight beams paused and then swung around and landed on her face. She blinked into the light. "I'm looking for Detective Sheridan," she announced.

A large shadow appeared behind the light and she heard Henry Sobol say, "Oh, for fuck's sake, it's you."

The flashlight dropped.

Susan wiggled her fingers at Henry. "Hi," she said.

"He's over there," Henry said, swinging his flashlight around to illuminate Archie, who sat on a fallen log just off the trail. Henry twisted his mouth wryly. "We're waiting for a bird expert," he said.

"Ornithologist," Archie called.

Susan could practically hear Henry rolling his eyes. "Whatever," he said.

She walked over to where Archie sat. He had a flashlight at his feet, shining off into the woods, so she could make out enough of him to see that he was soaking wet and covered in mud.

"Did you trip?" she asked.

"Do you know anything about birds?" he asked.

She put her hands on her hips. "Is that why you asked me out here?"

He picked up the flashlight and shone it in a bird's nest that he was holding on his lap.

"It's human hair," he said. "Blond. There's another body."

Susan leaned over and looked into the nest. She was confused. "You found a nest?"

"A kid gave it to me. He found it up the hill."

"A kid?" Susan said, looking around at the dark woods.

Henry walked up behind her. "He's gone," he explained.

"He disappeared," Archie said.

"The kid?" Susan said.

Archie looked up at Henry. "You call Search and Rescue yet?"

"Based on hair in a nest?" Henry shone his flashlight down Archie's mud-and-debris-covered body. "Are you okay?" he asked, lowering his voice. "Debbie called me, you know. After you stomped out in a cloud of self-pity."

"It was more a fit of pique," Archie said.

"She's worried about you," Henry said.

"You two should start a club." Archie stood. "I don't want to wait anymore." He called over the three uniformed cops who were standing with their flashlights. "I'm going to want shoulder-to-shoulder teams with flashlights. Take your time. We're looking for a female corpse."

"Archie," Henry said.

Archie shone his flashlight straight up the muddy hillside. "We're going up there," he said. "That's where the kid found the nest. So that's where we should start."

"Wait," Henry said.

"I'm done waiting," Archie said.

"No," Henry said. "Wait." He swung his flashlight around behind them and illuminated the face of a man.

Susan gasped.

All the cops turned and looked at her.

"Sorry," she said.

The man smiled. He was bearded and bespectacled and wore a hooded rain slicker. "Did someone call an ornithologist?" he said.

Archie waved his hand. "Here."

The man stepped forward. "I'm Ken Monroe. We spoke on the phone."

Archie took his hand and shook it. "Thanks for coming," Archie said.

"Sure." He grinned excitedly. "We don't usually get emergency calls."

I bet, thought Susan.

"What can you tell me about this?" Archie asked, shining his flashlight in the nest again.

Susan elbowed in as they all gathered around the nest.

Monroe lowered his head so he was only inches from the nest, and examined it carefully. Then he asked, "Where'd you find it?"

Archie gestured with his head up the hillside. "Up there," he said.

"It's a song sparrow nest," Monroe said.

Susan got out her notebook and wrote that down. "You can tell the kind of bird just by looking at the nest?" she asked. Nests all looked the same to her.

Monroe nodded. "Yeah, sure," he said. "See how it's shaped? Like a cup? You can see the rough outer layer of dead grasses and weed stems." He touched the exterior of the nest. "Some rootlets and bark shreds. If you look here, you can see it's lined with finer grasses and hair."

"I'm interested in the hair," Archie said.

"Some birds use it to pad their nests. It's uncommon, but not unheard of."

"So, like what?" Henry asked. "They get it from barber Dumpsters?"

Monroe frowned. "Dumpsters? Not likely. You said the nest was found here?"

"Up the hill," Archie said.

"Well, the hair came from nearby. Birds don't travel far for nesting material. Most nests get made in a couple of days. There's no advantage to flying long distances." Monroe looked up the hill. "No, this hair came from the woods. I'd say, within three hundred yards of here."

Susan felt goose bumps rise on her arms.

"Any idea how old the nest is?" Archie asked.

"No more than a year or two."

"How can you tell?" Henry said.

"Because nests disintegrate," Monroe explained. "If they didn't, we'd be standing on like a hundred of them right now."

"So all we have to do is search three hundred yards in every direction," Archie said.

Henry groaned. "That's a football field."

"Maybe we should call Search and Rescue," Archie said.

Henry looked at him for a minute and then pulled his phone out of his waist clip and started dialing. "Maybe I'll get a cadaver dog, too," he said.

Susan saw Archie smile. "Good idea," he said.

CHAPTER
10

The throbbing pain in Archie's abdomen was back. The rain was steady. It made everyone's skin look slick. It made the ground suck at their shoes. It had soaked through all of their clothing. Archie could feel the cold slime in his socks every time he took a step. His mud-caked pants batted at his calves. His hair stuck to his forehead. At least he'd had the presence of mind to hide the book behind a log. The last thing he wanted was for Henry to find him wandering the woods with a muddy copy of *The Last Victim*.

Archie focused on the small ball of light that his flashlight threw on the forest floor and turned his mind to the task at hand.

It was slow going. Three feet of ivy and morning glory vines blanketed everything in sight. He started left and then slowly worked the beam over the surface of the foliage inch by inch, forward, and then right. Henry was to his left, one of the patrol cops was to his right. Another patrol cop and four Search and Rescue volunteers were working in a line in the opposite direction. Even the ornithologist had been given a flashlight. So far, they had found a dead bird, half digested by ants, an empty Mountain Dew bottle, and some dog shit.

Susan had borrowed a flashlight, too, but was holding it in her teeth so she could scribble furiously in her notebook. Archie wanted her to write a story. He still had no leads on the identity of their Jane Doe, and coverage in the local media had been limited to a single paragraph in the Metro section of the *Herald*. He needed coverage. And he needed a lot of it.

Left. Forward. Right. Then Archie knelt in the mud and grime and began to pull the ivy and morning glory vines aside to look underneath them. The wet vines were heavy and hard to manipulate and Archie's hands looked raw and dirty, like he'd been buried alive and had clawed his way out.

He heard Henry say, "This is ridiculous."

And it was. They could come back in the morning. If there was a corpse out there, it could wait twelve hours. But Archie needed to know. If there was a woman dead out there, he needed to find her. He'd stay out there all night looking. At the very least, it was easier than going home.

He shone his flashlight at his watch. They'd been searching for almost an hour.

A dog barked. Archie looked up to see a dark figure on the path and the shadow of an animal. He swung his flashlight down toward the animal. The light reflected off its eyes, two silver orbs in the darkness.

"His name's Cody," the person with the dog said. "Mine's Ellen. Which one of you is Sheridan?"

"I am," Archie said.

She stepped forward, climbing up toward him, the dog a respectful few feet behind her. They shone their flashlights in her path to light her way, and Archie got a better look at her. She was a big woman, tall and slightly plump, with a long torso that dominated her body and a broad, masculine gait. She wore her hair pulled back in a ponytail and was dressed appropriately for the weather, with tall rubber boots, yellow rain pants, and a quilted down jacket. Ah, June in Portland.

When she reached Archie she held out her hand and he shook it. "Okay," she said. "This is how it's going to work. I'm going to let Cody off lead. He'll move around the area, looking for scents. If he finds something, he'll crouch down, like this." She looked down at the dog and said, "Cody, alert," and the dog sank down on his elbows and yowled. Ellen looked up. "I will praise him. Then you can move in and check out what he's found."

Archie had worked with cadaver dogs before. Once Gretchen had mutilated a man and left his heart and spleen in a shoebox, tied with a red ribbon, on a bed in a motel room in North Portland. Tied to the box was a typed gift tag addressed to Detective Archie Sheridan. The hotel staff called 911 within moments of finding the package. Gretchen had wrapped the organs in plastic but it had leaked and the box was soaked with blood. Archie opened the box and then brought in a dog to try to locate any other pieces. It had worked. The dog found the man's tongue in the ice machine, his penis in the key drop-off box, and the rest of him in the Dumpster of the restaurant next door.

"Assuming there are remains," Henry said, "how long is this going to take?"

"Could be minutes," Ellen said. "Could be days."

"Days," Henry said.

"Longer maybe," Ellen said. She bent down and unhooked the dog's lead. "Cody, go," she said.

The dog put his nose to the ground and

began rooting through the vegetation.

Susan stepped forward and took her flashlight out of her mouth. "How long have you been with Search and Rescue?" she asked Ellen.

"I'm not," Ellen said.

"She's a volunteer," Archie said. "We don't have the money to fund a cadaver dog unit. So people like Ellen take some training courses with their dogs and volunteer."

"I work at Home Depot," Ellen said.

"We found a body a few days ago about a quarter mile down the creek," Archie said. "Is that going to distract him?"

"Did you remove the remains?" Ellen asked.

"Yeah," Archie said.

"Should be fine," Ellen said. "There," she said suddenly. She turned her flashlight to Cody, who was crouching a few feet from where Archie and Henry had just been searching. "Good boy," Ellen said. She walked up behind the dog, clipped his lead back on, and gave his head a vigorous rub.

The area that Cody was indicating was covered with vines. Archie walked up and sank down to his hands and knees. "Shine your lights here," he said to the others. One by one they all stood around him, Susan, the ornithologist, Henry, Ellen, the patrol cops, the Search and Rescue workers, each shone a flashlight on the spot where the dog had knelt, until the ten yellow circles of light joined into one. Archie moved the ivy and morning glory vines aside with his hands. He started out slowly, methodically, careful not to disturb anything he didn't have to, and then began pulling at the vines, uprooting them and tossing them to the side. When he had cleared the area he sat back on his knees.

Susan leaned forward. "There's nothing there," she said.

Archie turned to the dog. "Should we dig, boy?" he asked, scratching the dog's head with his muddy hand. "Is it buried?"

Cody cocked his head and looked at Archie and then looked at the now bare spot of earth.

"I'll get the shovels," one of the Search and Rescue volunteers said, and he headed noisily for the path.

Archie looked at the mud. It was rough, thick with pebbles and roots. Archie picked up a pebble and rolled it between his fingers. It was light and porous. He touched it to his tongue.

"Why are you eating that rock?" Susan asked.

"It's not a rock," Archie said. Rocks were

dense and wouldn't stick to saliva. This was porous. "It's bone."

Cody whined and pulled at his lead.

Archie looked up at the dog. Anything that would chip bone like this wouldn't leave hair like what they'd seen in the nest. There was another body. "Let him go," he told Ellen.

She unclipped Cody's lead and he bounded off, nose down, about thirty feet up the hillside, and then crouched down.

Archie picked up his flashlight and scrambled after him, barely aware of the others behind him, their flashlights bobbing in the darkness. The hillside was thick with ferns, almost prehistoric in their enormity. He pulled himself up the slope by grabbing handfuls of fern fronds, using their root systems as leverage. Their tiny seeds stuck to his hands. When he got to Cody, he knelt down beside him and the dog licked his face. Then the dog whined again and nosed at a large fern that abutted a cedar bent cockeyed from the hillside. Archie reached out and pushed a fern frond aside and pointed his flashlight underneath.

"See anything?" Henry called from behind him.

"Yeah," said Archie.

The skeleton was partial, but it was definitely human. He could see a foot, the remaining skin dark and leathery, which is why it hadn't been eaten. The calf bones were picked clean above the ankle, so the foot looked odd, like a grotesque shoe. He swung the flashlight farther under the fern and saw what was left of a shrunken leather face, black lips, the cracked hide of a cheek, an eye socket, a half-crushed skull. And there, still rooted to the dehydrated scalp tissue, a tangle of blond hair.

"There you are," he said quietly.

Susan and Henry appeared on either side of him. Susan sank down next to him, her leg touching his. He was getting used to having her around.

"Three bodies all within a hundred yards," she said, pen pressed against her notebook. "Are they connected?"

"Maybe," Archie said. "Or maybe not." He looked up into the dark woods. It had stopped raining and the clouds had parted, revealing a bright shard of moon. In the distance, through the trees at the edge of the woods, he could make out the light of a house.

"Find out who lives there," he said to Henry. "And then find out if they have a wood chipper."

CHAPTER
11

Susan trudged after Henry. The ME had shown up, just behind the crime scene investigators and about a dozen other cops. The crime scene had been lit and taped off, and they were using sifters to separate the bone chips from the dirt. She wasn't allowed beyond the crime scene tape, and Archie was too busy to talk, so she had decided to trail Henry. Not that she'd been invited.

"Listen," she was saying to Ian on her cell phone. "I can get it in. I'll be there in an hour." She glanced at her watch, but it was too dark to see it, so she held her phone down to her wrist and read her watch by the phone's LCD light. Ten P.M. The outlying editions started printing at 11:00 P.M., but the metro area sunrise edition didn't go to press until 2:00 A.M. She had plenty of time. Plus, she wanted to keep Ian happy right now, at least until after the story about Molly and Castle ran.

Henry was hurrying up the long cement staircase that led out of the park up to street level. Was he trying to ditch her?

She held the phone back to her ear. "We're doing a spread on Castle's death," Ian was saying. "Eight stories. I can get you on the front page of Metro, below the fold."

"Below the fold?"

"There's a fire up near Sisters," Ian said. "That's the Metro lead."

She took the stairs two at a time. "Three bodies," she said, exasperated. "How is that not A-one? And who gives a shit about a fire in Central Oregon?"

"Spoken like someone without a second house in Central Oregon," Ian said with a snort. "And you don't know the bodies are connected," he added. "And they're nobody."

Bugs bounced off the yellow streetlights that lit the stairs. The bugs probably spent their whole life cycle doing that, Susan thought. Smacking against the grate that covered the bulb, again and again. "Nobody?" she said.

Ian sounded bored. "Word is the first girl was a prostitute. The other two probably are, too. Or homeless. No one cares, Susan. Dead politicians sell papers. Dead hookers don't."

"Castle was a sexual predator," Susan reminded Ian. She tried to make her voice sound steely with resolve.

"We're not running that story when the entire state is mourning him," Ian said.

Sometimes Susan couldn't remember why she'd ever slept with Ian. (He had let her hold his Pulitzer.) "You're a hypocrite, Ian," she said.

"While I have you on the phone," Ian said, ignoring her. "The fact checkers can't get ahold of Molly Palmer. They keep getting her voice mail. You have another number for her?"

Susan's stomach clenched and she forced some more bravado into her voice. "She's a stripper, Ian. She doesn't carry her phone on her when she's naked." She made a mental note to find Molly, before her skittishness cost Susan her story.

"I'm hanging up now," Ian said.

The line went dead and Susan pushed the phone back into her sweatshirt pocket and groaned in frustration. So much for keeping Ian happy.

"It's called a 'high-risk lifestyle,'" Henry said. He had turned to wait for her at the top of the stairs.

"What?" Susan said, jogging up the last few steps. She bent over for a minute to catch her breath. Her sneakers were covered with mud. She'd ruined more shoes in this job. . . .

"Prostitutes," Henry said. "Addicts. Homeless. They live 'high-risk lifestyles.' So we look hard for a couple of days after one of them gets stabbed in the neck with a fork, and then we move on to the more important cases involving honor students." He started walking away again, up the street. "You know how many black teenage gang members and hookers end up dead without more than a line of copy in your newspaper?"

"What about Heather Gerber?" Susan asked, struggling to get her notebook out as she caught up with him. Heather had been Gretchen's first victim. A runaway. A street kid. A prostitute. They had found her dead in the park, too. The *Herald* had certainly run stories about her.

Henry stuffed his hands into his pockets and picked up the pace. The sidewalk was wet and his shoes slapped against the standing water as he walked. "Your paper couldn't have cared less about Heather Gerber until Archie made the connection to the other bodies and everyone realized there was a serial killer loose. She was just another Jane Doe. Then Parker ran a story about her.

The kid's foster parents saw it. Turns out she'd been missing a year, and they'd never reported it. Just kept cashing the checks. You know who paid to have her buried?"

"No." The sidewalk was uphill. The street was parallel to the edge of the park and the houses on it abutted the forest. You couldn't build houses this close to the park anymore, but these were old and grandfathered in. Their porch lights revealed large wooden porches with porch swings and pots of geraniums. The air smelled like black-berries.

"Archie did." Then he added, by way of an explanation, "She was his first homicide."

"That case is still technically unsolved, isn't it?" Susan asked.

"Gretchen did it," Henry said. "She just hasn't admitted it yet."

A Subaru wagon parked on the street up ahead and a man in running clothes unloaded two large dogs and headed toward the park for a night jog. "Is that why Archie kept going back to see her, all that time? Because he wanted to close that first case?"

Henry was quiet for a moment. "No."

Susan wondered how much Archie talked to Henry about Gretchen. She'd seen the way he reacted when Gretchen had touched Archie's arm at the interrogation session

Susan had witnessed when she was writing the profile. Henry had been in the room in an instant, pulling Gretchen away from Archie, like she was something infectious. Susan had been terrified of her, and at the same time captivated by Gretchen and Archie's casual rapport. There was an intimacy to their relationship that was unsettling at best.

The sidewalk was old, buckled around tree roots, and Susan and Henry walked carefully, their eyes on the ground.

"We should never have agreed to the plea bargain," Henry said, almost to himself. "We should have let Washington State prosecute. She'd be dead by now."

"Archie closed thirty-one more cases," Susan said.

Henry stopped. They were at the house, a brown clapboard behemoth that looked like it had been built in the forties. She could see his face a little in the light of the streetlamp. He looked tired, shoulders hunched, his leather jacket shiny from the rain. "You didn't know him before," he said.

It was hard to imagine Archie ever being very happy.

"Parker wrote a lot about the Beauty Killer case, didn't he?" Susan asked.

"Hundreds of stories over the years,"

Henry said with a shrug. "Jesus, probably thousands."

Parker was old-school. He'd have used a typewriter if they'd let him. He probably had notes. Boxes of notes. They would be invaluable to someone who, say, wanted to write a book about the Beauty Killer case someday. Once the Molly Palmer story ran, she'd have some sway at the paper. She might be able to take a sabbatical.

"Do you remember him ever mentioning where he kept his notes?" Susan asked.

Henry looked at her for a moment and then raised his eyebrows and sighed. "I almost forgot," he said. He pulled a badge out of his pocket and snapped it open. Then he shone his flashlight at Susan's face.

She cringed, momentarily blinded, and lifted a hand over her face. "Forgot what?" she asked.

"That you care about stories more than people," Henry said. He snapped the light off. "Let me do the talking," he said, and he knocked on the door.

They waited in silence, while Susan fumed. She hadn't meant to be insensitive. She *did* care about Archie. She wasn't trying to write something trashy. That had been done already. She wanted to write a real book. A smart, compelling, illuminating book. Was that so terrible?

"I didn't mean to —" she started to say.

Henry held up his hand. "Stop," he said.

A porch light came on, splashing yellow light into the darkness. The front door opened and an elderly woman appeared. She wore her gray hair loose and was wearing a wool button-down shirt decorated with Indian totems.

"Yes?" she said.

Henry stepped forward and showed her his badge. "Hello, ma'am. I'm Detective Sobol. I was hoping to ask you a couple of questions." He smiled amiably. "Do you live here?"

"Yes, son," she said, her pale blue eyes alert and amused. "For fifty-four years now."

"Have you noticed anything strange lately?" Henry asked. He ran a hand over his bald head. "Activity in the woods?"

The folds in her face deepened. "Is this connected to the senator's death?"

"No, ma'am," he said. "We've found some remains in the woods."

"What sort of remains?" she asked.

Henry cleared his throat. "Human."

The old woman turned and craned her head back toward the park. Then she looked over at Susan. Susan tried to smile amiably, too. "Is this your wife?" the woman asked Henry.

Susan laughed out loud.

"No, ma'am," Henry said. "She's a reporter."

Susan held up her notebook and wiggled her other hand in hello.

Henry continued, shifting his weight uncomfortably. "Notice anything out of the ordinary? Hear anything? Smell anything?"

Missing any relatives, Susan thought but didn't say.

The woman considered Henry's questions. "Bill has been acting strange lately."

"Is that your husband?" Henry asked.

"My standard poodle," she said.

Susan saw the corners of Henry's mouth twitch up for an instant. "Strange, how?" Henry asked.

The woman frowned. "He just stands in front of his doghouse. Barks some. Won't let me near it."

"Do you let him run loose in the woods?" Henry asked.

"He jumps the fence sometimes," she said. "Always comes back, though."

"Where is Bill now?" Henry asked.

She motioned for them to follow, and then led them around down an old brick path that ran along the side of the house. She was wearing sheepskin boots, and Susan noticed Henry move close in behind her, in case the old woman slipped on the uneven wet bricks. The path was lit with solar yard lights that cast a pale blue glow, but did little to provide illumination. However, the woman was steady on her feet and didn't miss a step.

They came to a gate in the cedar fence that boxed in the backyard and the woman opened it, and the gate swung in with a rusty sigh. There weren't any lights back there and it was dark. Henry snapped his flashlight back on as the woman disappeared into the blackness.

"Ma'am?" Henry said.

A floodlight turned on, revealing an ivy-clotted backyard, and the woman appeared on her back stoop.

"Bill," she said to the backyard, "I've brought a friend to meet you."

Susan searched the yard for the poodle. The ivy from the park had crawled over the fence and snaked halfway across the yard. It was like some sort of intractable green tide. You could chop it back, sure, but it would just keep creeping forward, an inch a day, until it covered everything again. Susan heard a dog bark and she realized that the doghouse was half-covered with ivy, too. A large black poodle stood in the doghouse's open doorway. The dog had been recently groomed and his coat had been trimmed into a series of lumps and balls, a weird living topiary.

Susan saw Henry wince. "Is Bill friendly?" he asked.

"As a lamb," the woman said.

Henry shook his head, set his shoulders, and walked toward the doghouse.

Bill growled.

Henry stopped. "As a lamb?" he asked.

"Don't let him intimidate you, son," the woman said. "You don't have a cat, do you?"

"I have three cats," Henry said.

The woman clucked. "Bill doesn't like cats," she said ominously.

"Susan?" Henry called. "A little help?"

Susan had never had any pets. She hesitated. "I'm not good with dogs," she said.

"Get the hell over here," Henry said.

Susan walked slowly over to the poodle. "Hi, Bill," she said. "Good Bill." She reached out to let the dog smell her hand. "Nice Bill."

"You probably don't want to touch him," the old woman called from the porch.

Susan froze and the dog looked at her outstretched hand and bared his teeth. He didn't growl. He didn't make a sound.

"He's probably scared of your hair," Henry said, as he attempted to squeeze his large frame around the dog far enough that he could aim his flashlight around to see inside the doghouse. He got down on his hands and knees and managed to wedge himself halfway into the doghouse. Then he backed out, sat down next to the dog, and punched a number into his cell phone.

"Archie," he said into the phone. "It's me. The blonde." He rubbed his face with his hand. "Is she missing an arm?"

Susan heard Archie's voice say, "Yeah."

Henry glanced back over his shoulder into the doghouse. Then he looked at Susan. The dog growled and eyed them both suspiciously. "I found it," Henry said.

CHAPTER
12

The old woman's name was Trudy Schuyler. Susan had filled a few pages of her notebook with information about her. Her husband had died five years before. She didn't have a wood chipper. She didn't know a kid who fit the description of the kid Archie had seen in the woods. She had been a meter maid, but she had retired twenty years before. She had three grown children. The cops had taken the dog into custody so they could monitor its output, lest the furry topiary had managed to digest a clue or two while gnawing on the dead woman's radius bone. With this in mind, they had started bagging dog shit from the yard. That was about the time that Susan left.

There wasn't that much going on at the *Herald* building at 1:00 A.M. The ambulance chasers who'd been on hand to help put together the issue on Castle and Parker were all tucked neatly in bed. Even the janitors were done for the day. A security guard had let Susan in through the loading dock entrance. She had taken the elevator up to the fifth floor, where Ian was already huddled in his office with a copy editor, a headline editor, a designer, and a photo editor, all of whom had been called in to help pull the story together. They all looked tired and a little annoyed. Susan was trying not to look tired and annoyed. She was trying to look cheery. She had pissed Ian off enough already. And pissing Ian off was not going to get the Molly Palmer story published. Being nice might help. It was so crazy, it just might work.

The late filing was called a "hot chase," meaning that as soon as Susan was done with the story, they would stop the presses, slip in a new plate, and then continue the press run. She'd have a story in the Dead Senator issue after all. Just not the story she wanted.

Susan started to walk over to Ian's office, but Ian saw her through his office's glass wall. He held up a hand for her to stop, then pointed to his watch, and then to her desk.

She obediently walked over to her desk, threw her purse at her feet, set her notebook next to her keyboard, and called Molly Palmer. Nothing. If Ian was going to run the story, Susan knew it had to be solid, triple-checked, every *i* dotted. She left a voice mail. "Seriously, Molly," Susan said. "You need to call me back." She wrapped the phone cord around her finger, circling the knuckle so tight that the finger started to turn red. "It's going to be okay. He's dead. Let's go public with this." She thought of the ensuing press mayhem Molly was sure to endure. "You care about stories more than people," Henry had said.

Susan bit her lip. "If you want to drop out for a while, fine," she said into the phone. "But I need you to talk to some people first, okay?" Susan disentangled her finger and hung up. The lights weren't all on and the floor was quiet and you had to look hard to see across the room. Besides the huddle in Ian's office, the only other human being on the floor was a guy from sports, who sat wearing headphones and keyboarding something even he didn't seem interested in.

She began to type furiously. The Jane Doe. The two new bodies. The possibility of a Forest Park serial killer. It was the kind of story that Parker would have loved. Thinking of him made her pause, fingers poised over the keyboard, and she glanced up from her computer monitor to the lights on the West Hills outside the *Herald*'s large windows.

She glanced back at Parker's desk. There were two new bouquets of flowers. It was starting to look like a grave. Susan got up and went into the break room and dug around in the kitchenette cabinets until she found a glass vase, a coffee can, and three tall water glasses. She filled them with water and took a few trips to carry them back to Parker's desk. She did her best to arrange the wilted flowers in the vessels, but the stems were soft and the flowers drooped forlornly over the sides.

The flowers made her think of Archie Sheridan, whose yard was buried in floral arrangements during the ten days he was missing, and how Debbie Sheridan had once told her that she couldn't stand the smell of flowers anymore. They made her think of death.

Susan sat down in Parker's task chair, rolling in small circles, trying to get into his head, to figure out how he'd write the Forest Park murders story, when her knee bumped against Parker's desk's filing drawer. Each desk had one. They were always kept locked. Susan kept her key under a mug full of pens on her desk. She had learned that from Parker.

She reached out and lifted up the Hooters' mug of number two pencils that sat on

Parker's desk, revealing a tiny silver key. Then she put the key in the file drawer lock and turned it. It opened. Inside, toward the front of the drawer, were thickly packed files marked with names that Susan recognized as being connected to stories that Parker covered. She walked her fingers along the files until she came to a large, black three-ring binder that had been jammed in the back of the drawer. There was a label on the spine, and in Parker's slanted handwriting, the words "Beauty Killer."

Jackpot.

She pulled the binder out of the drawer, locked it, replaced the key, and carried the heavy binder over to her desk, just as Ian popped his head out of his office and hollered, "I'd like to get some sleep tonight."

"Almost done," Susan said. She slipped the binder onto the floor next to her purse, resting one foot on it protectively. Her face was flushed with excitement, but it was dark and Susan didn't think that Ian could tell.

CHAPTER
13

Archie still wasn't sure if he'd agreed to let Sarah Rosenberg treat him because he needed the help, or because he wanted an excuse to sit in the room where Gretchen Lowell had drugged him and taken him captive.

This was his Monday morning ritual. No more Sundays at the state pen with the Beauty Killer, but every Monday he spent an hour sitting across from Gretchen's big wooden desk. In one of her overstuffed striped chairs. He watched her grandfather clock, the time still stuck at 3:30. He looked between the heavy green velvet curtains, out to the cherry trees thick with green leaves outside her window.

Only none of it was Gretchen's. She had rented the house under a false name from a psychologist who was spending the season in Italy. It had been the last place the police could trace Archie to. But by then, Gretchen had already taken him to another house. The psychologist, Dr. Sarah Rosenberg, and her family came back; the carpet, onto which Archie had spilled his drugged coffee, had been replaced.

"I want to talk about Gretchen Lowell today," Rosenberg said.

It was their fourth session. It was the first time she had mentioned Gretchen. Archie had admired her restraint. He took a slow sip of the paper cup of coffee he held on the arm of the chair. "Okay," he said. He felt warm and pleasant, just high enough that he could relax, and not high enough that Rosenberg would notice.

Rosenberg smiled. She was lean with dark curly hair she wore back in a low ponytail, maybe a little older than Archie, though he probably looked older to anyone guessing. He liked her. She was better than the department shrink he'd seen for six months. But then, for some reason, Archie was always more comfortable talking to women.

"I want to talk about the six weeks you knew her before she revealed who she was," she said.

It was something the department didn't like to talk about, the fact that Gretchen had infiltrated the investigation for that long before she revealed herself. It didn't make them look exactly sharp. Archie sighed and looked behind Rosenberg, out the window. "She just showed up one day," he said. "She said she was a psychiatrist. She ran a couple of group counseling sessions. I also conferred with her about the profile." He rubbed the back of his neck and smiled. The smell of coffee wafted up from the cup. He brought the coffee because when he didn't he thought sometimes he could still smell the lilacs. "She seemed to have some insights," he said.

Rosenberg sat in the other striped chair, where Gretchen used to sit. She crossed her legs and leaned forward. "Like what?" she asked.

A squirrel bolted up one of the cherry trees, sending the leaves rippling. Archie took another sip of coffee and then rested it back on the arm of the chair. "She was the first person who suggested that the killer might be a woman," he said.

Rosenberg kept a yellow legal pad on her lap and she wrote something down on it. She was wearing black slacks and a green turtleneck and yellow socks the same color as the notebook. "What was your reaction to that?" she asked.

Archie noticed that his left leg had developed a restless bounce. He pushed his heel into the floor. "We had exhausted pretty much everything else," he said.

"Did she offer individual counseling?" Rosenberg asked.

"Yes," Archie said.

"Did she counsel you?" she asked.

He inched the pillbox out of his pocket and held it in his fist on his lap. "Yes."

"Just you?"

"Yes." If Rosenberg noticed the box, she didn't say anything.

"What did you two talk about?" she asked.

"The same stuff you and I do," Archie said. "My work." In fact he'd been more up front with Gretchen. He had shared everything. The stress of the investigation. The pressure it put on his relationship with Debbie. "My marriage."

Rosenberg raised an eyebrow. "It must have been quite upsetting to realize that you had shared all of those personal thoughts with a killer."

Quite upsetting. That was one way of putting it. The funny thing was, at the time, it had been nice to have someone to talk to. Too bad she carved people up for fun. "She was a good listener," Archie said.

"So you spent more time with her than the others did," Rosenberg said, her pen poised over the notebook.

"Yes," Archie said. "I guess so."

"Where did you have your counseling sessions?" she asked.

Archie lifted a hand. "Right here."

Rosenberg sat up and looked around her home office. "I understand why she would consult with you about a case here, but that's unusual. That she would actually treat you in her home."

"Why?" Archie asked. "You do."

"I'm a psychologist," Rosenberg said. "She said she was a psychiatrist." She wrote something on the legal pad, shaking her head.

"She wasn't really a psychiatrist," Archie reminded her.

Rosenberg looked up from the legal pad. "Did you ever suspect her?" she asked.

There went the leg again. Archie didn't bother to stop it. It felt good, somewhere for the nervous energy to go. He lifted his cup of coffee, but didn't take a drink. "About the time the paralytic drug she slipped in my coffee kicked in," he said. He set the paper coffee cup on the floor, opened the pillbox on his lap, removed a pill, and swallowed it.

"What was that?" Rosenberg asked.

"An Altoid," Archie said.

Rosenberg smiled. "I'm not sure you're supposed to swallow those."

Archie smiled back. "I was hungry."

Rosenberg leaned forward and then uncrossed and crossed her legs again. "I can't help you if you're not honest with me," she said.

Archie looked down at his hands. Sometimes he thought he could still see the faint tan line where his wedding ring had been. "I think about her sometimes," he said softly.

"About Gretchen Lowell," Rosenberg said.

Archie looked up. "I fantasize about fucking her," he said.

Rosenberg laid the pen down on the pad. "She held you captive for ten days," she said. "You were powerless. Perhaps your fantasies are a way of having power over her."

"So it's perfectly healthy," Archie said.

"It's understandable," Rosenberg said. "I didn't say it was healthy." She reached across and put a hand on Archie's forearm. She wore rings on all her fingers. "Do you want to get past this? To give up the pills? To get over what happened to you? To be happy with your family?"

"Yes," Archie said.

"That's the first step."

Archie rubbed the back of his neck. "How many are there?"

Rosenberg smiled. "One less."

■ ■ ■ ■

There were five Vicodin lined up like little piano keys on Archie's office desk. Archie swept them into his hand and washed them down with the dregs of the cold coffee he had left from his session with Rosenberg.

It was mid-morning and they were still waiting on the crime lab report on the new bodies. Archie glanced down at Susan Ward's story in the *Herald* in his lap. MYSTERY KID LEADS COPS TO NEW BODIES. It didn't even make the front page. It was in the Metro section, dwarfed by ongoing coverage of the senator's death. Maybe the mystery kid's parents would see the story and piece it together. Archie wanted to at least prove to Henry that he wasn't going crazy. In the meantime they had the standard poodle in custody. On the off chance he passed any clues.

Archie touched his right side, where his persistent cramp had returned. The Vicodin didn't seem to help.

He opened his desk drawer, and there was Gretchen. He'd gone back to the log the night before for the book. He'd told himself he didn't want to litter, didn't want one of the crime techs to find it, that he wanted the closure of lighting the thing on fire, et cetera.

121

Then why had he brought it to his office, brushed the mud off, and put it in his desk drawer?

Raul Sanchez poked his head in Archie's office door, and Archie slammed the drawer shut. Sanchez had foregone his FBI cap and windbreaker for a brown suit and tie. You almost couldn't tell it was a clip-on. "Meeting with the mayor," he explained. "They're already planning a public funeral for Castle down at the Waterfront. Speakers. Tents. The whole enchilada." He smiled at the enchilada line. "Traffic downtown is gonna be fucked."

"I'll make a note to be out of town," Archie said. Watching people weep over Castle was a little more than Archie could bear right now.

"You going to Parker's service?" Sanchez asked.

"Yeah," Archie said. Parker's funeral was that afternoon. No tents for that one. No crowd control. His family must have moved mountains to make arrangements that fast. Archie thought he knew why.

Sanchez hesitated, then rubbed the back of his neck. "His blood alcohol was .24." He looked up meaningfully at Archie, then scratched his bearded chin. "Thought you'd want to know."

Archie closed his eyes. "Fuck." They were getting him in the ground just in time.

"We'll wait until after his funeral," Sanchez said. "Make it public tomorrow."

"Thanks," Archie said.

Sanchez turned to go.

"You got my message about why Parker was meeting with Castle?" Archie asked. "Susan Ward's story?"

"Crazy shit," Sanchez said, turning back. He shrugged. "Doesn't change the blood test, though."

Archie sighed and leaned back in his chair, hands folded across his chest. The brass pillbox pressed against his thigh. Gretchen Lowell smiled in his desk drawer. "No," he said.

Susan fiddled with the white piping of her brown dress. She had decided against black. It was too funereal. The brown dress was vintage, A-line, cap-sleeved, with white piping and two big white buttons on the chest. She had clipped her turquoise hair at the back of her neck. It seemed too colorful somehow, disrespectful of the occasion.

There were a fair amount of people in the church, probably a couple hundred. Susan recognized many faces from the paper. The wooden pews were full, and it was standing room only in the back. The rain had passed and sun streamed in through the stained-glass windows, throwing colored trapezoids of light on the wooden floor.

Parker was at the front of the church, in a glazed ceramic urn.

Susan was sitting in the third row. She'd arrived early. Susan was almost never early. But she'd arrived an hour before the funeral, and after twenty minutes crying in her car in the parking lot she came inside and got a place up front.

She saw Derek, sitting in the back with some other city beat reporters. He tried to catch her eye, but she avoided him.

Then she saw Archie Sheridan come in with his family and sit a few rows behind her across the aisle. He was wearing a black suit and shiny black shoes and sat with his arm around his ex-wife, who was wearing a black sleeveless dress that showed off her lean, tan arms. His son was wearing a gray suit and the little girl was wearing a gray eyelet dress. They looked like a photo spread of what to wear to a funeral.

Susan looked down at her own ensemble. She looked like she worked at Mr. Steak.

The *Herald*'s publisher, Howard Jenkins, gave the eulogy. A few of the older reporters at the paper spoke. There weren't many left.

Most *Herald* employees over fifty were offered buyout options to retire so the paper could save on pensions.

Parker was an institution. Parker was a reporter's reporter. Parker was a muckraker, a local hero, a warrior for the afflicted, a champ, a gem, employee of the fucking year.

God, it was all such bullshit. Susan got up, squeezed past forty knees, feet, and purses, and walked as fast as she could out the door, into the hallway, down the carpeted stairs, and out of the church.

The old stone church had a courtyard that overlooked the park blocks. A few tables, fluttering with pink paper tablecloths, had been set up for the postfuneral reception. There was a large silver urn of coffee and a glass bowl of fruit punch. Several plates of deviled eggs sat spoiling in the sun. And bottles of Wild Turkey were lined up five deep. Susan smiled.

On the other side of the street, in the park, people streamed by, walking. Lunchtime traffic clogged the street. Susan's hands were shaking.

Archie Sheridan appeared at the door she'd just fled through. "You okay?" he asked quietly.

Susan turned her head, embarrassed, and dug through her purse. "I just needed a cigarette," she said, coming up with the yellow pack.

Archie walked down the stone steps and leaned against the church wall next to her while she found her lighter.

"Parker was legally drunk when he drove off the bridge," he said. "They're making it public tomorrow."

Susan held the lighter to the end of her cigarette. The flame licked and jumped, then flattened as she inhaled. It was bound to come up, but she was still sorry that it had. "Parker was *always* legally drunk," she said. "You know that." She dropped the lighter back into her purse. "He was an alcoholic."

Archie put his hands in his pockets and stared at the cobblestones. "His blood alcohol was .24, Susan."

Organ music started in the church. "When the Saints Go Marching In." Susan hadn't even known Parker was religious.

She shook her head. This was insane. They couldn't blame this on Parker. It was Castle. He was the predator, the asshole, the perv; Parker was a victim. "What about Castle?" she asked. "He could have still grabbed the wheel."

"Castle's tox screen came back clean," Archie said. "There's no lab test for suicidal impulses."

The organ music swelled as the side church door opened. A few people wandered down the stairs into the courtyard. Then a few more. Susan watched as they walked over to the deviled eggs and began eating them, seemingly without concern about salmonella. A sixtyish woman came up to Archie and he kissed her on the cheek.

"Margery," he said. "I'm so sorry."

It was Parker's wife. Susan had never met her, but she'd seen her in the church, along with her two thirtysomething daughters, and put it together. Parker had said that his daughters looked like his wife, and he was right. They were all thick-haired women with long necks and erect posture and large eyes that darted back and forth behind heavy bangs. Margery's hair was silver, her daughters' brown.

Margery wiped a smear of deviled egg off her mouth. "It was nice of you to come," she said to Archie. She hugged him, first lifting her thick braid and putting it back behind a shoulder. Then she smiled at Susan. She had pale blue eyes, like Parker's, and her pale skin paired with her silver hair made her look almost albino.

"You're Susan," she said.

"How did you know?" Susan asked. She reached up and touched her turquoise hair.

127

"Oh, right."

"Quentin thought the world of you."

Susan felt her eyes burn. "I liked him, too," she said. She slid a look at Archie, wanting him to signal to her that he would protect Parker's memory, protect his family from the implication that Parker was at fault.

But Archie was looking past them both to where Debbie stood with the two children near the exit of the courtyard.

"I've got to go," he said.

"Working a case?" Margery asked.

"It's my daughter's birthday," Archie said.

CHAPTER
14

The cardboard pirate hats came flat, so Archie had to fold them into shape and then fit them on each of the heads of the ten first-grade girls, securing them with elastic bands under their chins. There were Mardi Gras beads and Jolly Roger flags and chocolate wrapped up to look like gold coins. The girls mostly forwent the black plastic eye patches. Where Sara got it in her head to have a pirate-themed birthday party, Archie had no idea.

The girls were having a very complicated pretend sword fight in the living room with, apparently, the sofa standing in for a ship. Debbie was plying the parents with wine in the kitchen. Ben had sequestered himself in his room. Archie was on kid patrol, and stood with his arms folded, leaning against the doorway, watching the girl pirates go to war with the pillows.

Sara whispered something in another

pirate's ear and then came running over, slamming against his thighs. "Daddy," she said breathlessly. "We need you to be a bad pirate."

Archie knelt down so that he was her height. "I presume that you are all good pirates?"

"Yes," she said.

"And I'm supposed to fight you?" he asked.

Sara leaned forward with a concerned expression and whispered: "Do you know how to be a pirate?"

Archie stood and picked up a large rubber pirate knife that was displayed on the snack table and he put it in his mouth and said, "Arrrr," and charged the sofa. The little girls screamed and scattered and then swarmed around him giggling.

Then he heard Debbie's voice say: "Henry's here."

He looked up, still laughing, and saw Henry standing with Debbie in the doorway. "You're late," Archie said, smiling. Then he noticed that his friend hadn't taken off his shoulder holster. Henry knew the rules about guns in the house. So that could only mean one thing. "And you're not staying."

Sara saw Henry, too, and sprang from the sofa and ran over to him, wrapping her arms around his waist. "Henry!" she cried, delighted. Henry hugged her back and produced a small, poorly wrapped gift from his pocket and gave it to her. "I just wanted to drop this by," he said. "Happy birthday."

She beamed and wrapped her arms around his neck and kissed him and then scampered back to the sofa-ship.

Henry raised his eyebrows at Archie. "Can we talk?" he said.

Archie could tell from the heaviness of Henry's gaze that it was bad news. He had been happy for a minute, he thought. That was his mistake.

He handed the rubber sword to Sara and disentwined himself from the girls. They immediately fell behind him and began organizing a plank-walking.

Debbie stood in the doorway, next to Henry, arms crossed. As Archie walked over to him he felt the pain below his ribs start to throb.

"What's going on?" Archie asked.

Henry hesitated. "There's been an incident at the prison."

The pain was gone. Archie straightened up an iota. "Is she okay?"

Henry leaned forward and lowered his voice, so Archie had to strain to hear him above the girls' giggling. "She's in the infirmary. She was assaulted. It's bad, Archie. We've got a real situation."

Archie was suddenly aware then of Debbie standing beside them. She was perfectly still for a long moment and then, slowly, she reached her hand out and touched Henry's arm. "Don't," she said to Henry. "Don't do this. Not today."

Henry sighed and shook his head. "It was a guard," he explained. "We need her to tell us which one. She'll only talk to Archie."

"No," Debbie said. She turned to Archie. "It's your daughter's birthday party. Henry can handle it."

Archie took her hands in his and looked her in the eyes, the mother of his children, and he tried to explain: "She's my responsibility."

Debbie closed her eyes. And then let her hands fall away from his and turned to the girls. She clapped her hands.

"Who wants cake?" she asked.

The Oregon State Pen was a compound of fat-colored buildings sequestered behind a stucco-coated brick wall topped with razor wire. The prison was an hour south of Portland, in Salem, surrounded by twenty-two acres of green fields just off the highway. It housed both male and female inmates and was the state's only maximum-security prison. Archie and Henry had spent so much time there since Gretchen's capture that they knew every hallway, every guard.

The infirmary, a long, windowless room about forty feet by thirty, was in the center of the main building. The concrete walls were painted gray and the floor was a splatter-patterned linoleum. It was bare-bones. There were no pictures on the walls to make you feel better. The room had four beds, each with its own privacy curtain. The faint odor of sweat and blood and defecation permeated everything.

A prison nurse, dressed in scrubs, sat behind the nose-high desk near the door. He glanced up, saw their prison-issue ID badges, and glanced back down at the chart he was reading. Archie walked past to the back of the room, where he could see a guard. Gretchen always traveled with a guard.

He was not prepared for what he saw when he came around the curtain. Gretchen was restrained in the bed, her wrists and ankles secured with leather cuffs. Her head was turned to the side, and her eyes were closed. She was wearing a hospital gown and Archie could see deep bruises on both of her slender arms. Hematomas. The skin swollen, darkened with broken blood vessels. They had found her in her room like that. Curled up on the floor. A rape kit had been positive for semen. It made Archie sick to think about it.

"Give us a minute," Henry said to the guard.

The guard shook his head slowly. "I'm supposed to stay with her."

Henry tilted his head at Gretchen's prone body. "She's tied to a bed, Andy. Give us a minute."

The guard glanced at Gretchen's prone, bruised body. "I'll wait by the door, if you need anything," he said.

Archie moved around the bed to an aluminum chair and sat down. Gretchen didn't stir. He reached out and wrapped his hand around hers. Her hand felt cool and delicate.

Her eyelids fluttered open and she smiled when she saw him. "So this is what it takes to get your attention?" she said weakly. An IV morphine drip was taped to her arm and her cadence was slow and careful.

"Who did this to you?" Archie asked softly.

Her blue eyes moved to Henry. Archie knew she wanted Henry out of the room, but he wasn't about to ask him. He knew Henry wouldn't go.

"Tell me who did this," Archie said again.

She raised an eyebrow. "That would be a breach of prison etiquette."

"Oh, for fuck's sake," Henry said.

Archie shot Henry a look. "Let me worry about that," he said to Gretchen.

"Are you concerned about me?" she asked, appraising him. "That's sweet, darling. But your job isn't to protect me." She lowered her voice to a faux conspiratorial tone. "It's to protect people from me."

"Don't misunderstand my interest," Archie said. "You're a ward of the state. I'm an employee of the state. Until we've located everyone you've murdered, your well-being is in the state's interest."

"So romantic," she said with a sigh. She turned her head toward Henry. She had made an art out of ignoring him. She had never responded to anything he'd said, and had carried on whole conversations with Archie as if Henry weren't even present. "Tell me something, darling," she said, looking at Henry but talking to Archie. "Can you feel that your spleen is gone? Does it hurt?"

"Not anymore," Archie answered.

"I think about that," Gretchen said dreamily. "Having my hands inside you. You were so warm and sticky. I can still smell you, your blood. Do you remember?"

Archie ran a hand over his face. "I lost consciousness," he reminded her quietly.

She smiled. "I regret that. I wanted to keep you awake. I wanted you to remember. I'm the only one who's ever been that far inside you."

"You and the team of trauma surgeons at Emanuel."

"Yes." She laughed and the effort caused her to wince in pain.

"They told me that he broke four of your ribs," Archie said. His own ribs still ached sometimes, where Gretchen had driven a nail through his rib cage.

"Every time I breathe, I think of you."

"Tell me who it was," he said.

"You've moved back in with her, haven't you?"

The question caught Archie by surprise. Debbie often talked about Gretchen as if she were his mistress. But to Archie it sometimes felt like the other way around. As if, by moving back in with his ex-wife, he was cheating on Gretchen.

That was probably worthy of bringing up in therapy.

Gretchen was waiting for him to answer. Her beautiful eyes shimmered. She looked hurt. It was all an act, of course. Everything

Gretchen did was an act.

"Yes," Archie said.

She slid him a slow, wicked look and whispered: "But you still haven't fucked her."

Archie stopped breathing.

"That's it," Henry said.

Archie heard the door to the infirmary open and male voices and the smack of footsteps against the linoleum.

"Archie," Henry warned.

Archie saw the same thing Henry did — his and Gretchen's hands intertwined. But he still couldn't move. He saw Gretchen smile sweetly at Henry. It was a smile Archie knew. It meant, Fuck you. And still Archie didn't move.

Henry's voice was a harsh whisper: "Goddamn it, Archie."

It was like a switch had been thrown. Archie snapped his hand back and pushed the chair back a foot, threading his fingers behind his neck just as the warden and two guards entered.

"Gentlemen," the warden said. "I've got something you should see."

Henry waited until Archie and the others had cleared the curtain on their way out of the room. Then he lifted himself off the wall he had been leaning against and took a step toward the bed.

"It's funny," he said to Gretchen. "How he beat the shit out of you. And somehow didn't touch your face."

She stared back at him, expressionless, that way she had of seeing right through you. It wasn't just Henry. She didn't have time for anyone but Archie.

"You think this will get him back here?" Henry said. "That he'll be at your beck and call again? You're wrong. He'll see through it."

She just blinked.

He turned and took a step to catch up with the others.

"Henry," she said.

He froze at the sound of her voice saying his name. He turned back. She tilted her head and raised an eyebrow. "It will be interesting to see which one of us knows him better," she said.

Christ, she was smug. Henry had spent years blaming himself. For not suspecting Gretchen in the first place. For not finding Archie sooner. For endorsing the insane plea bargain that would send his friend into her clutches week after week. He had known Archie before. He knew how he had changed. The plea bargain wasn't worth it. It didn't matter how many bodies she could produce. Gretchen Lowell was a poster girl for the death penalty. He learned forward. "Whoever did this to you," he said flatly, "deserves a fucking medal."

Archie appeared around the curtain. "You coming?"

Henry straightened up, flustered. "Yeah," he said. He followed Archie around the curtain. Out of the corner of his eye, Henry thought he'd seen Gretchen wink at Archie, but he couldn't be sure.

CHAPTER
15

The guard hadn't been dead long. But it was long enough. He'd hung himself in the locker room, one of the few spaces in the prison without security cameras. It was a thin, long room, now crowded with people standing close, but not too close, to the body that was hanging from an overhead sewer pipe.

"His name is B. D. Cavanaugh," the warden said to Archie. "He's been here nine years. Clean file."

Hanging was the second most popular means of suicide in the U.S., after guns. Archie didn't see the appeal. It was too hard to control. Sure, if you were lucky, your spinal cord snapped, and you were dead in an instant. Even in the absence of a fracture, obstruction of the carotid arteries or vagal collapse could lead to a relatively peaceful death. Quick unconsciousness, followed by a massive coronary. But if you were unlucky, your neck didn't snap, and your carotid arteries kept pumping and you died a slow, agonizing death from strangulation.

The guard hadn't been lucky. His face was engorged and discolored, his eyes filled with blood, his tongue protruded between blue lips, and a stream of sweet-smelling urine ran down the tan pants of his uniform and pooled where his toe brushed the carpet below.

"He the guy who assaulted Gretchen?" Archie asked. The smell of urine mixed with the pungent floral-mothball bouquet of pink urinal cakes.

"He had access," the warden said. "He was on shift. And look at his hands."

The guard's fingertips were blue, and his forearms were webbed with fine red scratches.

The warden's gaze drifted to where the bulge of the guard's erection pressed against his pants. He cleared his throat. "You ever seen anything like that?"

"It's caused by blood pooling in the lower half of the body," Archie said matter-of-factly. "Tissues expand to their maximum capacity. It'll go down as soon as he's horizontal."

"So it's not a woody?"

"Get a penis swab," Archie said. "I want a

DNA match to the rape kit."

Archie wasn't sure what he'd expected to feel when faced with Gretchen's attacker. But he felt unsatisfied faced with this dangling corpse. Because he couldn't throw him against a wall? Arrest him? Because he couldn't be Gretchen's white knight?

Archie couldn't shake the feeling of responsibility for what had happened. Gretchen wasn't in the women's prison. She was on the solitary ward, which was on the men's section of the campus, so her guards were mostly male. Gretchen was slender, but she was dangerous. She had found a hundred different ways to kill people. But the guard was big, two hundred forty at least, and Archie could see how he might have overpowered her.

"He used a choke hold," the warden said. "Cracked her collarbone. The doc thinks she was unconscious through most of it."

"Jesus," Archie said.

"And then he offs himself?" Henry said with a snort. "Convenient." Archie threw him a look. "What?" Henry said. "You think she's not capable of setting this up?"

"She's a victim until proven otherwise."

Henry lifted his chin toward the body. "Divorced recently?" he asked the warden.

The warden nodded. "His wife left him last year."

Henry looked at Archie. "Fits her profile."

Gretchen had used the Internet to troll for lonely men whom she could manipulate. She traveled with them for a while, got them to kill for her, and then executed them. She'd done it at least three times. It wasn't out of the realm of possibility that she'd somehow convinced this man to die for her, or because of her. "He leave a note?" Archie asked.

The warden lifted his eyebrows toward the bathroom, which was directly off the locker room. Archie and Henry followed him in. The bathroom had two showers, three toilet stalls, a row of urinals, and a counter with two sinks and, above it, a mirror onto which someone had drawn, with a felt-tip marker, a heart.

Archie realized that he had subconsciously lifted his hand to the heart scar on his chest, the skin raised beneath the cotton cloth of his shirt. He forced his hand into his pocket, only to find the pillbox.

"It's her signature, right?" the warden was saying. "A heart?"

"Right," Archie said. He pulled the pillbox out, opened it, put three pills in his mouth and swallowed them. His hand was trembling. "You need to rotate all her

143

guards. It was a mistake to allow her contact with men. She's assigned women, from now on." He held the pillbox out to the warden. "Tic Tacs," Archie said. "Want one?"

The warden looked at Archie strangely and shook his head.

Archie glanced up at his own reflection, framed in the inked heart. "It's my fault," he said. "I should have paid more attention. I should have been here more."

"She's playing you," Henry said softly.

"I needed a break," Archie said to his reflection, trying to convince himself. "I can handle it now." He turned to the warden. "Go through the security logs. Review footage. Interview your staff. I want to know if they had a relationship."

The warden's ruddy skin colored with the realization of what Archie was driving at. "You think she was fucking him all along?" he asked.

Archie felt his stomach clench. It felt a little bit like jealousy. "You better hope not," he said.

CHAPTER
16

Archie had the TV on in his home office, without the volume. It was the first TV he and Debbie had bought together, for their first apartment, back in college. A twenty-seven-inch color Panasonic. It had seemed extravagant then. Now it just looked sort of old and clunky. Debbie had bought a flat screen for the living room. But Archie couldn't bear to part with the old TV. It had sentimental value.

He had turned on the local news in hopes that there would be some coverage of the remains in the park, but the news had been preempted by continuing coverage of the circus surrounding the senator's death. They were already talking about changing the name of the airport to Castle International.

Archie wondered what Molly Palmer thought of that.

He had pulled four cardboard file boxes full of missing persons reports out of the closet, and was unpacking the contents of one onto his desk. There were 108 files, all people who had gone missing in the Pacific Northwest between 1994 and 2005, the period when Gretchen was killing. Some were probably runaways, custody disputes, deadbeats. But some had been tortured and murdered, and only Gretchen knew which ones. Archie knew every photograph, every story. He had met with many of the families of the missing, looking for some clue, some indication that this person might have attracted Gretchen's deadly attention. Something in the way they dressed, or held themselves; a place they frequented. But that was the thing with Gretchen — there was no victim profile. She'd kill anyone.

There was something satisfying about looking at the files again. No one knew them better than Archie did. He couldn't identify a dead girl in a park, but this was something he could do. He had spent his career working the Beauty Killer case, one way or another. It felt good to be back.

He smiled to himself. He would meet with Gretchen on Sunday and she would give him the location of a body and another family would have answers. Another file would be closed. He and Gretchen could settle back into their routine. The thought made Archie

146

feel . . . happy.

He put two Vicodin in his mouth and got up to get some water in the bathroom across the hall to wash them down. When he opened the door to leave his office, empty glass in hand, he was surprised to see Henry standing next to Debbie, as if they were preparing to enter.

Archie stopped cold. "I didn't know you were here," he said to Henry. Archie glanced at Debbie for some sort of explanation. But she evaded his eye contact.

"I wanted to talk to Debbie," Henry said.

Archie turned the empty glass in his hand. "What's going on?" he asked slowly.

Henry leaned forward, glancing back toward the living room. The kids were there. Archie could hear a video playing.

"Can we talk in your office?" Henry asked.

Archie looked down at the glass, smooth under his hands. He could feel the pills — a hard knot in his throat — start to burn. "I was just getting some water," he said.

"I'll get it," Debbie said. She stepped forward and took the glass.

"Are you guys getting married?" Archie asked.

Henry didn't crack a smile. He glanced back toward the living room, toward the kids, and then back at Archie. "Let's go in your office," he said again.

"Okay," Archie said. He walked back into his office and went to his desk and sat down. The TV was showing color footage of Castle as a young man, when he was first elected into office. The missing persons files were stacked on his desk next to the empty box. He already had some ideas about how to approach Gretchen this time about her crimes, but he had a feeling that this wasn't the time to bring that up.

Henry didn't sit. He walked halfway into the room and stood. He ran a hand over his bald head. "I had Gretchen transferred," he said.

The pills in Archie's throat felt like a fist. "What?"

Henry looked Archie in the eye. "I put in a transfer order to have Gretchen moved to Lawford."

Archie searched Henry's face for some explanation. "But that's in eastern Oregon."

Henry didn't move. "You're not going to be able to see her anymore," he said simply. "You're off her visitor list. No contact. No letters in or out. No phone calls. No visits. Period."

Archie felt the room start to slip around him. He swallowed hard, willing the pills to go down, feeling the burn of his stomach

148

acid. But the pills held. He shook his head. "You can't do that."

"It's done," Henry said softly.

"I'll call the mayor," Archie said. He coughed and lifted his hand to his sternum.

"Are you okay?" Henry asked.

"I just need some water," Archie said, his eyes tearing.

"Debbie," Henry called. "The water?" He turned back to Archie, his big shoulders slumping. Archie had never seen him look sorrier. Or firmer. "I've talked to Buddy," he said. "We're on the same page on this."

Mayor Buddy Anderson had been the head of the Beauty Killer Task Force before Archie. He'd kept it funded when he was chief of police, and as mayor he'd made sure that Archie always had everything he needed. It wasn't altruism. Buddy knew the value of good publicity.

"What about the victim identification project?" Archie asked. They needed him. Buddy needed him. No one knew the Beauty Killer victim files like Archie.

"She can talk to someone else," Henry said. "Or not. It's not worth this."

"I need to see her," Archie pleaded. He hated how he sounded. Desperate. Frantic. Henry, Debbie, Buddy — they had all betrayed him. He looked up and saw Debbie stopped in the doorway, the glass in her hands. "Please," Archie begged.

Henry was immovable. "You can't. It's done. She'll be transferred tomorrow. She's in lockdown until then. It's over."

No. Henry couldn't do this. Archie had been the lead on the Beauty Killer Task Force. They couldn't just cut him out of the case. Archie stood and picked up the phone on his desk and punched in the prison number he knew by heart. The pills burned. Archie coughed. The TV droned on. Focus. "Hey, Tony. This is Archie Sheridan. I need to talk to Gretchen. I'm leaving now. Can you make sure she's ready?"

There was a slight hesitation. "She's in lockdown, sir. No visitors."

Archie closed his eyes. "Can you take a phone in to her?"

Another hesitation. Archie felt sorry for him. "We've got instructions not to let you talk to her," Tony said.

"It's okay," Archie said. He pressed the END CALL button on the receiver. "It's okay." The pills hurt like heartburn. It was a familiar pain. The drain cleaner that Gretchen had made him drink had burned through his esophagus. It had taken him months to recover from the surgery. He stood there for another moment with the receiver in his hand, and then he heaved it as hard as he could against the white wall of his office. It slammed into the drywall and then fell to the ground in two pieces, the batteries rolling on the carpet. Debbie gasped and dropped the glass of water she was holding. A moment later a framed commendation splintered and the glass fell to the ground in two sharp slices. Debbie dropped to the floor to pick up the water glass. It had fallen on carpet and hadn't broken. She looked helplessly at the soggy puddle of water soaking into the carpet.

At the moment, Archie hated her. "You knew about this," he said, coming out from behind his desk.

Debbie looked up, startled. "Henry just told me."

Her hurt expression cut Archie to the bone. He felt his legs grow weak and he sank to the floor in front of his desk. He hung his head and threaded his hands behind his neck. And still his only thought was of Gretchen. "I know I need help," he said. He felt desperate, his heart racing, like he might hyperventilate. His mind searched for anything he could say to change Henry's mind. It didn't matter what. "Cancel the transfer," he said. "I can pull myself together. Whatever you want.

But I need to see her."

Henry's voice was perfectly modulated. It was a tone Archie had heard him use a thousand times with suspects. "You went months without seeing her," Henry said. "You were doing better."

Archie's head pounded. He pressed the bridge of his nose with a thumb and forefinger. "No," he said with a sad laugh. "I wasn't."

Debbie walked over and knelt beside him. "Archie, we're doing this for you."

"I need her," Archie said, his voice barely above a whisper, the pills still stuck in his throat. "You think you're helping. But it will just make things worse."

Debbie put a hand on either side of his face. "I miss you so much."

He looked her in the eye. Her hands felt strange against his cheeks. Unfamiliar. "Leave me alone," he said. He looked up at Henry. "Both of you."

Debbie let her hands fall away and she got up and stood behind Henry, her hand on his arm.

"Archie?" Henry said.

Archie looked up. Behind Henry and Debbie, he could see the television; the car being lifted from the Willamette, the senator's weeping widow.

"I need your gun tonight," Henry said. "I'm going to sleep on the couch. You can have it back in the morning."

"Sure," Archie said. He reached up and picked his keys off the desk and tossed them to Henry and watched as Henry came around and unlocked the desk drawer where Archie kept his service revolver. Henry picked it up out of the drawer, flipped open the cartridge to make sure it was empty, and then closed the drawer.

Henry placed his big hand on Archie's shoulder and held it for a minute. "I'm sorry," he said.

Archie didn't know if he meant he was sorry about Gretchen or taking the gun or conspiring with Debbie. It didn't matter. If Archie were going to kill himself, he wouldn't use his weapon. He'd use the pills. Gretchen would have known that.

CHAPTER
17

Archie woke up stiff. It was a combination of the foldout couch in his office and not having taken his first pills of the day. Every day was like waking up with the flu. His first awareness was the stiffness in his legs and arms, the ache in his ribs, his throbbing head, and then Sara, standing next to the bed, dressed for school in a pair of red overalls and a pink T-shirt.

The TV was still on. An aerial shot of flames filled the screen. The local news had taken a break from the senatorial mourning to cover a forest fire somewhere in Central Oregon. Even the news moved on.

"Henry's making eggs," Sara said. He could smell the eggs then, the salt and fat wafting in from the kitchen. It made his stomach turn.

"You've got to get up," Sara said.

Archie rubbed his face and looked at his watch. It was 6:30 A.M.

Sara took his hand and began to pull.

He was wearing a pair of pajama pants that Debbie had bought for him a few Christmases ago, and no shirt, and as he sat up the blanket slipped and exposed his scarred chest. He felt the cool air on his torso, saw Sara's eyes widen, and then he looked down to see his mutilated body. He pulled his hand away from Sara's and lifted the blanket up to his armpits. He expected her to shrink away, but instead she leaned against him and wrapped her arms halfway around his neck. "I have scars, too," she whispered. She pulled back her hair to show him the paper-thin scar at her hairline from where she had fallen off a sled when she was three. "See?" she said.

Archie touched the scar on his daughter's head. It was so slight that it barely registered under his thick fingers; nothing like the chasms that marked his own skin. When he ran his hands over the topography of his own scars, he could imagine he was feeling the surface of another planet.

Archie kissed her on the forehead, the scar under his lips. "Go eat some eggs," he said. "I'll be up in a minute."

Only when Sara left the room and closed the door behind her did he pull back the blanket all the way and sit on the edge of the bed. He reached up and felt the heart-shaped scar, his heart beating underneath it. He liked the way it felt now, and he let his fingers slide over its surface for a long moment, before he reached for his pants, and the pills in the front pocket.

He glanced up at the crawl along the bottom of the TV. Two fires had merged.

Archie showered and shaved. The pills kicked in under the warm rain of the shower and by the time he was done shaving he felt a comfortable Vicodin buzz. The pills created a kind of dull roar in his head that muted the guilt. He thought, sometimes, about giving them up. But only first thing in the morning. Never once he was high.

He dressed for the day in brown pants and a brown button-down shirt, and then walked out into the kitchen. The kids had finished eating. Henry was standing at the stove, wearing Debbie's white chef's apron and making scrambled eggs. His head was freshly shaved. He was wearing a different set of clothes from the ones he'd had on last night. He'd planned ahead and brought an overnight bag.

Henry looked up at Archie and smiled. "You look like a UPS man," he said.

Sara ran from Debbie to Archie, slamming

her metal lunch box into Archie's thigh. Ben stayed where he was, next to Debbie.

Sara looked up at Archie. "I have a spelling test today," she said.

"You're in first grade," Archie said.

"Henry was quizzing me," she said.

"She can spell better than I can," Henry said.

Debbie walked up and put her hand on Sara's shoulder and kissed Archie on the cheek. "I'll see you tonight," she said. "Henry said he'd watch the kids. We can go out. Do something fun."

"Sure," Archie said.

Debbie nodded and then took Sara by the hand. "Let's go," Debbie said. "Ben, kiss your father."

Ben trudged forward and Archie bent down so his son could kiss him goodbye.

"I love you, Daddy," Sara said. *"L-O-V-B."*

"E," said Archie.

And they were gone.

Archie got a cup of coffee and sat down at the kitchen table. The kids' dishes still sat there, crusts of bread and egg goop and grease.

"My gun?" Archie said.

Henry walked over to one of the high cupboards over the stove and reached up and removed Archie's gun, and then walked

157

over to the table and laid it in front of Archie. "It's empty," he said.

Archie picked it up and held it for a moment in his hands and then slipped it into the leather holster on his waist.

"Do you want to talk some more?" Henry asked.

"Is she in transit?" Archie asked.

"Yep," Henry said.

"Then there's nothing to talk about," Archie said. Before Henry could respond, Archie's cell phone rang. He pulled it out of his pocket, snapped it open, and held it to his ear.

"It's me," Archie heard Susan Ward say. "I know who your Jane Doe is."

CHAPTER
18

The Portland city morgue was in the basement of a beige-colored stucco building in the north part of the city. The walls inside were painted beige. The linoleum was beige. The paper sterile gowns that Susan and Archie had to wear were beige. The room where they did the autopsies was in the basement. All morgues were in the basement. If you believed what you saw on TV. There was a line of steel gurneys, a lot of scales and devilish-looking containers, and four large drains in the floor for hosing down blood at the end of the day. About ten feet up, a bank of frosted windows let in a weird white light and someone had jammed a lot of houseplants up on a ledge below them. Spider plants. Rubber tree plants. Ferns.

"This place smells like nail polish remover," Susan said.

"Are you going to tell me who you think she is?" Archie asked.

Susan had arranged to meet Archie in the morgue parking lot. He was there, waiting for her, by the time she arrived, fifteen minutes late, which for Susan was early. She didn't see Henry.

"I just want to be sure," she said.

The body was under a black plastic tarp, the kind of thing you might throw over an outdoor woodpile. A morgue technician had just wheeled it in. Under her sterile beige smock, the technician was wearing corduroys and clogs and a turtleneck and wool socks, even though it was summer. It was probably always cold down there. Archie nodded at the technician and she unzipped the bag and folded down the thick plastic sheeting.

The dead woman didn't have a face anymore. Archie had warned Susan about that, but she still wasn't prepared. The woman's mandible was slack, so her lipless teeth were slightly agape, her darkened tongue like bruised fruit. The clotted blood remaining on her cheekbones and in her eye sockets looked like grape jelly. How medical examiners ever managed to eat, Susan didn't know.

She looked down and realized that her hand was clenching Archie's wrist. Her heart was racing and she felt a sort of heaviness in her throat. But she forced herself to keep looking. For something. Some clue. Something familiar.

And then she saw it.

"Oh, God," she said.

She felt Archie's wrist pull free and then his hand fold around hers, their fingers interlocking.

He said, "Tell me."

Susan wasn't crying. Not really. They were just tears. They slid down her cheeks and onto her mother's free-trade Peruvian black knit sweater. Her neck felt cold where the tears left salty trails. She shivered. This wasn't her fault, she told herself. Parker. The senator. None of it. It was a story. She was a reporter. There was a public right to know.

"It's Molly Palmer," she said.

CHAPTER
19

Archie stared down at the corpse on the slab in front of him. "You're telling me that this is your source on the Castle story?" he said. "That the woman we found dead the night before Castle went off a bridge was the same woman who was about to publicly disgrace him?"

Susan nodded.

Archie looked at the corpse's Halloween skeleton face, her marbled, bloated skin. "How can you tell?" he asked.

Susan reached up and pulled at a piece of turquoise hair. "I finally got ahold of her roommate last night. She said that Molly had taken off, left a note and just left. But first she dyed her hair. She was working as a stripper. And blondes make more tips. But she was giving it up." She let go of the piece of hair, but it remained twisted where she'd wound it around her finger. "So she dyed her hair red. It's called Cinnamon Glow. Her roommate found the box in the bathroom trash."

Victim identification based on hair color. Archie could imagine that meeting with the DA. Vidal Sassoon as an expert witness. "You won't be offended if I double-check with dental records?" he said. It was crazy. A hunch. Based on hair dye. But he could follow it up. Archie pulled his cell phone out and called Lorenzo Robbins. He got his voice mail and left a message detailing what he knew about Molly Palmer. She'd gone to high school in Portland. Chances were someone had X-rays on file. "When was the last time you spoke with her?" Archie asked Susan gently.

Susan shook her head. "I couldn't get ahold of her. But she was like that sometimes. I knew she was nervous about the story coming out." She pulled at the sleeves of her sweater. "She was blond. You said the woman in the park had red hair. Molly was blond."

"Did Molly use drugs?" They wouldn't have the tox screens for six weeks, but it was looking like an OD.

"Yeah," Susan said.

So she had red hair. She was missing. And she was a user. "Heroin?" Archie asked.

"She didn't do this to herself," Susan said,

her voice wavering. "Parker wasn't drunk." She laughed sadly. "Parker was always drunk. But he was never that drunk. Never drunk enough to steer off a fucking bridge." Her hands were entirely lost in the sleeves of her sweater now, her arms crossed. "Molly didn't take bad heroin. She was an addict. She would have had a source, someone trustworthy." Susan looked at Archie, her algae-green eyes large. "Someone killed her, Archie. Castle was humiliated. He must have gotten Molly to come down here to meet with him, and given her poison dope or something, and then he took Parker with him off that bridge."

Fuck. This was all he needed. "I need to see all of your notes on the Castle story," Archie said. "I need everything you have."

Susan flinched and shook her head. "I can't do that. I can't just turn over my notes to the police." She looked at the dead woman, head still shaking, fists in her sleeves. "Parker never would have done that."

Archie looked at his watch. It was almost nine A.M. To get to Lawford, they would probably transport Gretchen up I-5, then cut over on 84 East. That meant that they'd come through Portland. He could feel Gretchen. Nearer. "Did you drive?" he asked Susan.

"Yeah," she said.

"Can you give me a lift?" Archie asked. "I want to show you something."

Susan didn't move.

"Trust me, Susan."

Susan was quiet for a minute. Archie could hear water moving in a pipe overhead, like someone upstairs had flushed a toilet or hosed down a fresh corpse for autopsy. Then Susan unfolded her arms and pushed the sleeves up to her elbows. "Okay," she said. "Let's go."

Archie punched a number into his phone. When Henry answered he said, "I'll be late coming in this morning. I'm going to show Susan the boxes from Parker."

They were at Archie's house. Susan had been there once before, to interview Debbie Sheridan for Susan's profile on Archie and the Beauty Killer Task Force. Susan watched as Archie stood on the stoop. He held his keys in his palm for a moment, looking at them like they were something sad and precious before slipping them into the lock and pushing in the front door.

The house still smelled slightly of breakfast. Salt and grease. Eggs. Susan imagined the whole Sheridan family gathered around the kitchen table, clogging their arteries together and staring at one another adoringly. Once, when Susan was ten, Bliss had decided to start making breakfast. She spent the weekend baking homemade granola and fed it to Susan every morning that week. It had been a month before Susan had had a normal bowel movement.

"It's this way," Archie said, walking down a carpeted hallway.

"What is?" Susan asked.

"My office," Archie said.

She followed him into a large room. There was a desk, bookshelves jammed with books, an old TV, framed pictures and commendations on the walls, bulletin boards layered with papers, and a sofa bed still made up from the night before. She tried not to visibly react to the sofa bed. So, Archie Sheridan wasn't sleeping with his wife. Or ex-wife. Or whatever. It wasn't any of her business. Really.

He didn't offer any sort of explanation. He didn't even seem to notice. He walked over to the closet and carefully folded the accordion doors open. And he pulled a chain that turned on a light.

Inside, tacked on the back wall of the closet, were dozens of photographs. Some were snapshots. Some were morgue photos. They were all Beauty Killer victims.

"Jesus Christ," she said.

He didn't say anything. He just bent down and lugged out a big cardboard file box. And then another. And another. The boxes were made out of heavy-duty white cardboard and had cardboard lids and oval cutouts on the sides so you could carry them. On the end of each box someone had written, in red Sharpie, "Beauty Killer." Susan knew the cramped scrawl. It was Quentin Parker's.

"These are his notes," Archie said matter-of-factly, setting the third box on top of the second with a thud.

"How did you get them?" Susan asked.

Archie sat down behind his desk, picked up a pen, and began to rotate it between his fingers. "He lent them to me."

"Why?"

"He interviewed a lot of people. I asked if I could see the transcripts." He threw the pen up in the air and caught it. "To help with the identification project."

Susan glanced at the boxes and then back at Archie. "He gave you his notes?"

"He lent them to me," Archie said. "And now I'm lending them to you."

Susan walked up to the stack of boxes and ran her hand across the top one's lid.

167

Parker's notes. Almost thirteen years of research about the Beauty Killer case. Susan felt a smile spread across her face and then caught herself. God, she was such an asshole. Parker was dead, and she was picking over his corpse. She was no better than Ian or the rest of them. But she didn't take her hand off the box. "Parker once spent a month in jail because he refused to identify a drug dealer he'd profiled."

"I know," Archie said. His voice was so quiet she could barely hear him. "This was different. Gretchen had been arrested." He laid the pen at the base of a small frame propped up on the desk. Susan couldn't see the picture, but imagined his family, gathered around a Christmas tree, or lined up in front of a rustic fence. "I wanted her to admit she'd killed Heather Gerber," Archie continued. "The girl in the park, thirteen years ago. She refused. No one gave a shit about Heather." He adjusted the frame, repositioning the angle slightly. "Except for Parker."

"And you," Susan said softly.

Archie scratched his forehead, right above one eyebrow. He was still looking at the frame. "Gretchen had excised Heather's brain through her nose, using a crochet hook." He sounded tired, his voice affectless.

168

"You couldn't tell. Her head looked like the only thing Gretchen hadn't mutilated. The ME called me late at night and I went down to the morgue and he lifted off her skullcap and inside, where her brain was supposed to be, it was just mush." He scratched his eyebrow again. "It looked like cake batter," he said.

"That was your first homicide, right?" Susan sat on the edge of the desk and leaned forward over it so she could lay her hand on the inside of Archie's wrist. It was a crazy thing to do. Completely inappropriate. But she felt a sudden urge to reach out. She wanted to connect. She could feel his pulse in her palm.

For a moment, neither of them moved. And then he turned his hand and took her hand in his. She felt her heart quicken and a girlish itch to giggle so strong that she was almost afraid to look at him. It was awkward enough being in his private space, where he slept. But she forced herself to glance up and found him gazing at her so tenderly, that for a second she thought he might actually lean forward to kiss her. Instead he said, "I need to see all of your notes on the Castle story."

She laughed. She couldn't help it. Her eyes stung with tears. Her face burned.

"Archie," she said.

"Susan," he said. He tightened his hand around hers. "You don't want to get involved with me." As if to prove his point, he reached out and turned the frame on his desk. The picture he looked at on his desk every day wasn't of his family. There was no Christmas tree, no rustic fence. It was a school photograph of a teenage girl. Susan recognized her. She'd seen her image enough times. She was the Beauty Killer's first victim. Heather Gerber.

"Your Castle notes?" Archie said.

Susan caught sight of something out the window and froze.

"What?" Archie asked.

There were cops in the yard. There were two windows in the room and the beige curtains were half closed, but Susan could see, quite clearly, that there were cops in the yard. There were patrol cars on the street, their lights on, sirens off. The cops were moving toward the house. Archie turned in his chair to see what she was staring at and then stood.

"What's going on?" she asked him.

The doorbell rang. Not rang. It was more like someone had leaned on it, so it went off again and again, a frantic, persistent chime, followed by the sounds of someone's fist on the door.

Archie reached into his pocket for his phone, which Susan realized was ringing. He held it to his ear as he strode across the room toward the hall. Susan was still perched on the desk.

"Don't move," he said.

"Don't worry," Susan said.

She heard the front door open and heavy footsteps rush into the house. She looked out the windows again, and there was a uniformed cop, standing right behind the glass. He waved. Susan turned back toward the door just as Henry turned the corner into the room, his face beet red, his phone to his ear, his gun in his hand. He was followed by four uniformed cops.

"What the fuck?" said Archie.

Henry's face had a sheen of sweat on it. He didn't put away his gun. "Gretchen Lowell escaped about thirty minutes ago," he said. "She was last seen about ten miles from here."

Archie coughed once and then he leaned over and vomited on the cream carpet.

CHAPTER
20

"Check the house," Henry barked. "The yard. Everywhere."

Archie could hear the sound of people moving through the house. Doors opening. Rooms being cleared. This wasn't happening. The sour taste of vomit in his mouth made his stomach turn again. She knew where he lived. They'd shown the house on the news enough goddamn times during his captivity. She could find him. God, he should have stayed away. He felt a hand on his shoulder. The touch sent a current down his arms and he jumped, startled, and opened his eyes. It was Claire. Archie didn't even know when she had come in.

Her expression was calm, in control, but her eyes darted, taking in every detail in the room. He saw her register the sofa bed, Parker's Beauty Killer boxes, the macabre collage of Gretchen's victims in the closet.

She had her service weapon in her hand, a nine millimeter, with double action. It was a big, accurate gun and Claire pointed it at the carpet, but her arm was extended, elbow slightly bent, so if she had to, she could fire in an instant. "We'll find her," she said.

Archie turned away. Susan appeared at the door with a towel from the hall bathroom. She walked over, her face pink, knelt, and started to sponge up the vomit from the carpet.

"Leave it," Archie said. "It doesn't matter."

But Susan kept pressing the gray towel into the carpet. Her hands were shaking. "It's okay," she said. He saw her glance around, taking in all the guns, the frantic energy of the cops in the room. She pushed the towel harder into the carpet. "It's okay," she said again, barely audible.

"Susan," Archie said, louder. "Leave it."

She looked up at him, lifted her hands from the towel, and nodded.

"Debbie and the kids?" Archie asked Henry.

"I've got units on their way to pick them up now," Henry said.

Archie nodded, his heart starting to slow. "What happened?"

"We have no fucking idea," Henry said, his face reddening, hand behind his neck. "They stopped to gas up just south of 205. She was practically hog-tied. There were two sheriff's deputies traveling with her. A clerk noticed that the truck hadn't moved from the pump, and went to check on it. He found a female sheriff's deputy dead. Gretchen and the male deputy were gone."

Archie shook his head. He had no doubt that she had convinced that male deputy to help her. That he was now dead. Even with the shit beaten out of her, Gretchen was dangerous. If she was even as hurt as she'd seemed. "Fuck," Archie said.

She had planned the whole fucking thing. They were fools. They were all the biggest fucking saps in the whole fucking universe. He sat on the edge of his desk and slowly, softly, he started to laugh.

"This is funny?" Henry said, not amused.

"She had it planned," Archie explained. "She wanted to be transferred. Don't you get it? The assault at the prison. She wasn't playing me." He pointed a finger at Henry, Henry who would do anything for him, who would transfer a prisoner, end the identification project, if he thought Archie was coming unhinged. "She was playing *you*."

Henry squinted at him and Archie saw a flicker of realization in his friend's eyes.

174

Henry ran an angry hand over his bald head. "She knew how you'd react," he said. "And she knew what I'd do."

"Of course she did," Archie said.

"Enough," Claire said. "We need to get you into protection."

But Archie didn't move. "How did she kill her? The sheriff's deputy? She doesn't usually kill people quickly. How did she do it?"

Claire glanced at Henry. "She cut her throat," Claire said.

"She had a knife?" Archie asked.

"We don't know," Henry said.

Susan stood up from where she had been sitting on the carpet. Her hands had stopped shaking and she pulled at a piece of turquoise hair. "I don't mean to be mercenary," she said. "But has this been released to the media?"

"We're keeping it quiet for now," Henry said. "The mayor's afraid of a panic."

"She's going to kill someone," Archie said. He looked from Henry to Claire, trying to make them understand. "She likes to kill people. She hasn't gotten to kill someone, slowly, the way she likes, in almost three years. We've got to warn people."

Claire looked at her watch. "We need to go," she said to Henry.

"No," Archie said, shaking his head, staying firmly planted on the desk. "She needs to be able to find me."

"That's actually the opposite of what needs to happen," Claire said.

"Do you want to catch her?" Archie asked.

"She's probably on her way out of the country by now," Henry said.

Archie's phone rang. He pulled it out of his pocket and looked at it. The caller ID read UNKNOWN CALLER. "No," Archie said, "she's not."

"Hello?" he said into the phone.

Gretchen's voice purred back, "Hello, darling."

The relief swept over him like a wave, washing away the anxiety, the nausea, the fear. He slid off the front of the desk to the floor. His fingers were cold around the phone, but his body felt hot, the back of his neck suddenly wet with sweat. Then he realized, he wasn't afraid of her.

He was afraid of never seeing her again.

"It's good to hear from you," he said.

CHAPTER
21

Archie tried to shut out everyone in the room, to focus only on the telephone pressed against the side of his face, only on Gretchen. He was aware of Claire's hand on his shoulder. He could see Susan Ward open her notebook and place a pen against it. He could see Henry on his phone, ordering a trace on the cell. They would need two minutes to trace the call, if she was calling from a landline and they didn't have to get cell carriers involved. Archie looked at his watch and started counting.

It was 10:46 A.M.

"Do they have you in protection yet?" Gretchen asked.

Archie swallowed hard. "Gretchen, you have to turn yourself in."

He could almost hear her smile through the phone. "You'll miss me, won't you? Like I've missed you." Her voice turned cold. "All those Sundays you stayed away."

"I'll visit you," Archie said. His stomach burned, his head ached. "I want to. You know I do."

"Empty promises."

Archie could still see Henry on the phone. He had to keep her talking. He fumbled for the pillbox in his pocket and took out four pills and put them in his mouth. Claire handed him a glass of water from his desk, and he swallowed them. "You faked the rape?" he asked Gretchen.

"No," she said. "I just showed him what he was capable of."

Archie's mind turned to the heart scrawled on the bathroom mirror at the prison. "Did you kill him?" he asked. He handed the glass of water back to Claire and she set it back on the desk next to the photograph of Heather Gerber. It was 10:47.

"Does it matter?"

It was just the beginning, Archie knew. If Gretchen was out, the carnage was just beginning. "The missing sheriff's deputy?"

"Dead. Dead. Dead."

"Turn yourself in," Archie said. He pressed the fingers of one hand into his right temple, trying to slow the pulse of blood that beat against his skin. Susan was taking notes, recording everything. He didn't care. "I'll do anything you want," he said.

"You know what I want." She let that linger in the air between them.

"Tell me," he said.

"I want you," she said. "I've always wanted you."

The warm pulse under his fingers quickened. He pressed against it harder. "I can't."

"I'd love to talk all day, darling. But I've got to go. It's almost time for morning recess."

Ten forty-eight A.M. Archie looked up. Henry was on his phone, and Archie watched as his face colored. They had a location. Henry hung up and punched another number into his cell phone and started talking. "This is Detective Henry Sobol with the Portland Police Department. Do you have lockdown procedures? Okay. I need you to lock down the school."

Archie turned his attention back to his phone. "Gretchen?" he asked. "Where are you?"

He could hear Henry continue, his voice commanding, urgent. "We have reason to believe that Ben and Sara Sheridan are in danger. Do you know who Gretchen Lowell is? We believe she may be in your building."

Archie felt disconnected from his body. He didn't know if it was the pills kicking in, or just shock. But a peaceful numbness settled in his brain, making his head feel dark and heavy. None of this made sense. Gretchen couldn't have escaped. This couldn't be happening.

He could still hear Henry. "She is, and I can't stress this enough, very dangerous. Do not approach her. Just lock down every classroom. No one gets near any of the kids. I have police on their way. Understand? Good."

"Gretchen?" Archie said again. The numbness was lifting, reason rushing in. His hand clenched around the phone.

"I'm only interested in them," she said sweetly, "because they remind me of you." And then he heard it, through the phone. Five sets of two schoolbell rings. The signal for lockdown. She was at his children's school. She was going to kill them. She was going to kill the last thing that mattered.

"Goodbye, darling," she cooed, and the phone went dead.

Susan saw the phone fall from Archie's hand. It was light and bounced once on the carpet before settling on its side, the blue LCD light holding for a moment and then going dark. The room smelled like vomit. No one but Susan seemed to notice it.

Archie stood.

She knew it had been Gretchen on the phone. She had heard Henry call Archie's children's school. She had pieced it together. Media blackout or no, she was going with the story. A master's degree in creative writing. Five years of newspaper journalism. And still, the only question she could manage was, "What's going on?"

Henry took four steps toward Archie and put a big hand on either of Archie's upper arms. Archie's knees buckled and for a moment it looked to Susan as if Henry were the only thing holding Archie upright. "I've got units on their way to the school," Henry told Archie.

"I've got to go there," Archie said. "I've got to go there now."

Henry seemed to waver and then he said, "All right."

Susan closed her notebook and stepped forward. "Me, too," she said.

Henry didn't even hesitate. "No," he said.

Susan wasn't going to take no for an answer. She waved the notebook. "Your media blackout is over," she said. "You've locked down a school. Every news van in town is on its way. They're already live with it. I'm your best bet to controlling the story. Right now, all you're going to get is hysteria.

181

Is that what you want?" she asked. "Hysteria?"

Henry's voice dropped. "I want to catch her before she kills someone else," he said.

Susan lowered the notebook, and looked him in the eyes. "I can help you do that."

Claire said, "She can ride with me."

Henry stooped in front of Archie and picked up the phone he had dropped and stood up and handed it to him. Archie took it and looked at Henry and nodded.

Then Henry turned back to Susan. He squinted and wiped some sweat off his forehead with the flat of his hand. Susan could taste the smell of vomit in the back of her mouth.

"Don't get shot," Henry said.

CHAPTER
22

William Clark Elementary School was 1.4 miles from the house. Archie had trip-metered it once. Ben had insisted. Something to do with a bet with a friend about who lived nearer. One point four miles. It seemed farther. It was twenty minutes if you walked it. It took eight minutes to drive in the morning. Six minutes in the afternoon because traffic was lighter. With the lights and sirens on, it took four. That was what lights and sirens bought you: two minutes. One hundred and twenty seconds.

It could make a difference.

Archie knew the protocol for locking down a school. Students were instructed to stay in their classrooms. To push desks into the center of the room, and to stay away from the windows. Hallways were cleared. To control access, every door was locked except for the front door. Teachers turned off their classroom lights and instructed students to get down on their hands and knees. Just another day of public education. It made the old duck-and-cover drills seem quaint.

Archie imagined Ben and Sara in their respective classrooms, terrified, and he hated himself. His phone rang and he snapped it open, his heart sinking a little when he saw the number. He had hoped it would be Gretchen.

It was Debbie.

"Are you safe?" he asked.

"I'm at your office," she said, her voice steel. "Are you at the school yet?"

He glanced out the window. A school zone sign warned motorists to reduce speed to twenty miles an hour. Henry was ignoring it. "Almost."

"You protect them, Archie," Debbie said, choking on the words. "You kill her." Her voice was a desperate whisper. "Promise me."

"I'll protect them," Archie said.

"Kill her," Debbie pleaded.

The car squealed to a halt, jumping the curb in front of the school. Eight squad cars were already there, their lights on, sirens eerily quiet. "We're here," Archie said. The school, built in the nineties, was a modern one-story brick-and-glass structure that looked more like a junior college than an elementary school. It was a privileged suburban district, a refuge for parents fleeing Portland's cash-strapped schools. A safe, enviable alternative.

Until today.

Archie snapped his phone shut and unholstered his gun. Henry was already out of the car, his badge out, barking orders, shouting at the uniforms to enter the school. Archie turned the safety off on his weapon and got out of the car. The adrenaline made the pills work faster, and Archie felt the soothing tickle of codeine in his shoulders and arms.

Just in time, he thought.

CHAPTER
23

Archie didn't remember putting on the bulletproof vest from the trunk of the car, but he must have, because he and Henry were both wearing them as they moved toward the school. He didn't usually like the way those vests felt, the weight pressing against his sore ribs, but today he didn't notice.

In a school lockdown drill, the police secure the premises. They do not enter the building until the perpetrator in question has been located and the situation assessed. Schools, by definition, come with a couple hundred potential hostages and you didn't want kids shot because you rushed it. Of course the drills presumed that the mad gunman was another kid. Kids are unpredictable. Kids with guns are extremely unpredictable. And no one wanted to have to shoot a kid, even one with a gun. So, secure, assess, wait.

The drills did not take into account Gretchen Lowell. She was predictable. She would kill until someone stopped her.

"We go in," Archie said.

"Yeah," Henry said.

The responding Hillsboro patrol cops had made contact with someone in the administration office. She was afraid but calm. The school was quiet. Lockdown procedure was in place.

A plaque above the front doors read EDUCATION IS NOT THE FILLING OF A PAIL, BUT THE LIGHTING OF A FIRE.

"Yeats," Archie said.

"What?" said Henry.

"Nothing."

They drew their weapons and, followed by six flushed and unsettled suburban cops, they entered the school.

The front doors opened onto a wide carpeted hallway. A life-sized papier-mâché tiger, the school's mascot, stood in mid-stride, facing the doors. It was painted burgundy with orange stripes. A sign next to it read DO NOT CLIMB ON ME.

Archie had been to that school a few hundred times. Ben was in second grade. Sara was in first. Both children had gone to kindergarten there. There had been parent-teacher meetings and art shows and fundraisers and PTA meetings and basketball games and drop-offs and pickups.

That was a lie.

Debbie had been to the school a few hundred times. The nature of Archie's job kept him away. He had to work early and stay late, so Debbie dropped the kids off. Debbie picked them up. Debbie went to PTA meetings. Archie tried. He attended as many events as he could. He had never missed a parent-teacher meeting. But he had not tried hard enough. He would, he promised himself now, try harder. If they were still alive, he would try harder.

"Ben's in room six," Archie said to Henry. "That way." He pointed past the tiger. "At the end of the hall. I'll get Sara." He turned to the patrol cops. "The rest of you move in pairs, secure as much of the school as you can."

The patrol cops stood motionless for a moment, looking at one another. The only woman among them cleared her throat. She was young. She'd probably been a cop for only a year or two. "What should we do if we find her?" she asked.

"Shoot her," Henry said.

"No," Archie said quickly. "She's dangerous. Don't confront her. If you see her, you radio me." He touched the walkie-talkie on his hip.

Henry motioned with his fingers at two of the patrol cops, the woman and a middle-aged man whose age bespoke a decided lack of ambition. "You two go with him," Henry said. "And if you see her, shoot her."

They split up and Archie led his small posse away from the grinning tiger, left down the hall, in the opposite direction Henry headed to go to Ben's classroom. Sara was in room 2. It wasn't far. Just past the hall wall display of construction-paper dioramas of beach balls and sailboats and sun. Summer break was days away and Sara had already started begging to go to horse camp. They came to her classroom door. Beyond it Archie could see a pint-sized drinking fountain against one wall. A Spider-Man backpack lay unattended on the ground next to it.

God, it was quiet.

Archie tried the doorknob. It was locked. He pounded twice on the door with his fist. "It's the police," he said, his voice startling in the silence. "I need you to open the door."

He heard movement inside and the door opened. Mrs. Hardy, Sara's first-grade teacher, stood in the doorway. She had been a teacher for thirty years and her red hair had only recently started to fade to a light gray. She held a copy of *Green Eggs and Ham* clutched to her sweater.

Archie lowered his gun, but kept his finger where it rested on the trigger guard. His center of gravity was shifted forward on the balls of his feet. He was relaxed. They taught you that. Keep your breathing steady. If you're relaxed, you shoot better. There was a moment, when two thirds of the lung's capacity had been exhaled, when you were most steady. It was called the "natural respiratory pause." During normal breathing, you had a window of about two to three seconds, but it could be stretched to up to eight seconds to allow time to aim and squeeze the trigger before lack of oxygen began to affect aim.

If you breathed slow enough. If you didn't think about your children. If you stayed relaxed.

"I'm Detective Sheridan," Archie said, looking past the teacher. "My daughter, Sara, where is she?"

"I know who you are, Mr. Sheridan," Mrs. Hardy said. She stepped aside and turned on the classroom lights and Archie could see the kids sitting in a circle in the center of the room. They were motionless, eyes on him, faces pale.

Archie didn't see Sara. He stepped farther

into the room, toward the children. "Sara?" he called. The panic he had been fighting surged. His heart raced. He felt the heat rise under his skin. His throat constricted. He took another step toward the children.

Stay relaxed.

He felt Mrs. Hardy's hand on his elbow, stopping him. "The principal came and got her," she said. "To keep her safe."

Archie gasped, a strangled sigh of relief that nearly doubled him over.

Mrs. Hardy tightened her grip on his arm. "You're frightening the children, Mr. Sheridan," she said.

He saw himself then. The bulletproof vest. The weapon. The patrol cops at the door. His daughter's classmates stared at him silently, a few lower lips starting to tremble. They weren't scared of the lockdown. Or of Gretchen Lowell.

They were scared of him.

He lowered his weapon.

"Has anyone else been here?" he asked the teacher. "A blond woman?" Archie searched for some other word to describe her and came up with nothing. "Beautiful?"

"No," she said.

Archie took a step backward toward the door. "I'm sorry," he said stupidly.

A little boy in an Elmo sweatshirt stepped

forward. He reached out his hand. "Can I hold your gun?" he asked.

Jesus Christ, thought Archie. "It's okay," he said. "It's okay, everyone. I'm sorry."

The patrol cops followed him back out into the hall where Archie immediately peeled off his vest and let it drop to the floor. It fell on the carpet with a thud.

"What are you doing?" the older patrol cop asked.

"It's a school," Archie said. "We're in a fucking school, for Christ's sake."

Henry came around the corner with his weapon drawn. His eyes darted, scanning the hallway; his shaved head glistened with sweat. "The principal came and got Ben," he said.

"Sara, too," Archie said. "The office is this way." Archie holstered his weapon and turned to the patrol cops. "Put your weapons away. Go door to door." They looked at him, not understanding. "Calm. Them."

The older one looked at the woman. "But what if the Beauty Killer's still here?" he said.

"She wants me," Archie explained. "Or my children." He ran a hand through his hair. "Go."

Archie started jogging for the principal's

office, Henry a step behind him. "She's fucking with us," Henry said as they ran. "This whole thing. It's not right."

There was a poster of a frog on the administration office door with a slogan that read LEAP INTO LEARNING. Archie slammed the heel of his fist against the frog's face three times. "It's the police," he said. "I need you to unlock the door."

The door opened and the office secretary appeared, her eyes wide behind thick glasses.

"Ben and Sara Sheridan?" Archie asked.

She tilted her head toward a door marked PRINCIPAL.

Archie reached the door just as it opened. Archie had met Principal Hill only once, at a fund-raiser. He was a black man in his mid-forties. He had a master's degree in education. The school board had recruited him from Philadelphia, and everyone had been excited because he'd once played a year on a major league baseball team. He came to the door with a heavy wooden bat in one hand. His other arm was wrapped around Archie's daughter's shoulders. Ben was standing next to her.

Archie slid to his knees and both Ben and Sara ran to him and he took them in his arms.

"What the hell is going on?" Principal Hill

asked, lowering the tip of the bat to the carpet.

Archie held his children close, breathing in the smell of their hair, tasting their skin with his kisses. "It's okay," he told them. "It's okay now. I promise."

Out of the corner of his eye he saw the bat fall to the carpet and looked up to see Principal Hill raise both his hands and take a half step back, his eyes focused behind Archie.

Archie heard the gun a moment before he felt it press against the back of his neck. A single metallic click. The sound of someone turning off the safety of a semiautomatic.

"Let go of the children," a voice commanded. "Now."

CHAPTER
24

The sun felt good.

It was a funny thing to notice, Susan realized, given the current situation. But that was the thing about Oregon; it rained most of the year, so when the sun came out, you noticed it. Gretchen Lowell was loose. Archie Sheridan's children were in danger. And she was having a sun moment.

Not that there was anything she could do. The school was surrounded by cops. Susan counted five fire trucks. What, did they think the school might burst into flames?

Susan had lost sight of Claire. She had left Susan behind in the car as soon as they'd arrived, and Susan couldn't get near the school without a police escort. There she was, the first reporter at the scene, and not only could she not get close to the school, she had forgotten her pen.

So she was sitting on the hood of Claire's Festiva scribbling notes with a stick of

Chanel kohl eyeliner. It may have been the most expensive writing implement she'd ever used. The mid-morning sun was huge and egg-yolk yellow. That was nice. She wrote that in her notebook, "egg-yolk yellow." Underlined it.

She squinted up at the school. SWAT had rushed in five minutes before. They had been in there awhile. Five minutes, when you were watching a building, was a long time. Susan felt her stomach tighten with anxiety. She saw a heavyset man in a Hillsboro PD uniform walk by on the other side of the tape, and slid from the hood of the car with her notebook.

"Hey!" she called. "Susan Ward. With the *Herald*. What's going on in there?"

The cop walked by her quickly without even the usual seething glance of disregard.

The TV media had started to arrive. Charlene Wood from Channel 8 was first, bursting from the passenger seat of the Channel 8 van, and staking her claim for her live shot. She was tall and skinny with legs that looked like piano legs and black hair that she always wore parted on the side and curled under at her shoulders. Everyone loved Charlene. Ian claimed that she kissed him once at a KGW holiday party, but Susan didn't believe him.

A SWAT member jogged by, a walkie-talkie in each hand.

"Susan Ward," Susan shouted at him. "*Oregon Herald.* Can you tell me what's going on in there?"

He looked right at her and walked away toward the command center the Hillsboro PD had established directly in front of the school.

Susan's phone rang. She glanced at the caller ID. It was Ian. For the fourth time in ten minutes. He wasn't going to be happy.

"Anything?" he said. "We need an update for the Web site."

"SWAT arrived," Susan said. "They're inside the school."

"I know," Ian said. "Charlene Wood is live with it on Channel 8. Anything else?"

"You're fucking kidding me," Susan said, glancing over at Charlene, who was broadcasting live in front of the command center, her piano legs poked into black high heels. "She just got here."

"Well, she's scooped you," Ian said. "Find something. I want Web updates every ten minutes. We've got a photo team on the way."

"Every ten minutes?" Susan asked.

"You can call them in. Don't make me wait. Welcome to the information age, babe."

Something was going on in the school. Susan hung up the phone and pressed forward. More cops were streaming inside. Portland PD. Hillsboro PD. State cops. FBI. How did they all get here so fast?

Susan pressed against the thin strip of plastic crime scene tape and tried to record everything she saw. A few parents had arrived and stood sobbing next to a female patrol officer. They were young. Susan's age. Tears streamed down one father's face. But his wife was stoic, solid, her arm draped around the man's shoulder. Susan felt bad for them. Their suburban lives menaced like this. She knew that losing a kid was a parent's worst nightmare. She couldn't relate, but their fear was so naked that it made her glad for a second that she didn't have kids. She was safe, at least, from that kind of helplessness.

She heard the sound of children before she saw them. Their voices floated on the air like birds. And suddenly there they were, streaming from behind the building, in rows, boy-girl, smiling at the activity. Like it was just another fire drill.

The cops were evacuating the back of the school. That was a good sign, right? Susan searched the crowd for any sign of Archie. Nothing. She had seen pictures of his children, and didn't see them in the crowd, either.

Her phone rang again. Crap, she wished Ian would leave her alone. She picked it up.

She heard her mother's voice say, "Hi, sweetie."

"Bliss," Susan said, annoyed. "I'm working."

"You got chocolates from Archie."

"What?" Susan asked, shaking her head slightly to try to make sense of her mother's statement.

"Chocolates. With a card from Archie Sheridan."

Susan giggled despite herself, lifting her hand to her mouth. "Seriously?"

The parents she'd been watching shouted out. A single word: "Max." A small boy looked up from the schoolyard and ran to them.

"They're in a heart-shaped box," Bliss said.

The boy got to his parents and they lifted him into their arms, both of them how crying. Ordinarily, Susan would be all over a story like that. Parents and child reunited. *Herald* readers loved that. Good news. Happy family. Tragedy averted.

But Susan's notebook had fallen from her hand and lay on the grass below.

She tried to speak, but a knotting sensation gripped her chest. She forced herself to take a breath and then tried again. "You didn't eat any of the chocolates, Bliss, right?"

There was no response.

"Mom?" Susan said.

CHAPTER
25

Archie lifted his arms straight out and then bent them at the elbows and locked his fingers behind his head. Ben and Sara stepped away from him, trembling, eyes fixed behind him, terrified. A stream of urine darkened Sara's red overalls. Her cheeks reddened.

"I'm sorry, Daddy," she whispered, her eyes on the ground.

"It's okay," Archie said just before he was slammed facedown on the floor. He felt a large hand grind the side of his face into the carpet and a forearm press against his shoulder blades. He knew the move. It was a tactic they taught you at the academy to subdue a suspect.

Hillsboro SWAT.

"We're cops," Archie said.

"Yeah, fuckheads," he heard Henry say. "Notice the Kevlar?"

A walkie-talkie crackled. Sirens wailed

outside. Archie thought he could hear at least one helicopter. If Gretchen had been there, she was long gone by now.

"Shit," he heard another voice say.

"Look around my neck," Archie said. He felt the forearm on his back shift and then his neck burned as someone tugged the beaded chain that his badge hung from. Then the forearm and hand lifted and Archie sat up.

He immediately crawled a few steps toward Ben and Sara. They didn't run to him this time. Sara squirmed in her wet pants and Ben pulled her close to him. Archie stopped moving toward them. Principal Hill knelt behind Sara and put a protective arm around her. She flinched, still riveted by the SWAT officers.

There were five of them in the office, all wearing black jumpsuits, gloves, thigh holsters, and head wraps, their weapons drawn. Henry was just standing up, from where they had positioned him on his knees. He grabbed the badge that hung around his own neck, over his bulletproof vest, and thrust it toward one of the SWAT officers. "What the —" Henry glanced over at Ben and Sara and faltered. "Heck?"

"Sorry, sirs."

"You find her?" Henry asked. They all

knew which "her" he meant.

"No. We've secured most of the school. I don't think she's here."

Archie turned back to his children. He held an arm out for Sara to come to him, but Ben just pulled her toward him more tightly. Their small chests rose and fell, the sound of their breathing audible. Ben wiped his nose with the back of his wrist. "You're scaring her," he said.

Archie lowered his hand, and felt his children slip farther from his grasp. Gretchen was never going to kill them. Not when she could still use them to hurt him. "Gretchen's not here," he said softly.

The woman behind the front counter, the school secretary, lifted a quaking hand to her mouth. "She said she was your wife."

"What?" Archie asked, turning.

The secretary was in her fifties. Her blond hair was permed and she wore a smock over a turtleneck, like an oversized kindergartener. She'd been the secretary there ever since Archie could remember, but he didn't know her name. "She said she was your wife," the woman continued. "I knew you were divorced from their mother." She motioned vaguely at the children, one hand still held in front of her mouth. "She said that she was their stepmother. That they had forgotten their lunches. She asked to make a call from the phone, right there. I was working at the copier, so I couldn't hear. And then in the confusion of the lockdown she disappeared." She looked from one cop to the next, and then shrugged sadly. "She had a short brown wig on. I didn't recognize her." Then she lowered her hand from her mouth and leveled it until she was pointing at the far end of the counter, where two lunch boxes sat side by side like bookends.

Archie stood up and walked over to them. They were both plastic. One had a Dora the Explorer theme. The other was Batman.

"Should we call the bomb squad?" one of the SWAT officers asked.

Archie ignored him, reaching for the Dora the Explorer lunchbox and opening it. When he saw what was inside his gut clenched, and he fumbled for the next lunch box and opened it. He forced himself to stay rigid, not to let his children see his reaction. He had scared the shit out of them too much already today.

"What is it?" Henry asked.

The two plastic boxes lay open, the dark meaty flesh inside glistening under the office's fluorescent lights. The blood puddled and slipped on the lunch boxes' colorful plastic interior shell. Archie could smell it, the coppery sweet tang. He knew now what had happened to the missing male deputy, the poor sap who had helped Gretchen escape, probably even bought her the fucking lunch boxes.

Archie's voice was steady. "It's a human heart," he said quietly. "I think it's been cut in half."

And judging by the smell, it was fresh.

CHAPTER
26

"Mom?" Susan said again.

There was a pause. "I might have eaten one."

Susan couldn't breathe. "Mom," she said, as calmly as she could. "You have to throw up."

"What?"

"Listen to me," Susan said, her voice rising. "The chocolates are poisoned. Make yourself throw up. I'm going to hang up now and call nine-one-one." She squeezed her eyes shut. "Promise me."

"But I don't feel nauseous."

Nauseated, Susan thought. But she didn't say it. She opened her eyes. "Bliss, promise me."

"Okay," Bliss agreed hesitantly.

Susan hung up and dialed 911. "I think my mom's been poisoned." She rattled off Bliss's address. "She ate a chocolate. I think Gretchen Lowell sent me poisoned chocolates."

"Yeah," the 911 operator said. She sounded unconvinced.

"I'm not crazy. My name's Susan Ward. I write for the *Herald*. Please send paramedics."

She hung up and looked around frantically. More kids were streaming out of the school now. All sorts of cops were jogging in. Something had happened in there. All hell had broken loose.

Susan didn't care. "I need some help," she cried. "Someone."

She ducked under the tape and headed toward the school.

"Get behind the line," she heard someone bark.

Susan felt the tears start to slip down her face. "Gretchen Lowell," she cried. "She sent chocolates to my house." She looked around frantically for someone, anyone, who could help her. But everyone was focused on the school. "My mother ate one," she yelled. "I need help." She looked for Archie, for Henry, for someone she knew. "I need Archie," she screamed at a Hillsboro patrol cop. "Where's Archie?" The cop looked back at her blankly. "Please," Susan begged. She was running now. "Someone. Help me."

Claire Masland appeared. She was there in

an instant, out of nowhere, her arm around Susan's shoulders.

"Susan?" she said. She took Susan by the shoulders, just as Susan's knees started to buckle. "Calm down. Tell me what's going on."

Susan had to take a deep breath before she could talk. "My mom just called. A heart-shaped box of chocolates came to the house addressed to me. The card said they were from Archie. She ate one. My mom ate one." She gripped Claire's shoulder and looked at her hard, so she'd understand. "Archie wouldn't send me chocolates."

"Your mom's at home?" Claire asked.

"I told her to make herself throw up," Susan said. That would help. That's what they always made people do on television. "But she never does what I tell her to."

Claire lifted a walkie-talkie to her mouth. "I need a bus sent to — what's your address?" Susan told her. Claire repeated it into the walkie-talkie. "Female in her fifties. Possible poisoning." She turned to Susan. "Let's go." She pointed a finger at a white male patrol cop with a dark blond Afro. "You," she hollered. "Art Garfunkel." She shouted Bliss's address at him. "Follow me."

They got in Claire's Festiva and Claire

flipped the siren on the hood on. The schoolyard was crowded with parents, cops, emergency vehicles, and news vans, but once that siren went on a path cleared and Claire was able to careen out of the chaos. Susan dialed her mother's landline, but the phone just rang and rang. Maybe Bliss was busy vomiting. Maybe she was unconscious on the floor. Susan was the target. If anything happened to Bliss, it would be her fault.

She let the phone keep ringing, holding it tight against her ear, her eyes closed so it was the only sensation. Maybe her mother could hear it; maybe she would know that Susan was on her way. "God, I'm stupid. I thought he sent me chocolates," she said to Claire, hiding her face. She used her sleeve to wipe the tears from her cheeks. Her skin felt clammy and cold. She wanted her mom. She opened her eyes, and looked over at Claire. Claire was steering the car around the fast traffic on 205, past the car dealerships and the malls and the mortgage companies. Her gun was on her lap. She could probably mud drywall and target shoot and change the oil in her car. "Do you have someone?" Susan asked her.

"Yes," Claire said.

Everyone had someone. "All I have is my mom," Susan said.

"We'll get there, sweetie," Claire said. "I promise."

The ringing stopped. For a second Susan thought that Bliss had picked up, but then an operator recording came on the line. "The party you are trying to reach is not available. . . ." No shit. She hung up. The moment she did, her cell phone rang and she snapped it to her ear, expecting to hear Bliss on the other end.

"It's been ten minutes," Ian said. "Anything?"

"Nothing," Susan said.

CHAPTER
27

Archie held Sara close as they moved out of the administration office. Henry was behind them, Ben in his arms. Eight members of the Hillsboro SWAT team flanked them, four on either side. Their weapons were drawn, fingers on their triggers, knees bent. Archie knew that Gretchen was long gone, but no one was taking any chances. They were ready to shoot. Archie could hear the sound of children's voices coming from a classroom. They were singing. *There was an old lady who swallowed a cat. Imagine that, she swallowed a cat.* Some teacher was trying to keep her students busy. Their voices and the footsteps of the cops were the only sound. Archie held Sara's head down on his shoulder. Her wet pants were cold against his arm. *She swallowed the cat to catch the bird. . . . She swallowed the bird to catch the spider. That wriggled and jiggled and wiggled inside her.* He could hear Sara then, eyes still squeezed shut, face pressed against his shirt. She was singing, too. *She swallowed the spider to catch the fly.* The front doors opened, and they stepped out into the light.

Emergency vehicles ringed the perimeter of the school. Patrol cars, ambulances, fire trucks. Behind them, news vans. Two helicopters overhead. They had evacuated the back of the building and children stood in groups in front of the school. Many parents had already arrived, but most would just now be hearing about the siege, leaving work, speeding to the school, their worst fears burning in their chests. They would arrive to find their children safe. They would take them in their arms and carry them home and they would weep with relief and they would move on.

Archie envied them.

Jeff Heil, a detective on Archie's squad, fell in step with Archie, guiding them toward the street. Heil was light-haired. His partner, Mike Flannigan, was dark-haired. They were both medium build and square-jawed and clear-skinned. Archie called them the "Hardy Boys."

Heil didn't say anything. He just led Archie by a light touch on his elbow, keeping such pace with Archie that the two were almost pressed together. Heil was using his body,

Archie realized, to shield Archie and his children from the news cameras.

Archie heard the mayor before he saw him. Buddy was barking orders at some patrol cops, telling them to move the press line back. His yellow tie flapped against his dress shirt as he swept toward Archie.

"Are you okay?" he asked.

"I want to see Debbie," Archie said.

"She's in the car," Buddy said. He walked them across the grass to a waiting black Town Car with city plates. The SWAT team moved with them. Archie could hear the distant sound of media shouting his name. He held Sara closer and glanced back at Henry and Ben. Ben's face was pale, but he held his head up, eyes trained on the activity that surrounded them. Archie could still hear Sara singing. *But I dunno why she swallowed that fly. Perhaps she'll die.*

A tall Japanese man opened the back door of the Town Car. Archie recognized him as part of the mayor's security detail.

Debbie sprang out of the car, hands over her mouth. When she saw them, she burst into tears and the hands fell and opened wide. Sara lunged from Archie toward her mother, falling into Debbie's arms.

Debbie fell to her knees and wrapped her arms around Sara, so that their entire bodies were touching. Henry unwrapped Ben's thin freckled arms from around his neck and set the boy down and Debbie held an arm out for him and he fell into their hug.

Debbie looked up at Archie. Her eyes were red, her face pale. "Did you get her?" she asked.

"I'm sorry," Archie said. Debbie closed her eyes for a moment and then loaded the children into the backseat of the car with her. Archie turned back to Heil. "Make sure all my lines are tapped," he told him.

Heil glanced back at Henry.

"Did it as soon as we heard she was loose," Henry said.

Of course he did. "Right," Archie said. He climbed into the backseat. Sara was on Debbie's lap, Ben in the middle. Ben had taken Sara's hand and held it in both of his. Sara stared out the tinted window at the distant television cameras.

"We've got to go," Heil said, getting in up front in the passenger seat.

Henry leaned in the open door toward Archie. "Who would Gretchen go after?" he asked.

Archie thought about it, tried to distance himself emotionally from the question. "Debbie," he said. "The kids. Anybody who means something to me." He looked past

Henry, at the police cars, the children, the school. There weren't that many people left he allowed into his life. But Gretchen knew him well enough to intuit who they were. He'd made it easier by taking one of them down to meet her. He looked for Susan now, in the crowd, the shock of aqua hair. But he didn't see her.

"Where is she?" he asked Henry.

"Who?" Henry said.

"Susan," said Archie. "Find her. Make sure she's okay."

From inside the car, Sara's voice was tiny. *No, I dunno why she swallowed that fly.* She looked up at her mother and smiled, her apple cheeks dimpling. "You think Gretchen is pretty, right?" she asked.

Debbie threw Archie a withering look and then rested her head in her hand like she had a headache. "Sara," she said calmly. "Shut up."

CHAPTER
28

"I'm glad you're fine, Bliss," Susan said, twisting around to face her mother in Henry's Crown Vic. Her mother hadn't said much since Henry had picked them up at the hospital. Susan and Claire had arrived at the house after the ambulance. The only ingredients in the chocolates, it turned out, was the stuff you made chocolate out of. Gretchen's motive had been to terrorize, not kill.

"I wish we'd known that before they pumped my stomach," Bliss said. "With a hose. In the yard." She pulled at a bleached dreadlock. "In front of the neighbors."

Susan looked out the windshield and crossed her arms. "Maybe this will teach you not to open my mail," she said.

Henry sighed audibly as he slid the car in front of a hundred-year-old brick building in the cultural district of downtown Portland. The front door of the building was framed with Corinthian-style columns and a hunter green awning featured a white crest with the letters AC.

"You're fucking kidding me," Susan said.

"It's safe," Henry said, getting out of the car. He walked around and opened the passenger door for Susan to get out.

"It's the Arlington," said Susan. "It's a social club for capitalist geezers."

"The mayor's a member," Henry said, opening the back door so Bliss could climb out of the backseat.

"I think I've protested this place," Bliss said, climbing out of the car and looking up at the brick façade. "Do they still make women wear skirts?"

Henry's face steeled. "We can control access. You'll be comfortable."

Susan was still sitting in the car. "I'm not staying here," she said, crossing her arms.

Henry squatted down next to her and gripped her upper arm hard. "This isn't a joke. Do you not think that she won't kill you?"

"That's a double negative," Susan said. "You should keep it simple. 'She will kill you.' Direct. Scary."

Henry glared at her. "Archie's worried about you. It will make him worry less if you are nearby." He ran a hand over his shaved head. "And that will make me worry less."

"Archie's staying here?" Susan asked.

"Yep," Henry said.

She reached over and released her seat belt. "Why didn't you say so?"

Henry sighed again and led Susan and her mother through the club's oak double doors. The wainscoting and crown molding were white, but the walls were painted incongruously with a light salmon that had been sponged on in an attempt at texture. An ornamental table, festooned with flowers, squatted in the middle of the entryway below an enormous shiny brass light fixture. A grand staircase led upstairs, its treads covered in blue carpet. The once grand fireplace had been fitted for gas and the oriental rugs were threadbare. Susan had heard about the Arlington Club, but this was the first time she'd been inside. It was a little disappointing.

She looked around for power brokers and saw only a single old man sitting on a sofa in front of the gas fireplace reading the *Wall Street Journal* under a painting of Mount Hood that hung on the wall in an old gilt frame.

The only sounds were hushed voices and clinking silverware from the restaurant upstairs.

A tall, skeletal man appeared from behind a desk at the back of the room. He was dark-haired and wore a suit and his tie was affixed to his shirt with a silver stickpin. Henry flashed the man his badge. The man waved his hand. "Please put that away." He slid a look over at the old man reading the paper. "The members."

Henry shut the badge and bent his head at Susan and Bliss. "This is Susan Ward and her mother, Bliss Mountain."

Bliss leaned toward the clerk. "My given name was Pitt," she explained.

The clerk glanced down at Bliss's Indian tunic pants, red rubber Crocs, and the breasts that hung free underneath her vomit-stained QUESTION EVERYTHING T-shirt.

"They'll be staying on the sixth floor," Henry continued.

The man's face was frozen in a half-desperate, half-welcoming expression. "Yes, sir. Good afternoon, ma'am. Right this way."

"I'm twenty-eight," Susan said. "And I'm single. So you don't have to call me 'ma'am.'"

"Yes, well." His forehead creased as he pushed the button for the elevator. "You'll be 'ma'am' while you're with us."

Susan narrowed her eyes at Henry.

CHAPTER
29

The pain in Archie's flank had become so constant he could almost block it out, like the ticking of a clock. Almost. Then he would breathe and the pain would bloom into a sharp ache and he had to steady himself to keep from wincing. So he took more pills. It was ironic, he knew, that the very chemicals causing his pain were the only thing that gave him any respite from it.

They had been given a two-bedroom suite. It was painted baby-shit yellow. Squash, Debbie had called it. She was with the kids now, getting them to sleep in the twin beds of their new baby-shit bedroom. She was scared. And more than that, Archie knew, she was furious.

"Do you want to watch TV?" Claire asked. She had come directly from the hospital and had been sitting there for over an hour, pretending to look interested in a coffee table book on Portland's bridges that she had found in the room.

"You don't have to stay here," Archie said.

"I'm your security detail," Claire said.

Three dead bodies in the park. Gretchen on the loose. And his people were busy minding him, instead of out there doing their jobs. "There's a uni in the hall," Archie said.

Claire turned another page of the book. "I am more ferocious than he. Did you know that the Hawthorne Bridge was built in 1910?"

There was a knock and Claire leaped up to get the door.

"It's me," they both heard Henry's voice say. Claire opened the door and Henry walked in pulling a large suitcase. He rolled the suitcase against the wall and rubbed his shoulder.

"Did you get everything?" Archie asked. He and Henry both knew he meant the pills.

"I packed a few sets of clothes for the kids, for you, and for Debbie. We can drive one of you by in the next few days for more. Toiletries," Henry added, "are in the outside pouch."

"Susan?" Archie asked.

"Just got her settled," Henry said. "Along with the mother." He rubbed his shoulder some more. "It took five trips to get all their crap upstairs."

"What's the latest?" Archie asked.

Henry leaned against the baby-shit wall and crossed his arms. "Manhunt of the century. Five agencies. Us. State cops. FBI. Coast Guard. National Guard."

"Who's coordinating the Feds?" Archie asked.

"Sanchez." There were some take-out boxes of half-eaten Thai food on the coffee table. "Pad kee mao?" Henry asked Claire.

"With tofu," Claire said.

"You know I like chicken," Henry said.

"I was ordering for me," Claire said.

"I'm not saying I won't eat it," Henry said. He picked up a box of noodles and a pair of used chopsticks to shovel in a few mouthfuls. "Sanchez will be by later," he said, chewing. "He's getting things set up in the field. Her picture's all over the media. The whole world knows what she looks like. We're going to catch her."

"What about the heart?" Archie asked. He couldn't rid himself of the image of the severed heart in those bloody lunch boxes.

Henry wiped some grease off his mustache with his hand. "They think it's male," he said.

Claire glanced up from the book. "How do they know?"

"It had a tiny penis," Henry said.

No one laughed.

"I'm just trying to lighten the mood," Henry said.

Archie saw Claire shoot Henry a look.

Henry looked at the floor and took another bite of food. This time he swallowed it before he spoke. "How are the kids?" he asked Archie.

It was a question Archie couldn't answer. The kids had clung to Debbie all afternoon. Sara wouldn't even go into the bathroom without her. But they had barely spoken to him.

Archie cleared his throat. "I need to get back to work," he said. "Susan ID'd our first Jane Doe from the park as Molly Palmer."

Henry leaned forward, chopsticks poised over the paper takeout box. "Jesus Christ."

"Yeah," Archie said, closing his eyes and rubbing the bridge of his nose. "Keep it quiet for now."

"Who's Molly Palmer?" Claire asked.

There was another knock at the door, three hesitant, evenly spaced raps. "Officer Bennett, sir," a voice said.

Henry reached over and opened the door, and Officer Bennett's head appeared. He wasn't as dirty as he'd been after he'd slid down the ravine at the Molly Palmer crime scene, but he still had that startled, anxious expression. He looked at Archie. "Susan Ward wants to see you, sir."

"Consider her announced," Archie said.

Susan walked into Archie's room. Her turquoise hair was wet and combed straight back and tucked behind her ears, making her look much younger. She was wearing sweatpants and a University of Oregon sweatshirt and lugging a large box.

"Are you and your mom okay?" asked Archie.

Susan didn't answer. She just carried the box over and set it on the coffee table in front of Archie.

"What's that?" Archie asked.

"All my notes and tapes on Castle," Susan said. "Someone killed him. Someone killed him and Parker. And Molly. And probably that blond woman in the park." She looked around the room at the three cops. "Find out who."

CHAPTER
30

It was two in the morning and Henry and Claire had finally gone home. The Arlington during the day was quiet. The Arlington at night was cryptlike. Archie was going through the contents of Susan's box. There were discs with digital recordings of interviews that Susan had had with Molly Palmer, people who'd known her as a teenager, and a variety of people connected to the case, including the senator's former and current staffers, and even the mayor. Susan's story was going to be big. And a lot of people knew it was in the works.

Archie listened to one of the recordings on his laptop while he leafed through the twelve reporter's notebooks that Susan had included in the box. Her scribble was almost illegible, and punctuated with random notes on that night's take-out order or band names she wanted to remember.

Then he saw a name, underlined, and

followed by a question mark. John Bannon?

That was a name from the past.

What did Susan know about John Bannon? And what did John Bannon know about Molly Palmer?

The bedroom door opened and Debbie came out, wearing an Arlington Club robe. She walked over and sat on the arm of the sofa next to Archie. "You going to come to bed?" she asked.

"Soon," Archie said.

Archie saw Debbie notice his cell phone, sitting within immediate reach on the coffee table. Her face darkened.

"Expecting a call?" she asked.

The truth was that Archie had been glancing at the phone every few minutes, willing Gretchen to call again. "Maybe," he said.

Debbie leaned forward and held down the phone's off button until the light went out. "Let the bitch leave a message," she said, tossing the phone on the cushion beside him. Then she turned to Archie and touched his face gently with her hand. It smelled like shea butter. "You need to get some rest," she said.

Archie nodded. "Okay," he said. He put his hand on the curve of her hip and kissed her lightly, but long, on the mouth. As he did he reached behind him, found the phone, and turned it back on. As she led him into the bedroom, he glanced back, finding reassurance in the phone's green light blinking in the darkness.

Archie awoke to Debbie's voice and her hand on his bare shoulder. They had slept together naked side by side in the same bed. It had felt good to fall asleep next to her, her breath a steady heartbeat in his ear. It had felt almost normal. Except that they hadn't touched, both careful to keep their arms at their sides as they slept, lest they accidentally brush against the other.

"Buddy's here," she said.

Archie struggled to surface from his grogginess. The sun streamed through the wooden blinds and striped the baby-shit walls with light. "What time is it?" he asked.

"After nine."

"Jesus." Archie hadn't slept in past eight since Ben was born. He tried to remember dreams, but recovered only darkness. Still, he did not feel rested. Debbie was dressed, wearing a pair of jeans and a long-sleeved white T-shirt that must have been in the suitcase Henry had packed. She looked fresh and awake, her freckles a fine dust on her unmade-up face.

"I'll be out in a minute," Archie said.

Debbie left the room and Archie sat up and put his feet on the floor. His right side throbbed with each breath and he held it as he stood up to walk to the bathroom. As he made his way gingerly across the carpeted floor he felt a numbing sensation in his hands. He lifted them to look and found the fingers swollen, his nail beds white. He unzipped the outside flap of the suitcase and pulled out a grocery bag full of prescription bottles and dug through them until he found Vicodin and a diuretic. The Vicodin would help the pain, the diuretic would eliminate the swelling. He took four Vicodin and two of the diuretics. He had cut back to two Vicodin first thing in the morning. But his restraint was seeming less necessary.

He took off his watch, noticing the red indentation it left on his swollen wrist, and stepped into the shower. He woke up a couple of times a week with an erection that betrayed his dreams about Gretchen, but not today. Today he was merely exhausted. After the shower he brushed his teeth and shaved and then got dressed in yesterday's pants and a shirt from the suitcase Henry had packed. It was one of those Teflon dress shirts that didn't wrinkle. Debbie had bought him five of them in varying earth tones. When he pulled it on, he looked almost put together. If you could get past the death-warmed-over thing.

"Anything?" Archie asked immediately, as he entered the suite's living room. Buddy sat on the couch next to Debbie. Henry sat in an adjacent armchair. He could hear the sounds of cartoons coming from Ben and Sara's room. A TV in the living room showed a silent split-screen image, Gretchen on one side, him on the other. Then his children's school filled the screen, with the headline BEAUTY KILLER TERROR.

"Not yet," Henry said.

Buddy sat forward a little on the couch. His brown suit jacket was folded immaculately and placed carefully over the couch back beside him. "The public is worried about you. They want to see that you're okay."

Archie had never gotten used to that, the idea that the public wanted anything from him. "You want me to issue a statement?" he asked.

"I want you to go on TV," Buddy said.

Archie saw both Debbie and Henry tense. "TV," Archie said.

"I've got Charlene Wood downstairs. She just needs ten minutes. I think it would buy us some comfort in the marketplace." Buddy had always talked like a politician. Even when he'd been Archie's boss on the task force. It was like he'd just glanced up from reading Plato's *Republic*.

Archie glanced at his cell phone lying silent on the coffee table next to a room service tray with a pot of coffee on it. He leaned forward, trying to ignore the pain under his ribs, and poured himself a cup of lukewarm coffee. The heavy white mug felt clumsy and strange in his swollen hand, but no one seemed to notice.

"I don't think this is a good idea," Debbie said.

Archie took a sip of the coffee. It was bitter in his mouth, or maybe that was the Vicodin. He did not want to be on TV. He did not want to indulge what were surely Buddy's reelection instincts. He did not want to piss off his ex-wife.

On the other hand, if he played it right, he might be able to force Gretchen to show her hand.

"Okay," Archie said. "Invite her up."

CHAPTER
31

Charlene Wood sat with her knees together and crossed her feet at the ankles, facing Archie and Buddy, who now sat side by side on the sofa. Buddy had put on his suit jacket. Two young crewmembers wearing KGW caps had erected a background screen behind them, to disguise the location from the few viewers who might recognize the Arlington Founders Suite.

"Are you ready?" Charlene asked. She looked thinner than she did on television, and hungrier.

"Absolutely," Buddy answered before Archie could open his mouth. Buddy had been caked and powdered and sprayed and now Archie saw him lick his top teeth. It was a trick Buddy had taught him when Archie had taken over leadership of the task force all those years ago, so your lip wouldn't stick to your teeth when you talked on camera. Archie had thought

Buddy had been kidding.

"We're going to go live," Charlene said.

Archie looked down at his hands. The swelling had gone down a little bit. But his side still throbbed, despite the four Vicodin and the two more he'd just taken. He wanted to be higher. He needed to look like he was sick. He *was* sick.

Now he needed to sell it.

Charlene turned to the camera, tilted her chin down thoughtfully, and lowered her voice. "Thanks, Jim. I'm here with Mayor Bud Anderson and Gretchen Lowell's so-called last victim, her former pursuer, Detective Archie Sheridan." She turned to Archie and reached out and touched him lightly on the knee. "Detective, can you tell us what went through your mind when you heard that the Beauty Killer had escaped?"

Archie kept his face composed, irrespective of the ludicrousness of the question. "I was sick," Archie said. "I felt concern for the community." He wanted to do something with his hands, and settled on folding them in his lap. "Gretchen is very dangerous. She should not be approached. It's important that she be returned — alive — into state custody so we can finish our work identifying her victims."

"I just want to reiterate," Buddy said, "that

we are doing everything in our power to apprehend Gretchen Lowell. We will catch her."

Charlene reached out and touched Archie's knee again. Debbie was standing behind her, out of camera range, and Archie thought he saw her roll her eyes.

"How are your children after yesterday's trauma?" Charlene asked.

"They're well," Archie said. "Considering. But," Archie added, and he felt Buddy shift a little beside him, "I'm saddened that this is distracting me from my work investigating who is responsible for the murders in Forest Park." He looked up, directly into the camera. "If anyone out there knows of a blond woman who has been missing for two to three years, please call your local police precinct."

Charlene's eyebrows quirked quizzically at the change of subject, but she was enough of a journalist to at least ask the obvious follow-up. "And the first body?"

"We've identified her," Archie said. The pain in his side had grown to a fire. "Her name is Molly Palmer."

Archie had called Molly's parents from the bedroom after his shower. Molly's father had answered the phone. "She's been dead to us for fifteen years," he'd said. They had

233

another daughter, the father explained, a lawyer. Very successful. Two kids. A husband in investment banking. It was always smart to have a spare.

Buddy's entire posture went rigid. He cleared his throat with a little cough. "To stay on topic," he said, "I again just want to reassure the public that we are doing everything possible to protect them."

Archie lifted his hand to his throbbing side, and pressed it against the cloth of his shirt. His stomach turned. He looked up. The camera was still rolling. Buddy was blathering on. Archie tried to steady himself, to brace himself on the edge of the coffee table, to make it look real. It wasn't hard. The pain and nausea were there — it was just a matter of surrendering to them. He glanced up at the television camera again, waiting for Buddy to pause, to give the cameraman enough time to react. Finally, Buddy took a breath and Archie slipped forward off the sofa onto his knees.

"Oh, my God," Buddy said.

"Keep filming," Archie heard Charlene bark.

Debbie was there in an instant, her hands cupping his face. "Archie?" she said. She laid him on the carpet. "Archie?" she said again.

She leaned over him, her face just above his, pinched.

Archie took her hand in his and squeezed it. "Give it a minute," he whispered.

She tilted her head, confused.

Henry stormed between Archie and the camera. "The interview's over," he said.

Archie heard Charlene say, "Archie Sheridan has collapsed. We'll update you with more information as soon as we have it. Jim, back to you." The camera must have stopped filming because then she added, "Fucking shit."

"Go," Henry said. "Now. Everybody out."

"Should I call for paramedics?" Buddy asked.

"No," Archie said from the carpet. "Fergus."

Henry manhandled Charlene Wood and her crew out the door, leaving their backdrop screen where it sat behind the sofa.

Archie heard the kids' bedroom door open and a moment later Sara was kneeling beside him. "Daddy?" she said.

"I'm fine," Archie said. He lifted his free hand and wiped a tear from Sara's pink, wet cheek. "I'm fine."

Sara looked down and immediately noticed what no one else had. "What's wrong with your hand, Daddy?"

Archie pulled himself up into a seated position. Ben was standing at the end of the sofa. "Take your sister back into your room," Archie told him. Ben held his hand out and Sara glanced once at her father before obediently standing up and following Ben into the suite's second bedroom.

"What's going on?" Debbie asked, her voice flat.

"Shh," Archie said. "Please. Everyone. Quiet."

"Archie?" Henry said.

"Just wait," Archie said.

He closed his eyes, willing himself to hear the noise.

And then there it was. His cell phone.

Gretchen had been watching the news.

CHAPTER
32

"Are you all right?" Gretchen asked.

Archie waved a hand at Henry, and Henry immediately snapped open his cell phone to get a trace on the incoming call.

Archie's heart banged in his chest, and he had to struggle to keep his voice conversational. "Worried about me?" he asked.

"You looked swollen, darling," she said. "It's the edema. Your liver's shutting down."

He glanced down at his free hand. The palm was scarlet; the flesh of his fingers tight with fluid. He closed his fist and hid it under his armpit. "I want to see you."

He could hear her breathing. Her long, light breaths only made his breathing seem more strangled. "Soon," she said.

"Then you're still in the area?" Archie asked, glancing up at Henry to make sure he had heard.

She took another breath, exhaled. "I want

to be close to you."

"Where are you?" Archie asked.

"Where are you?"

Henry looked at Archie and shook his head. Archie knew what that meant. Gretchen was on a prepaid cell phone. Untraceable. She would hang up and go about her merry business and there was nothing they could do to stop her. "Gretchen," Archie said. "Don't kill anyone else, okay?"

"Does it hurt?" she asked.

Archie's hand found its way to his flank, the dull burning pain behind his ribs. "Yeah."

He could almost hear her smile through the phone. "Good."

The line went dead and Archie sat with the phone in his hand, only then realizing that he had been gripping it so tightly that his fingers ached. He set the phone down on the table and forced his cramped fingers straight. He hadn't worn a wedding ring in almost two years, but his hand still looked naked without it.

Henry, who had been pacing with his hands threaded behind his neck, stopped and slammed a fist into the baby-shit wall. The sound of his flesh hitting the plaster caused everyone in the room to turn. "Shit,"

Henry said, withdrawing his hand and shaking it. A hairline crack in the plaster marked the impact.

Buddy sat on the arm of the chair. "No one knows about the calls." He looked back and forth at each of them. "It doesn't leave this room."

Debbie, who had been sitting on the sofa, her hands balled in her lap, stood and walked into the kids' bedroom without a word.

Archie had so much to say to her, to explain, but it would have to wait.

The door to the suite was flung open and Archie and Henry turned. Susan Ward stood in the doorway. She was wearing all black and her turquoise hair glowed like the top of a flame against her flushed, angry face. "You gave an interview to Charlene-fucking-Wood?"

CHAPTER
33

"When did you ID the Jane Doe?" Buddy asked softly.

Susan looked livid. "That was my scoop. I was the one who identified her. It was my story." She looked at Archie sitting on the floor, then at Henry holding his hand and the spider crack on the wall beside him. "What's going on?" she asked.

Archie pulled himself up and sat down on the sofa where Debbie had been. The cushion was still warm. "I needed it on TV," he said to Susan.

"Are you sure it was her?" Buddy asked Archie.

Susan's mouth opened. "You knew?" she said, her eyes narrowing at Buddy. "You knew about Castle and Molly?"

He shrugged defensively. "I'd heard the same rumors that everyone else had over the years."

"But you knew her name," Archie said softly.

"It was an affair," Buddy said to Archie. "Jesus, don't be so self-righteous. All the time you and Debbie have been together, you've never thought about fucking around?"

The adrenaline of Gretchen's call was lifting, and Archie felt sick again, stomach acid rising in his throat.

"She was fourteen," Susan said.

Buddy's face colored. "I thought she was older than that," he said. "Eighteen."

A phone started to ring. For a split second Archie thought it might be Gretchen again, but the ring was wrong. He leaned his head back on the sofa and closed his eyes. His head hurt. His side throbbed. His skin felt like it was crawling with ants. "Susan ID'd her. We matched dental records. It's her." He glanced back at the second bedroom, where Debbie and the kids were. The door was still closed. He looked back at the others.

The phone was still ringing.

"Is someone going to get that?" Archie said wearily.

"It'll wait," Buddy said, tapping the leather phone holster on his belt. He stood. "This is a political shit storm, my friends," he said. "If the affair gets out."

"It's not an 'affair' if the girl is fourteen and the man is fifty," Susan said. "It's statutory rape."

Archie sighed. Did he have to spell it out? "It's more than that, Buddy," Archie said. It was a motive for murder.

Susan took a tiny step forward into the room. Her voice was just above a whisper. "You think Castle killed Molly?"

Henry, who had been holding his injured knuckles to his mouth, lowered his hand. "Jesus," he said.

"No," Buddy said. "I worked for the man. He wasn't capable of murder."

Susan bit her lip. "He was capable of fucking a fourteen-year-old and covering it up for fifteen years," she said.

"This is your fault," Buddy said, shoving a manicured finger in Susan's face. "If you'd let the thing rest —" He caught himself, clenched his hand and withdrew it. "Anyway, the story isn't out yet." He nodded to himself a couple of times. "If we're lucky, no one will connect Molly Palmer to the senator."

"She was his kids' babysitter," Susan pointed out. "Besides, I'm standing right here." She waved. "Hello. Journalist."

Buddy waved his hand in the air, like he was swatting away a bee. "It will still take the

242

press a few days." He turned to Susan. "Until then, embargo it."

Susan's face scrunched up in offense. "You can't tell me to embargo a story."

"I already did. You think it was the *Herald*'s idea to not run the thing after the senator died?"

"That's censorship." Susan looked helplessly at Archie. "That's government censorship."

Archie leaned forward a little, hoping to stem the black burn of pain that had been building under his ribs. It didn't work. Buddy's ringing phone was driving him crazy.

"You okay, Archie?" Henry asked.

Archie looked up at Buddy. "Did you call Fergus?" Fergus had been Archie's doctor from the minute they'd first wheeled him into Emanuel, after his ten days with Gretchen. He was one of the best trauma surgeons in the U.S. And he was discreet.

"His answering service was going to send him over," Buddy said.

"I thought you were faking," Henry said, coming around the sofa and kneeling beside Archie. "To get her to call."

Archie watched behind Henry as the hairline crack in the plaster wall began to spread, inching up the baby-shit wall, a tiny heart-shaped fissure. "Half faking," Archie said.

CHAPTER
34

Fergus moved his cold hand along the bare skin over Archie's rib line. Archie's shirt was open and he was sitting on the bed. Buddy had taken Debbie and the kids downstairs to get something to eat. Henry and Susan were in the living room.

Fergus pressed his fingers into Archie's scarred flesh. "Your liver's failing," Fergus said.

She had to be right.

Fergus moved his hands up and felt the lymph nodes under Archie's jaw. His hands weren't getting any warmer. He usually wore a bow tie, but today he wore khakis and a golf shirt. "Cirrhosis," Fergus said. "I won't know how severe it is until I run some labs."

There it was. There was a farmer's market on Saturday in the park across the street and Archie could hear the faint sound of milling crowds and a Grateful Dead cover band.

"The pills?" Archie asked.

Fergus looked at Archie over his glasses. "You need to give them up."

"I'm in pain," Archie said.

"There is a chance," Fergus said, taking off the glasses and rubbing the lenses with his shirt, "that if you stop taking the pills right now, your liver will be able to repair itself." He held the glasses up toward the light streaming through the wooden blinds and examined them. Then returned to cleaning them. "If you keep taking the pills, you will either need a liver transplant or you will die." He put the glasses on and looked at Archie, his expression grave. "And they don't give liver transplants until you've been clean for six months."

Archie started buttoning his shirt. "That seems reasonable of them."

"This isn't a joke."

Archie looked up at Fergus. Archie felt bad for him. He'd treated him since the beginning. Saved his life. Bent the rules. Written him prescription after prescription. "Slow it down," Archie said.

"Stop taking the pills," Fergus said. "Stop drinking. Keep taking diuretics for the edema. Stay away from salt. If you notice swelling in the abdomen we can insert a needle through the abdominal wall to remove fluid from the abdominal cavity."

"How bad is it going to get?" Archie asked.

Fergus rolled up Archie's sleeve, pulled a rubber tourniquet out of his medical bag and tied it around Archie's forearm. "If you start vomiting blood or notice changes in mental function, you call me or you go to the ER."

Archie nodded.

"I can't prescribe a medication I know is killing you," Fergus said, tapping a vein in Archie's arm. "I'll write you a few more scripts, so you don't go cold turkey. And I can get you the name of some treatment facilities." He retrieved a syringe from his bag, popped the rubber stopper off the end, and slid it into Archie's arm.

Archie watched as his blood slowly filled the syringe. He'd seen more blood in the past few years than he'd ever thought possible. "I don't want anyone to know about this."

Fergus slipped the syringe out and pressed a cotton ball over the bleeding needle wound. "You're going to need someone to take care of you," he said.

Archie allowed himself a wry smile, but by the time Fergus looked up it had faded. "I have someone in mind," Archie said. It was a relief, really. Because if he was going to die, he had nothing to lose. If he was going to die, he could catch her.

CHAPTER
35

Susan was standing at the end of the hall watching a bee tap at a window that overlooked the street. Outside she could see people carrying produce from the market, walking dogs, riding bikes, circling for parking. The bee smacked against the glass again. The skinny cop with big ears from the night before sat in a chair under a painting of an ugly old man. He looked up and smiled. "He's been at it for an hour," he said. "The bee. It's an old window." He reached up and scratched at one of his big ears. "Bees use UV rays to see. New windows have UV protection. But old ones? The UV goes right through the glass. So the bee can't see it."

Susan extended her hand. "Susan," she said.

"Todd Bennett," the cop said. "You can call me Bennett," he added. "Everyone does."

"You know a lot about bees, Bennett,"

Susan said, opening her cell phone.

"I know a lot about windows," Bennett said.

Susan wasn't in the mood to talk about glass, or bees, or even protopunk feminist singer-songwriter poets of the 1970s, and she was almost always in the mood to talk about them.

She punched in a *Herald* number and extension.

Ian picked up the phone at his desk. "Features," he said. His voice made Susan's skin crawl. She could taste him in the smooth timbre of it, his skin, his soap. Don't sleep with the people you work with, her mother had told her. In fact she'd said, "Don't shit where you sleep," but Susan had known what she meant.

Susan was trying to be better about that. It was one of the reasons she'd broken up with Derek.

Susan turned away from Bennett and spoke in a low tone. "Ian," she said, "when are you running the story about Castle and Molly Palmer?"

Ian paused. "When the time is right."

The bee smacked against the window again. "Meaning?"

"People are still grieving," Ian said.

Susan wanted to laugh or maybe jam the

heel of her palm into Ian's xiphoid process and drive it into his heart. "You fucker," she said. "You're not going to run it, are you?"

His voice grew smoother. "Be patient, babe."

"Don't call me babe," she said. The bee was on the outside windowsill now, readying itself for another sortie. It fluttered its wings. "I'll take it somewhere else. Someone will run it."

"You got a contract with us," Ian said. "Break it, you lose your job. We're the only daily in town." He laughed and Susan decided that instead of his xiphoid process, maybe she would go for the bridge of his nose and blind him. That way he'd live to rue the day he'd crossed her. "Who are you going to work for?" Ian continued gleefully. "The *Auto Trader*?"

Ouch. "So you're going to let them kill the story? Just like that?"

"He's dead. What does it matter? You're brilliant. The Castle story is over. Everyone wants Gretchen Lowell now. And you're right in the middle of it."

"I'm trapped at the fucking Arlington," Susan said, more loudly than she had intended. The bee smacked against the window again. "Give it up," Susan said. "Shoo."

"What?" asked Ian.

Susan covered her face with a hand. "I was talking to a bee," she said.

"Oh," Ian said. He made a little clucking sound. "I'm covering the manhunt. Woman hunt. Whatever. But we'll set up a blog for you on the Web site. You can update it every day from the Arlington."

"A blog?" As far as Susan was concerned, the *Herald*'s Web site was a wasteland. Susan glanced over at Bennett. He was reading a copy of *Portland Monthly*. The cover had a photograph of Oregon's high desert and a headline that read THE BEST EXOTIC GETAWAYS. Maybe he was reading an article about windows.

Gretchen Lowell or not, Susan needed to get out of there. She was not going to write a blog. Not if they were going to kill the Castle story. She owed that, at least, to Molly Palmer.

"Listen, babe," Ian said. She could hear the familiar tap-tap-tap of him typing on a keyboard. "I've got to run. I've got copy on the school siege to file."

The bee was gone. Maybe it was dead. Maybe it had given up and flown away to some pollen-swollen paradise. Susan didn't know. "You know how I said your penis was average-sized?" Susan told Ian. "I lied."

She snapped her phone shut. She missed Parker. Parker would know what to do. Parker would make sure the story got published. Parker would get it on A-1. She dropped the phone back into her purse and walked back to her room, right past Bennett, who, she noticed, didn't make eye contact, which meant that he'd overheard every word of her conversation. He was sitting directly across from Archie's suite, number 602. And next to Susan and Bliss's room, number 603. Archie and his family had a suite. She and Bliss were sharing a single room. Two twin beds. A desk. A TV. And a bathroom with no tub.

Susan wanted a bath right now. More than anything.

She opened the door to her room and there, in the small space between the end of the beds and the far wall, found her naked fifty-six-year-old mother standing with her legs together, arms raised, palms together. Her mole-dotted skin was pale, the flesh loose around the midsection and upper arms. Her breasts swung laterally as she reached down and touched her toes. Her bleached dreadlocks hit the carpet like a bundle of rope.

Susan quickly closed the door behind her. "Bliss," she asked. "What are you doing?"

Susan's mother jumped back into a plank position, so that her body was flat, her arms and toes on the floor. Her nipples brushed the carpet. "Sun salutations."

"You're naked. You're naked in the Arlington."

Bliss stretched into upward dog, keeping her toes on the floor but stretching her torso up, so her arms were straight and she was looking up at Susan. "I always do naked yoga," she said. She bent back into downward dog, lifting her dimpled bare butt cheeks in the air and arching her back, and then moved one leg up between her hands, bent her knee and sank into warrior pose, so she was in a lunge with her arms extended above her head. "It's very freeing."

Susan's mother had a tattoo of English ivy that began below one breast and snaked down to her upper thigh. As Susan followed the tattoo with her eyes, her jaw dropped. "What did you do to your pubic hair?"

Bliss lowered her arms into the proud warrior pose, extending one in front of her and one behind. "I had it waxed," Bliss said. She spread the flesh of her abdomen so Susan could make out the design that had been carefully created in the rounded thatch of gray pubes. "It's a peace sign. Bodhi did it at the salon."

"Oh, my God."

Bliss lifted her arms up again, sank a little lower into the pose, and closed her eyes. "It's an illegal war, honey," she said.

Susan spun around and opened the door to the hallway. There was Henry. And Debbie. And Archie's two kids. They all turned and looked at Susan. And beyond her, clearly visible through the open door, Susan's lunging naked mother.

"Namaste," Bliss said with a wave. She stepped forward and bent all the way over, her dreadlocks piling again on the carpet.

Henry, Debbie, Ben, and Sara all stood motionless for a minute.

"I like your tattoo," Ben said to Bliss.

"Thanks!" said Bliss, stepping back into plank position.

Susan stepped into the hallway and closed the door behind her. Bennett still sat in the chair, the *Portland Monthly* open in his lap. Ben and Sara each held on to one of Debbie's hands. Henry raised an eyebrow.

"Nice lunch?" Susan asked, trying to sound casual.

"Try the smoked salmon salad," said Debbie. "It's delicious."

The hallway was quiet. The only sound was the noise of the cop's magazine pages turning too fast for him to actually be reading.

"Where are you going?" Henry asked Susan.

Susan was wearing skinny black jeans, a black tank top, and a black belt. Her purse and her shoes were red patent leather. "To work," she said.

Henry shook his head. "You can't leave. You're under protection."

"I have stories to write," Susan said. Her voice sounded too desperate, so she tried to rephrase it, make it sound more important. "Journalism. Newspaper journalism."

"Write in your room," Henry said. "Where you're safe."

Susan glanced back at the closed door that separated them from her naked mother and then back at Henry. "I need to get out of here," she said between clenched teeth.

Henry sighed. "I'll talk to Archie."

Great. Trapped at the Arlington. Gretchen gets out. And Susan gets locked up. That was fair. Susan stole another glance at Bennett. She couldn't get past Henry. But maybe that guy. "Okay," she said.

Henry looked at her for a minute, then nodded. He put a hand on Debbie's lower back and led her and the two kids through the door to Archie's suite.

"Was that a peace sign?" Susan heard Debbie ask Henry as they disappeared through the door.

CHAPTER
36

Archie held Sara in the crook of his arm on her bed, amid a menagerie of stuffed animals. Henry had brought them from the house and they were wedged in every available space, a rolling topography of faux fur, paws, and tails. His body felt light and relaxed from the pills and it was all he could do not to doze off next to her.

"Read it again," she said.

He had just finished reading Sara the Winnie-the-Pooh book *Now We Are Six*.

"It's time for bed," he said.

Ben was in the next bed, reading a Lemony Snicket book.

Archie kissed Sara on the head. Her hair was the same shade as her mother's. He loved the smell of her and he kept his face against her head for a moment, savoring it. He couldn't remember the last time Ben had let him kiss him good night.

"I love you," he said. There were moments,

like this, when he was perfectly, beautifully happy. And he still didn't know if it was real. Or the Vicodin.

He put his feet on the floor and searched for his shoes.

Sara's flat little hand gripped his arm. "Stay with me," she said. "Until I go to sleep."

"Sure," Archie said, happy to stretch the moment out. He leaned back on the bed, crossed his feet, and put his arm back around his daughter. A plastic nose from some buried stuffed animal pressed against his back.

Her eyes didn't waver from him as she fell asleep, her eyelids growing heavier and heavier until, with a sliver of white, she finally gave it up.

Archie waited another few minutes and then disentangled himself and put on his shoes.

Ben put his Lemony Snicket on the bedside table and rolled over so he wasn't facing Archie. "Good night, Dad," he said to the wall.

"Good night," said Archie.

He expected to find Henry and Debbie where he'd left them in the suite's main room, but they weren't there.

"I'm in here," Debbie called from the bedroom.

She appeared in the doorway, clad in the white Arlington robe she'd taken to wearing. Archie bet if they ever moved back home, the robe would find its way into her suitcase.

"When did Henry leave?" he asked, coming into the room and sitting on the bed.

She walked into the bathroom and started brushing her teeth. "Fifteen minutes ago," she said, the toothbrush in her mouth. She scooped some water into her mouth, rinsed, and spat in the sink. "He said to say goodbye."

He watched her reflection from where he sat. She was beautiful. Sara would be beautiful like that, too, when she grew up. The brown hair, the freckles, the watchful eyes. Debbie rinsed her toothbrush and dried her mouth with a white hand towel. Then she saw him watching her and turned around, resting her back against the sink.

"What?" she said.

"Nothing."

"I'm glad you're all right," she said softly.

Archie shrugged. "Just stress, I guess," he said.

"You scared me," she said.

"I'm sorry," he said. He finished the sentence in his head: For everything.

She gave him one of her concerned crooked smiles. Debbie would survive him. It would be hard. But she would be okay. The kids would be okay. They would probably be better off in the long run.

"Why are you looking at me like that?" Debbie asked.

He held his arms out toward her. "Come here," he said. Maybe it wasn't the pills. Maybe he was actually happy.

She walked barefoot over to him and he reached out and untied her robe and let it fall open. He stood and reached inside the robe and slid his hand down the bumps of her ribs to the round curve of her hip.

She inhaled sharply and bit her lip. "It's been a long time," she said.

Archie pulled her toward him and kissed her on the neck, inhaling her. "Tell me about it," he said. He pushed the robe off her shoulders and it fell behind her on the floor and she stepped away from it into his arms.

He knew her. Her breasts, the left one just a little larger than the right. The constellation of moles on her pale stomach. The small pad of pregnancy fat on her upper abdomen.

He kissed her on the mouth and backed onto the bed, pulling her on top of him. She tasted like peppermint toothpaste. She moaned and reached down to unbuckle his pants. He stopped her, taking her hand by the wrist and lifting it to his mouth so he could kiss her fingers. He willed himself to respond. He wanted to make love to her. He did love her. But his body resisted. It had been like that since Gretchen. He didn't know if it was the physical trauma of what he'd been through, or if he was just so poisoned by his lust for Gretchen that his body wouldn't betray her, wouldn't get hard for anyone else.

He was going to make love to his wife. He was going to do this one last time. Even if it meant cheating just a little. So he decided to let Gretchen into his mind just for a moment. He closed his eyes. And there she was. God, she was beautiful, her blond hair and milky white skin, her mouth open, wanting him. He tasted Debbie's earlobe, and it was Gretchen's earlobe. He ran his hands through Debbie's hair, and it was Gretchen's hair. He felt instantly hard. He could feel Gretchen unbuttoning his pants, slipping her hand inside his underwear, taking hold of him. It was good. He wondered why he hadn't done this before. She covered his neck with butterfly kisses like Debbie used to do. But that wasn't what he wanted. He pushed his tongue into her mouth, pushed the waist of his pants down, and flipped her over and pushed himself inside her. He was rough and the force of him caused her to take a breath and it turned him on more. He thrust as hard and as deeply as he could. He couldn't stop it. He wanted to fuck her harder than anyone ever had before. Any of the men she'd had. The men who'd killed for her. The men she'd killed. He wanted to reach the center of her.

He heard, from somewhere far away, his wife say, "You're hurting me."

And then he came. His whole body shook with it, his back muscles spasmed. All the rage and stress and grief he kept bottled up was screwed up on his face. And he opened his eyes.

"Jesus Christ, Archie," Debbie said. She was trembling, her eyes huge.

Archie pulled out of her and rolled off her onto the bed. He could taste, in his mouth, a faint trace of peppermint. "I'm sorry," he said, disgusted with himself.

Debbie was quiet for a long time, sitting on the bed. She held the sheet tight around her torso, her knuckles white where she gripped it. "You see your therapist," she said finally. "Tomorrow." She got up and headed into the bathroom, taking the sheet with her. She turned on the faucet and looked in the bathroom mirror at Archie's reflection, as Archie stared back at hers. "Or I will fucking drag you to her myself."

CHAPTER
37

"Are you smoking?" Susan asked.

It was dark in the room. Susan had been asleep until the smell of cigarette smoke had wrenched her from a perfectly lovely dream in which she and Archie Sheridan were having an adventure in a city that looked a lot like Atlantis. Susan lay there for a few minutes, inhaling the damning evidence of her mother's midnight smoke break.

"Mom?" she said.

Her mother didn't answer.

Susan reached over and flipped on the bedside lamp. It cast a triangle of light that revealed Bliss hunched over the side of her bed, her naked back to Susan, holding a cigarette just below the edge of the mattress to hide the telltale glowing tip.

Bliss's blond dreads were tied back in a jumble that fell almost to her waist. She glanced back at Susan. "Just a puff," she said, holding up her cigarette. "I couldn't sleep."

Susan sat up. "No," she said. "You can't smoke in here. It's no smoking. You'll set off the fire alarm. Hold it out the window."

Bliss drew the cigarette to her mouth and took a drag. "The windows don't open," she said.

Susan threw her head back in frustration. "Mom," she groaned.

Bliss sighed and stretched across the bed to grind the cigarette out in an empty glass on the bedside table. She was wearing black cotton underpants and red-and-orange striped knee socks. "You are such a cop," she said.

Susan glanced at her watch. It was just past three A.M. This could be her chance to get the hell out of there. She got out of bed and crept toward the door to the hall. She was wearing her I SMELL BULLSHIT T-shirt and underpants. Not exactly escape clothes, but this was recon. She opened the door a crack and peered out. Bennett looked up instantly from his chair and waved.

Fuck, that guy never went home. He didn't even nod off.

Susan waved back, trying not to look too disappointed. "Can't sleep," she explained. Then she ducked back into the room and flung herself back onto her bed.

"I may get fired," Susan said. "That girl I was writing about, Molly Palmer. She's dead. That was her body they found Saturday in the park."

Bliss looked up, interested. "How did she die?" she asked.

"They don't know," Susan said. "They thought it was an OD. But the senator's dead. And Parker. Again, tragic accident. But it's got to be connected. And the *Herald* doesn't want to run the story. Ian said it was because Castle had just died and they wanted to wait a few days to attack him. And now he says they can't run it without Molly to verify her story." Susan had promised Molly that everything would be all right. She had promised her a lot of things. She would have said anything to get her to talk. "I think he's getting pressured," Susan said.

"You have notes?" Bliss asked. "Tapes of interviews?"

"I gave all my story material to Archie," Susan said.

Bliss raised an eyebrow. "You gave the only evidence you have to support your story to the police?"

Susan bit her lip. She hadn't really thought of it that way. "Yeah," she said.

Bliss reached over and turned off the

bedside light, throwing the room back into darkness. "Sometimes," she said, "I think all those protests I took you to as a kid didn't teach you anything at all."

CHAPTER
38

"Is all this really necessary?" Sarah Rosenberg asked. She had agreed to see Archie first thing in the morning and her hair was still wet from a shower, a tangle of brown curls that left dark stains on the shoulders of her gray turtleneck. No makeup. A mug of coffee sat on a coaster on an end table next to her striped chair. The mug had a big red heart on it and the words WORLD'S GREATEST MOM.

Archie took a sip of his own paper cup of coffee. Henry was sitting outside the door to Rosenberg's home office. Two squad cars were parked out front. A patrol cop was on the porch. "It's in case you try to murder me," he said. The green velvet curtains were drawn. He couldn't see the cherry trees.

Rosenberg's eyebrows knitted in concern. "Are you all right?" she asked.

There was no faking it. He'd seen himself in the mirror that morning. His skin looked like paraffin wax. There were dark circles under his eyes. His hands trembled. "No," Archie said.

"How is your family?" Rosenberg asked.

Archie glanced at the grandfather clock. Still three-thirty. Someday he was going to pay to get that clock fixed himself. "Just giddy," Archie said.

Rosenberg was quiet for a moment. She picked up the mug with the heart on it, took a sip, and put it back down. Tea, Archie realized from the smell. Not coffee. "I read about what happened at the school," Rosenberg said. "That must have been difficult for you."

He didn't want to believe that Gretchen would kill his children. Terrorize them, yes. But would she be able to actually murder Archie's own flesh and blood? "She killed a little boy once," Archie said softly. "It was notable because she's only killed a couple of children." Who was he kidding? "That we know of." He put his elbow on the arm of the chair and rested his chin in his hand. Rosenberg sat, spine and neck erect, watching him. "Ten years old," Archie continued. "He disappeared on the way home from playing at the park near his house. She made him drink drain cleaner and then she skinned him with a scalpel."

That had been in Washington State. He'd driven up for the autopsy. "Then she left his body, hog-tied, in his own backyard for his mother to find."

Rosenberg's posture didn't change. "You've seen a lot of violence," she said simply.

Archie took a sip of his coffee. It was a long time after his ten days with Gretchen that he could swallow anything without it burning his damaged esophagus. "It's hard to drink drain cleaner," he said. "You end up vomiting a lot of it back up. For the amount in his system, she would have had to hold him down, to force it down his throat." Archie got out the pillbox. He didn't even try to hide it. He opened the box and tapped a couple of pills into his hand. "I was lucky," he said, putting the pills in his mouth. "She only fed it to me a few teaspoons at a time."

"You weren't lucky, Archie," Rosenberg said. "And you didn't do anything to deserve it."

That was just it, though. He had.

"I need to catch her," Archie said. He couldn't make his family happy, but he could keep them safe.

"How?" Rosenberg asked.

Archie smiled, remembering the engraving over the entrance to Ben and Sara's school.

" 'Education is not the filling of a pail, but the lighting of a fire,' " he said.

Rosenberg didn't say anything.

"Yeats," Archie said.

"I know who said it," Rosenberg said. "I'm just not sure how it applies."

"She'll keep killing," Archie explained. He was growing more and more comfortable with his plan, convincing himself that it wasn't mad. "She can't stop herself. She burns everything she touches. How do you put out a fire? You feed it, and let it burn itself out."

"Or you run as fast as you can, and call nine-one-one," Rosenberg said.

"Or that," Archie said.

CHAPTER
39

Debbie Sheridan answered the door in a white terry-cloth robe with the words ARLINGTON CLUB stitched in gold thread on the breast. Susan's room hadn't come with a robe. Her room hadn't even come with shampoo.

"Archie isn't here," Debbie said.

Susan tried to crane her neck past Debbie to see if the box she'd given Archie was still where she'd left it. She could hear the kids' voices inside. "I gave him a box of notes that I need to look at," Susan said.

Debbie seemed unimpressed by Susan's predicament. "You'll have to come back later," she said, closing the door.

Susan blinked at the closed door four inches from her nose. "Okay," she said. She was going to go back to her own room, but as she brushed her fingers against the doorknob, she reconsidered and turned and headed for the door to the stairs.

"Where are you going?" she heard a voice call. Bennett.

Susan turned back to face him. "Do they ever give you time off?"

"I volunteered to work double shifts," Bennett said. He was sitting in the chair. He didn't even look tired. "Where are you going?"

"Out?" she said.

Bennett stood up, carefully marked his place in the magazine he was reading and set it on the chair, and walked over to her. "You're supposed to stay upstairs," he said, eyes narrowing.

Susan splayed her fingers in agony. "I need to have a cigarette," she said.

"Bad habit," Bennett said.

Susan smiled. "Have you ever been profiled? I could write a story about you. For the paper." She fluttered her eyelids. "Something heroic."

"I have one assignment," Bennett said, crossing his arms. "To sit here in this hallway and make sure you and Detective Sheridan are safe."

Susan reached into her pocket and produced a pack of cigarettes and wiggled them. "I could share," she said.

"I don't smoke," said Bennett.

"So what am I supposed to do?" Susan asked.

Bennett reached into his own pocket and pulled out a weathered-looking pack of Big Red. "Gum?"

"Archie's not here," Susan told Bliss when she got back into the room.

"It took you long enough. Where did you get the gum?"

Susan's phone rang. It was the *Herald*. She picked it up.

"Just met with editorial," Ian said. "They're excited about the blog." He paused dramatically. "I've got the headline — SAFE HOUSE DISPATCHES. You have content yet?"

"Is the paper under pressure to bury the Molly Palmer story?" Susan asked.

Ian was quiet. She listened to him get up and close his office door. Finally, he said, "Yes."

"Are you fighting for me?" Susan asked. "Behind the scenes?"

"I know you won't believe it," Ian said. "But yes."

She believed him. Not because he wasn't an ass, but because he was a journalist first. And then an ass. "I'll do the dispatches," Susan said. "But I want print. No more of this Web bullshit. And I'm only doing it because I want you to run the Castle story."

"More people look at the Web site than read the paper," Ian said.

"Oh," Susan said. "I'll post something in the next half hour."

It was dark by the time Susan posted that day's final blog. The police had determined that Gretchen had been having an affair with B. D. Cavanaugh, the guard who'd killed himself. And Gretchen had killed the female transport guard and taken off with the male one. If he was still even alive. Since Susan was sequestered she had to do all her legwork over the phone and by e-mail. With her mother on the bed next to her watching daytime TV. Bliss didn't have a TV in the house on principle, and whenever she was around one she was completely transfixed.

Of course there were constant TV news updates about the manhunt for Gretchen. The way the TV newsies talked about it, you'd think they wanted her to get away.

Susan closed her laptop. Gretchen Lowell on the loose. Archie Sheridan just down the hall. There she was in the thick of the biggest story of the year. Her blog had gotten over a million hits. She should have been thrilled.

But she couldn't get Molly Palmer out of her head.

Susan slid the laptop onto the bed. Her legs were still warm from it.

"You're going to get thigh cancer from that thing," Bliss said, her eyes still trained on the TV news.

Susan stretched. "There's no such thing as thigh cancer," she said.

"Not yet," Bliss said.

Susan felt stiff and tense and a little stir-crazy. "I need a cigarette," she announced. "Will you distract Nurse Ratched?"

Bliss flicked her attention off the screen to Susan. "Who?" she asked.

"The cop in the hall," Susan said.

"How?" Bliss asked.

Susan pulled on her sweatshirt. "Talk to him," she said.

Bliss's face creased with concern. "What should I say?" she asked.

Susan shrugged. "Ask him about windows," she said.

Charlene Wood was yammering away on the television, as the screen showed images of the Beauty Killer's victims.

"Are you sure it's safe for you to go out?" Bliss asked.

Susan stowed her cigarettes and a lighter in the pocket of her sweatshirt. "Keep an ear out," Susan said, pulling up her hood. "If Gretchen Lowell tries to get me, I'll scream."

It wasn't even hard. Bliss went out and talked to Bennett and Susan was able to slip right down the stairs. Bennett was too engrossed to notice. Maybe he'd heard about the peace sign.

Susan was free and she had nothing to do. She didn't have her notes. Ian wanted her at the Arlington for the blog, and as long as he had power over the Castle story, she wanted to keep Ian happy.

Susan lit a cigarette and inhaled. That first drag was the best. Her whole body relaxed a little. It was a bit like sex that way, always a relief. She tried to tell herself that she smoked because she liked smoke breaks — those forced little interludes of solitude and contemplation — but the truth was, she liked the nicotine.

The downtown ornamental streetlights had just come on and a couple of seagulls that had wandered in from the coast were squawking in the park. Portland was an hour from the Pacific, and Susan didn't know why the gulls came so far inland, but they were always there, padding around the river, shitting on the esplanade, wandering the parks. A kid covered in tattoos and piercings flew by on a skateboard and the gulls barely gave him a glance.

It was in the high sixties, warm for evening, and pretty. The nighttime Pacific Northwest sky was a blend of pastels. There were lights on in some of the downtown buildings, late-night workers or cleaners or clandestine office affairs.

Susan took another drag off the cigarette. Maybe she was wrong. Maybe the second drag was the best.

Molly had smoked Kools. Susan wondered if her estranged family was going to have a funeral service. If they did, Susan pledged to herself that she would bring a pack of Kools and put it in the casket.

A voice said, "You can't smoke here, ma'am," and Susan looked up to see the ghoulish Arlington Club concierge moving toward her waving his hand like a fan.

She glanced behind her to see if he was talking to someone else. Susan was, after all, standing outside. On a public sidewalk. Not bothering anyone at all. And she'd told him not to call her "ma'am."

The concierge kept waving his hand. "Ma'am?" he said.

Susan took another drag off the cigarette. "Why not?" she asked.

"You'll disturb the guests," he said, as if it were obvious.

She gestured, with her cigarette, to the dark brick façade of the building, its green awning, the park, the cars on the street. "I'm outside."

"But they have to pass you," he said. He opened the big glass doors to illustrate. "Coming and going."

Susan looked down at her cigarette. It needed ashing. But she was afraid to ash on the sidewalk in front of this guy. He'd probably make her clean it up. "Where am I supposed to go?"

He pointed across the street to the park.

Susan relented and ducked across the street and found a wooden bench that faced the Arlington. That part of the park had a decorative public water fountain and a low concrete wall with a medallion bearing Simon Benson's profile on it. The fountains, so-called Benson Bubblers, were all over downtown Portland. The story was that Simon Benson, a turn-of-the-century Portland lumber baron, had the bubblers installed to discourage his workers from drinking beer in the middle of the day. Susan didn't know if his plan had worked, but a hundred years later there were signs all over the park warning that alcohol was prohibited.

Susan ashed her cigarette on the hexagonal cobblestones beneath her feet. She smoked American Spirits. Molly was dead. And Susan was smoking. She needed to get back to Molly Palmer. The blog could wait. Writing a book about Gretchen could wait. She needed to stay focused. She needed to find a way to get the *Herald* to publish Molly's story. She was growing more and more certain that Molly's death wasn't an accidental overdose. She needed to find out who killed her. And she needed to find out who was trying to cover it all up.

She was pretty sure that one line of inquiry would lead to the other.

A shaggy-haired homeless man came and sat down next to her with a bundle of *Street Roots* newspapers. He stank of grime and body odor, but Susan was determined not to react to it. He dropped the newspapers between them on the bench, sniffed the air, made a face, and turned to Susan.

"Do you mind?" he said.

"What?" she said.

"Not smoking."

CHAPTER
40

The beaver was three feet long and had been stuffed standing on its back paws, its tail a plate-sized flap on the carpet, head turned, as if he had just caught sight of something dangerous out of the corner of his eye. He'd been dead about a hundred years and his fur was molting, but there was a spark of fear in his black glass eyes that made him look almost lifelike. Archie could relate.

The beaver stood beside the maître d's station in the Arlington Club Restaurant. Archie felt bad for the maître d', because the restaurant was for members and guests only, and Archie had never seen more than seven people in there at a time. Mostly the maître d' spent his time leafing through the leather-bound reservation book and, when he wasn't doing that, picking up the tiny feathers that fell from the stuffed pheasant on the mantel and drifted to the carpet below.

Debbie glanced up at the buck's head hung

above the door to the dining room. "This place gives me the creeps," she said. There was only one other table occupied for dinner, and the clanking of their silverware carried more than their voices.

"It won't be for long," Henry said. "A few more days."

Debbie looked at Archie as if she wanted some kind of confirmation, a nod, something. They hadn't talked about the previous night. What could he say? Sorry?

Archie looked at his plate.

After his visit with Rosenberg he'd spent a few hours at the task force offices trying to help with coordinating the manhunt, and the rest of the day at the Arlington Club, trying to seem normal for his children. Claire was upstairs with them now, so Archie and Debbie could have some time together. But they couldn't even do that without Henry.

The food was all right. Archie took another bite of salmon drizzled in cilantro pesto, still avoiding Debbie's gaze. Salmon was pretty much all they served. Salmon cakes. Salmon salad. Salmon fillet. Salmon steak. It was Copper River season, when hundreds of fishermen flocked to the head of the three-hundred-mile rugged Copper River in Alaska to try to catch the fish going upstream to spawn. That's when the fish were rich with fat. The farther on their journey you caught them, the more damaged and tasteless they became.

Archie's stomach churned and cramped. He had cut back on the pills before. He knew how the withdrawal started. He put down his silver fork and his white cloth napkin, pushed his chair away from the table, and stood up. "I'm going to the bathroom," he said.

Henry stood, too, intending to go with him.

They were too worried about him, and not worried enough about catching Gretchen. If it had been up to Archie, he'd have called in the army. But it wasn't up to Archie. With the exception of his therapy field trip he'd spent the day under lock and key at the Arlington, not making eye contact with Debbie.

Archie sighed. "Are you going to watch me take a shit?" he asked.

Henry looked around at the vacant restaurant, the restroom within sight at the end of the room, then shrugged and sat.

"Thank you," Archie said.

The men's room had stalls with doors that shut. Classy. Archie finished up and washed his hands. The liquid hand soap smelled like lilacs. Or maybe he was just imagining it. He felt bleary from lack of sleep. His eyes looked yellow in the bathroom mirror. He used a real towel to dry his hands and dropped it in a straw bin below the marble counter.

The kid was waiting for him outside the bathroom door. He wasn't a real kid. He was twenty, probably. Archie could see the hole in his lip from where he wore a piercing when he wasn't at work. His white busboy jacket was starched flat and as he got close to Archie, Archie caught the harsh waft of fresh cigarette smoke.

The kid talked out of the side of his mouth, like he had a secret. "Your friend's looking for you," he said. "She said to wait and tell you when you were alone."

The kid had a new piercing on the top of his ear, in the cartilage. It was just a tiny silver stud, lost under his hair and so small the restaurant management probably hadn't noticed it. Archie wouldn't have noticed it either except for the thin tear of blood that ran down the outer fold of the kid's left ear.

Those sorts of piercings took a long time to heal.

"Where is she?" Archie asked.

"In her car in the alley." The kid gestured behind them, toward a swinging steel door, as if it were nothing, as if he were giving directions to the mall. "Back there. Through the kitchen."

Archie realized then from the sly spark in the kid's eye that the kid thought that Gretchen was his mistress.

"You're bleeding," Archie said.

The kid's eyebrows shot together and then he reached up with his left hand and touched the ear, wincing as he did. He lowered his hand and looked at it, the streak of blood evident on his fingertips. "Gross," he said.

"Do you have any plans tonight?" Archie asked the kid, imagining the hours of interrogation the kid faced at Henry's hands.

"No," the kid said.

Archie walked away, toward the door that led to the kitchen, away from Henry, away from Debbie, away from everything. "Good."

CHAPTER
41

The last person Archie expected to find on the other side of the door to the alley was Susan Ward. She glanced up from where she was standing, next to a green Dumpster, snapped the cigarette from between her lips, and said hello, as if she weren't surprised to see him at all. For a long second Archie was confused. Then he saw past her, farther up the alley, where the brake lights of a silver Jaguar hovered in the dusk, like sleepy, sinister eyes.

"Are you okay?" Archie asked Susan.

Susan ashed her cigarette in a large restaurant-sized can that had once held stewed tomatoes, but now held the ashes of a thousand smoke breaks. "Yeah. This is the only fucking place I can smoke." She gestured to the side of the Dumpster, which reeked of spoiled food. "Watch the urine."

The fact that Susan was there was a coincidence. Dizzy from relief, Archie stumbled, and had to reach out and grab on to the Dumpster to catch himself.

"Yikes, drink much?" said Susan. She smiled, red lipstick on her teeth, and sucked in another lungful of tobacco smoke. Cigarette butts lay everywhere on the concrete below, like matchsticks dropped in a children's game. Cigarette butts were excellent sources of DNA.

"Give me one," Archie said.

Susan hesitated. "Seriously?"

Archie held out a hand. It was shaking slightly, but not enough for anyone but him to notice. Susan pulled a cigarette out of her yellow pack and handed it to him.

"Have you ever been a smoker?" she asked.

Archie took her black plastic lighter and lit the cigarette and inhaled. The smoke burned his lungs, but he didn't cough. He glanced over to where the Jaguar still idled up ahead, its engine almost silent. It was the only good car the British had ever built. "Nope," he said. "Tried a few times. Never took. I remember the first one, though. That's always the one you remember. First cigarette. First kiss. First corpse in a park."

Susan raised her eyebrows. "O-kay." She was wearing black leggings, brown boots, a T-shirt advertising a band that Archie didn't recognize, and a hooded sweatshirt, and her turquoise hair was up in pigtails. "Hey," she said. "I know I just gave it to you, but I need that box of notes from the Castle story back."

Her request barely registered. Archie had other things on his mind. "I've got to go," Archie said.

Susan glanced back at the scratched fire door that led into the kitchen. "Where's Henry?"

"They'll be fine," Archie said more to himself than to Susan. He took a few steps toward the car and then turned around and looked at Susan and smiled and dropped the cigarette.

"Archie?" he heard Susan call, her voice rising a pitch.

He kept walking toward the car. When he reached it, he turned back again. He opened the passenger side door. Susan stood with her hands on her hips, head cocked to one side. Between them, the cigarette he had dropped glowed orange on the pavement. He hadn't stepped on it, hadn't ground it out. He hadn't wanted to risk ruining their chance of getting his DNA off it.

He didn't wave goodbye to Susan. It seemed too ghoulish. Instead he just turned away from her, and moving steadily, gently, climbed into the car.

The nausea had lifted now and he was almost relieved, certain that this was the best plan. Besides, the cigarette would help them later.

If they had to identify a body.

The car moved instantly.

He felt her hand on his upper thigh before he heard her voice. "Hello, darling," she said.

He looked over at her. Her blond hair was tied back at her neck, her left hand was at twelve o'clock on the wheel. She was ravishing and terrifying and strangely full of life. If it worked, it would be worth it. If not, well, what the hell.

"Hello, Gretchen," he said.

CHAPTER
42

The dashboard of the Jag was a walnut veneer, so shiny Archie could see his reflection in it. It was blurry and he looked away from his haggard face.

"Take the bullets out of your weapon and the battery off your phone and toss them out the window," Gretchen said. Her voice was glass, mellifluous, like music.

Archie turned to her. His heart was pounding, adrenaline pulsing through his body. It was nice. It made him feel high. "That's littering," he said.

Gretchen smiled sweetly. He had missed looking at her. She was thirty-four but seemed both younger and older somehow. The flawless skin. The perfect features. It was like looking at a painting in a museum after you'd only seen the postcard; the print in his memory could never live up to the original. "The police looking for you will find them by morning," she said.

He took his phone out of his pocket, popped the back off, and removed the flat blue battery, and then lifted his gun out of his holster and let the bullets fall gently from the chamber into one hand. Gretchen pushed a button somewhere and his window slid open and he held his hand out the window and let the bullets and the battery fall to the street. The bullets bounced, snapping against the cement.

Gretchen turned left off the park blocks toward the river. "Nice car," Archie said.

"I had some money set aside," she said. "In another name." She moved her hand slightly up his thigh. It was only a millimeter, but it felt farther. "Look in the glove compartment," she said.

He opened the car's slick glove box. Inside were five large amber prescription bottles of pills.

"Remove the pills," she said. "And put your gun and phone inside. There's water in the cup holder."

Archie followed her instructions. The gun and the phone were useless now anyway. He picked up the bottle of water next to his left knee in the car's cup holder and unscrewed the cap. Then he opened one of the pill bottles. Even in the dim light of the car, he knew what they were, the shape and feel of the pills. He tapped four out of the bottle and then swallowed them with water.

She picked up three little yellow pills from the car's change drawer and handed them to him.

"What are they?" he asked. They were on Bill Naito Parkway now, heading south. The river was to their left. In the seventies there had been a freeway adjacent to the river, but they'd decided to tear it down and build a park that stretched the length of downtown at the water's edge.

"We have a long drive ahead of us," Gretchen said.

She didn't want him to see where they were going. That was a good sign. If she had been planning on killing him right away, it wouldn't have mattered.

"Am I going to wake up strapped to a gurney?" he asked.

"No."

He put the pills on his tongue. They were bitter. But not like the Vicodin. It was a different taste. He took another swallow of water to wash it from his mouth.

"I've missed you, darling," Gretchen said.

Archie smiled and leaned his head on the side window and watched as they pulled onto I-5 headed south. "Yeah," he said.

CHAPTER
43

"What kind of car was it?" Henry said.

Susan fumbled for another cigarette, her hands trembling. Henry had burst out of the alley door, a moment after the silver car had disappeared. And had been yelling at her ever since.

"I told you," Susan said. "It was silver." She thought about paint, picturing the paint samples her mother brought home and tacked to various walls for years while she decided. "But not blue silver; not glacier or metallic; not neutral." She searched her mind for any further explanation, wanting to help any way she could. "It was silver with a splash of gray, like that silk blouse with the French-cut sleeves I sometimes wear. Expensive silver. Platinum." Then it came to her. "A shade lighter than the Macbook Pro."

Henry did not seem to appreciate her efforts at specificity. The veins in his forehead pulsed. "Was it a new car?"

"Yes?" Susan said. He was making her nervous. She looked at her pack of cigarettes. Only two left. Crap, why couldn't she pay better attention to things?

Henry put a hand on her arm, so she looked up at him. "Was it an American car? A sedan? Did it have a license plate? Bumper stickers? How many taillights?"

Susan felt her eyes fill with tears. "I don't know." She lit her cigarette. Behind Henry, across the alley, Susan could see Debbie standing at the door to the kitchen. The two cops who had been on rotation upstairs stood with her. Three patrol cars had already arrived, filling the darkening alley with flashing lights.

"You're a reporter, for Christ's sake," Henry said.

"I don't know about cars," Susan said. She took a strangled breath, followed by a drag on her burning cigarette. "I know about clothes and music and agritainment."

"Agritainment?" Henry said.

"I did a story on it," Susan explained.

Henry closed his eyes. "What did he say?"

They'd been over this. "I told you, he said, 'They'll be fine,' that's it," Susan said.

"Fuck," Henry said loudly.

Susan watched as Debbie broke away from

the other cops and ran toward them. Debbie kept her hand over her mouth, like she was trying to keep a sob from escaping. "What's going on, Henry?" Debbie said through the hand. "Is it her?"

Susan automatically lifted her cigarette out of Debbie's proximity. Then glanced at it. "The cigarette," Susan said. "He tossed his cigarette there." She pointed to a spot ten feet down the alley.

Debbie shook her head. "Archie doesn't smoke."

Susan walked over to the spot where Archie had dropped the cigarette, followed by Henry and Debbie. Scanning the ground, Susan found it quickly, burned to the filter. She could still smell it.

Henry squatted, took a Ziploc bag out of his pocket, turned it inside out, and picked up the cigarette, turning the bag back so the cigarette was inside it.

"What's happening?" Debbie asked.

Henry looked at the cigarette and rubbed his forehead with a big hand. "You moron," he muttered. He looked up at Debbie. "Not you." He rubbed at his face again. "Archie wanted us to have a DNA sample. But we don't need one." He sighed. "Because we have his spleen in a bottle of formaldehyde in an evidence room downtown."

Debbie started to shake. "We were happy," she said to no one in particular. "We loved each other." She gasped and her shoulders jutted forward, and she lowered her hand from her mouth to Henry's shoulder to steady herself.

"Oh, God," she said to him. "What do I tell Ben and Sara?"

Henry didn't answer.

"So what happens now?" asked Susan.

"We find them," Henry said simply.

A patrol cop walked up, leading a young man in a white busboy's jacket. "This kid says a blond woman told him to tell Sheridan to meet her here," the cop said.

The busboy reached up and touched his left ear. "What's up, dudes?"

Henry, who was still in a squatting position, looked up wearily. "What kind of car was she in?" he asked the busboy.

"A silver 2007 Jaguar XK coupe with chromed Sabre wheels," the busboy said.

Henry turned to Susan. "See how easy that was?" he said.

CHAPTER
44

Susan took a swig of cold coffee out of the mug on her desk. It was six hours old and tasted like bark, but she didn't care. She leaned back in her task chair. It was four A.M. and the fifth floor of the *Herald* was bustling. Rumor was that Howard Jenkins himself was in his office downstairs. Even the interns had come in. Gretchen Lowell taking off with Archie Sheridan? That was big news, and all the usual suspects wanted in on it. Never mind that there was a fire raging in Central Oregon, a small plane missing off the coast, and the usual collection of bad news. Gretchen sold papers so fast even Hearst himself would blush. The *Herald* hadn't seen this much action since Archie Sheridan had been kidnapped. The first time. "Someone put more coffee on," Susan said.

No one in the newspaper offices moved.

Susan wadded up a piece of paper and

threw it at Derek, who sat surfing the Internet three desks over.

"Hey!" Derek said, rubbing his ear where she'd hit him.

"Put some more coffee on," Susan said.

Derek got up and slumped off toward the break room.

Susan had been at the *Herald* all night. She had insisted that she be allowed to work, with the agreement that she'd return to lockdown to sleep. Gretchen Lowell was on the run. Susan was convinced that she was the last thing on the Beauty Killer's mind. Bliss remained at the Arlington. She still felt endangered, she said. Susan was pretty sure she just liked the room service.

Susan sat at her computer. She had worn the *L* and the *S* off the keyboard and her palms had left permanent dirty prints on the laptop's white hand rests. She had a PC desktop at the paper, but she didn't use it. It was a Pentium II. Parker, who'd had as much seniority as anyone on the floor, had a Pentium III, and they were all just waiting for a tasteful moment to make a play for it.

The *Herald* had broken the story of Archie Sheridan's disappearance on the Web site eight minutes before Charlene Wood had gone live in the alley. That was something at least. It was the longest Susan had gone without pestering Ian about the Castle story. Instead, she had written a longer personal account of the events in the alley. Ian liked to do that *New York Times* thing where the reporter always refers to himself in the third person, as in "According to this reporter the car in question was silver," or "This reporter was outside smoking a cigarette and witnessed the event."

Susan thought it made her sound like an asshole. So she ignored Ian and wrote the piece in the first person, but left out the smoking.

They had been able to control it. She had agreed with Henry to omit the part about Archie getting into the car on his own. For now. As it was, the public story implied that Gretchen had again taken him by force. Which was possible. She could have had a gun. Susan couldn't see. It wasn't lying. It just wasn't fully exploring all the scenarios. And God knew the press did that all the time.

Ian came over and sat next to her on her desk. He sat too close to her. He'd done that when they were sleeping together and she'd liked it. It had felt naughty. She had thought it was their little secret. Now she wondered if everyone in the newsroom had known. Probably.

"There's a press conference at six," Ian said. He was wearing jeans and a T-shirt he'd bought at the MoMA gift store. "You want it?"

"Yes," Susan said. Was he just trying to keep her distracted?

"Then go home," Ian said.

Susan didn't want to go home. And she sure as hell didn't want to go back to the Arlington. "I'm waiting on a source," she said.

"Go home, Susan," Ian said gently. "Get some rest. Take a shower. Put some clothes on. Be at the justice center at six." He put his hand on her shoulder. "I know that Sheridan is important to you," he said.

Susan's back stiffened as she realized what he was thinking. "I'm not sleeping with him," she said quickly.

Ian lifted his hands. "It's none of my business."

"No," Susan said. She shook her head. "Don't make it tawdry." She didn't like him thinking of Archie like that, like he was just another one of her inappropriate crushes. "He's my friend." She reached under her desk and pulled her laptop cord free from the power strip with a jerk of her hand. "It's not like how it was with us."

Derek appeared with a *Herald* mug in each

hand. One had a plastic stir stick and so much milk it looked like Nesquik. The other coffee was black. He handed her the black one.

"Dark and bitter, right?" he said.

CHAPTER
45

Susan stood with her hand poised, ready to knock, an inch from the door to Debbie Sheridan's room at the Arlington. Bennett was in his chair watching her encouragingly.

She had almost worked up the nerve to follow through with it — she wanted to see how Debbie was doing, but didn't want to seem like a stalker — when the door fell away and there stood Henry Sobol. Susan caught a glimpse of Debbie, red-eyed, on the couch, with her children curled up on either side of her, before Henry closed the door behind him.

"It's not a real good time," he said, his tone leaving little room for argument.

Susan ran her raised hand through her turquoise hair. "What's the latest?" she asked.

She could tell that Henry hadn't slept, either. He was wearing the same clothes he'd had on the night before, and his shaved head had five-o'clock shadow. His voice was thick and flat. "There's a press conference at six," he said.

"It's not your fault," Susan said. She regretted the words as soon as they were out of her mouth, but continued awkwardly. "That you weren't with him. He would have found a time to slip away if that's what he wanted."

Henry's blue eyes darkened. He glanced back at the closed door and lowered his voice to a growl. "He didn't slip away. She took him by force. Got it?"

Susan took a tiny step back. "Yes."

Henry's big eyebrows lifted and then he turned and started to walk away.

"I want in," Susan said, surprising herself.

Henry stopped. "What?"

Susan set her shoulders back a little. "I want in on the investigation," she said. "That's my price." The words spilled out before she could stop them. "I can help. I'll stay out of the way. I just want to do something."

Henry closed his eyes for a moment. "Don't pull this bullshit right now."

"I will go public with everything," Susan said, gaining confidence. "Unless you allow me access to the investigation. I know Archie. I know a lot about the BK case. I can help find them." In that moment, she even believed it. Molly was dead. The Castle story was stalled. But she could help with this. She could do this. "I have to help find them. Please."

Of course Susan would never have betrayed Archie. But she was banking on the fact that Henry wouldn't risk that. She wanted him to agree, and at the same time she wanted him to call her bluff. Because if he agreed, it meant he didn't trust her.

"Okay," he said. "You're in."

Susan hadn't been to the task force offices since the After School Strangler case had ended. It was in an old bank on the east side that the city had bought and turned over to the department as extra office space. The bank was one story and square, and centered in a parking lot. There was an ATM on the east side of the building where you could still get cash.

They had done a little work on the place: ripped up old carpet, pulled out the cashier's counter, and installed desks and flat-screen computers. But it still looked like a bank. It still had the old vault. The old bank clock still read TIME TO BANK WITH FRIENDS. It was still lit with fluorescent lights bright enough to count every pimple of a bank robber's face off surveillance tapes. Not very flattering. Susan pulled at her T-shirt. She'd left right away with Henry, no time to change. Now she was regretting not taking the time to put on a bra.

Claire Masland sat down next to Susan at the conference table in the bank's old break room. The room was packed with cops. No one had slept. They smelled like a sports team. Susan lifted a paper cup of coffee to her mouth. She had gotten the coffee from an air pot on the counter. It was hazelnut. What kind of cops drank flavored coffee?

"New Kids on the Block?" Claire said.

Susan looked down at her T-shirt. "It's ironic," she said.

"Okay," Henry said. "Let's get started." He leaned over and unrolled a map of Oregon onto the conference table. It was covered with different color Post-it notes. "Roadblocks are marked," he said. "We've got bulletins at all airports, bus stations, train stations, and shipyards. We've got both their photographs on the wire. Media coverage." He rubbed the back of his neck and looked up at the group. "What are we missing?"

Jeff Heil examined the map over Henry's shoulder. "You think she's still in the state?" he asked skeptically. The map featured only a sliver of Washington above and California below, and to the right, the edge of Idaho, pressing against Oregon, the border forming a vague human profile gazing toward the Pacific.

"She didn't go far last time," Claire said.

"Maybe we should search all the basements in Gresham," someone else said.

Henry shook his head and looked down at the map. "Don't think I've ruled it out," he said. His shoulders rose and fell with a deep breath. Then he looked up around the room until his eyes rested on Lorenzo Robbins, from the ME's office. He'd come in while Henry was talking, and was standing just inside the door. "What do we have on the heart?" Henry asked him.

Robbins crossed his arms and leaned back against the door. Several manila folders were stuck under one armpit. Susan didn't know him, but she'd seen him around. His dreadlocks made him easy to recognize. "It's a human male's. Mid-thirties. We matched it to a DNA sample taken from the missing transport guard's house. Name's Rick Yost."

"Can you tell how he died?" Henry asked.

"He didn't die of a heart attack," Robbins said.

Henry sighed heavily and moved on. "Anything from the cell phone battery and ammo?" he asked Mike Flannigan.

Susan suddenly felt more awake. She sat up a little. The fact that they'd found a cell phone battery and ammo hadn't been released to the media. She raised her hand.

Henry saw her hand in the air and winced. "We found Archie's phone battery and a handful of bullets in a gutter near the park," he explained. "Can we wait on questions?"

Susan lowered her hand and picked up her cup of hazelnut coffee.

"Just his prints," Flannigan said. "He must have tossed them from the car."

Susan hated hazelnut coffee almost as much as she hated vanilla coffee, which was almost as much as she hated all flavored coffees. But she took a sip and swallowed it anyway. Just Archie's prints. He'd gotten into the car of his own free will. And then thrown the battery and ammo out on his own.

"Okay," Henry said, rubbing the bridge of his nose. "We keep that quiet for now." He looked around the room at the assembled cops. He looked tired, Susan thought. His blue eyes were bloodshot; the stubble that peppered his bald head was gray. "Let's get ready for the press conference," he said.

He stepped away from the table and the cops all got up and started to move out of the room. Susan stared at her coffee. Then she felt someone brush her arm and she looked up and saw Lorenzo Robbins standing between Claire and her. He thrust a manila folder at Claire. "This go to you now?" he asked. "It's my findings on the park bodies."

Susan twisted around. "The case Archie was working?"

Robbins looked to Claire. Claire shrugged. "Go ahead," she said. "She practically works here now."

"It was a couple," Robbins told Susan. "One male, one female, in their late twenties. Been dead about two years."

"Huh," Claire said matter-of-factly.

Susan looked between Robbins and Claire. "So are they related to Molly's murder or not?" she asked.

Claire took the folder from Robbins and leafed through its contents. "I don't know. There are a lot of fucked-up people in the world, and it's a great place to dump a body."

"So what are you going to do?" Susan asked.

Claire closed the folder. "It's a cold case. It can wait a couple of days."

Susan thought of Molly's body on the slab in the morgue. "Molly's murder isn't cold," she said.

Claire moved close to Susan. She was shorter than Susan, but she was stronger, and Susan had to fight the instinct to take a small step back. The room had cleared out except for a few cops who still stood around the map. But Claire still lowered her voice. "Archie's out there with Gretchen Lowell," she said to Susan. Her voice was calm, her eyes level, but there was something unrelenting in her posture that gripped Susan by the throat. "She's had him all night. How many nails do you think she has in him by now?"

Susan wasn't going to give up that easily. "Molly's death may be related to Parker's and the senator's murders," she said.

Claire rolled her eyes in frustration. "They weren't murdered, Susan. They went off the road. It might have been suicide. It might have been an accident. But we don't have any evidence that it was anything more than that."

Susan shook her head. "Gretchen Lowell dumped Heather Gerber there. Some killer dumped a couple there two years ago. And now Molly Palmer?"

"Just because you hear hoofbeats, doesn't mean it's a zebra."

"What does that even mean?" Susan asked.

"It's almost always a horse," Claire said, hands splayed. "The hoofbeats." She ran a hand through her short hair. "I've got to clean up. Henry wants me at the press conference."

The press conference. "Me, too," Susan said. "Give me a minute." She turned and started to pack up her notebook, in the process knocking over her cup of coffee, which spread across the table, splattering the map. Susan gasped in horror and lunged for some napkins on the counter next to the microwave.

"Jesus," Claire said. "I'll meet you out there." She turned and left the room.

Two cops still hovering next to the map, one of them Mike Flannigan, lifted the map off the wet table. Susan flung the napkins onto the puddle of coffee on the table and then ran over and began to dab up the coffee off the map, which the two men had laid out on the carpet.

She'd managed to splatter coffee all the way into Central Oregon. Santiam Pass. Bend. Prineville. She fumbled with the napkins, careful not to disturb the Post-its that marked roadblocks. As she soaked up the coffee, she noticed there wasn't a Post-it at the intersection of I-5 and Highway 22. "There's no roadblock on 22," she said.

"Twenty-two doesn't go anywhere," Flannigan explained. "Just up into the mountains." He took the map from Susan and began to carefully roll it up. "There's a fire up there."

"I thought they were getting that under control," Susan said.

"Wind changed," Flannigan said. "Fire's almost four hundred acres. We don't need a roadblock. The Forest Service closed 22 this morning."

CHAPTER
46

When Archie woke up he was on his back on a bed. It was dark, but the door was open and light poured in through what looked to be a hallway. A ceiling fan spun overhead, the fixture loose, so that it knocked softly against the ceiling as it rotated. The ceiling and walls were cedar, like in a cabin. There was a wooden dresser and a framed picture of an old rodeo poster and a window with a shade that was drawn. He was alone, but he could smell a fire burning. She was there somewhere.

He had been asleep awhile. He could tell because his body ached and he felt cold and jittery. He needed more pills. He put his socked feet on the carpet. She had taken his shoes off and he saw them sitting side by side next to the bed and he reached down to put them on. His head pounded and he had to pause for a moment before he could move. Then he put his feet into his shoes and tied them and sat up. He glanced for the pill bottles from the car but they weren't on the dresser or the bedside table. The closet door was cedar plank. He opened it and found it full of clothes. He wondered who they belonged to and then realized that they were all new. She had bought them for him. She was either planning on his being around awhile, or she wanted him to think she was. Corduroys. Tan pants. Blue button-down shirts, white button-down shirts, sweaters, and a few professorial sport coats. It looked just like his closet at home. Predictability was always one of his flaws.

He turned and walked to the window and opened the shade. It was dusk or early morning. He saw only trees. Ponderosa pines. They didn't grow west of the mountains. She'd taken him east. Into the high desert. Maybe they were still in Oregon. Maybe not.

There was music. Classical. It was faint but definitely coming from somewhere in the house. He glanced back at the window. He could open it. Climb out. Walk away. They could be miles from anywhere. But he could still do it. He could still abandon his plan, still leave her. Try to get home.

He considered it for another moment, before he turned back toward the light streaming from the open door and walked into the hallway. There were several doors. The hallway was also cedar plank. The hallway floor was gray carpet, the kind of speckled industrial stuff you'd put in a rental or vacation house. The music was coming from down the hall, where the hallway opened into a living space.

He walked toward it.

There was a bank of windows in the living room that looked out onto a deck and more trees. The light had darkened another notch. It was evening, not morning. A staircase with a wrought-iron banister led up to a loft that overlooked the living room. There was a leather sectional and a fireplace with a huge stone mantel. A fire crackled and growled in the fireplace. Gretchen was sitting in a leather chair next to it, a laptop on her lap. Her hair was loose and she wasn't wearing makeup and the glow of the fire made her flawless skin look angelic.

She glanced up at him and smiled. "Your pills are in the kitchen," she said. She looked to the left, and he followed her gaze to where the floor lifted a step and he could see a kitchen that opened out onto the main room. The pill bottles were lined up on the counter by the sink. He walked over and opened a few cupboards before he found a glass. He filled it with water from the sink and took four Vicodin. Then reconsidered and took one more.

"Do you want a drink?" he heard her ask.

He turned around and saw that she was standing up now, next to a small rattan bar. She was wearing a gray cashmere sweater and fitted gray slacks and was in her stocking feet. She held up a bottle of something.

This wasn't real. This wasn't happening. "Sure," he said.

"Scotch okay?" she asked.

"Sure," he said. He didn't move, his hands behind him, holding on to the edge of the counter.

He watched her as she poured the drink, scooping ice from an ice bucket then pouring the alcohol over it, no water. Her glossy blond hair settled on her shoulder blades, swinging slightly as she moved.

She turned back and held the glass out toward him, arm extended.

He stood there another moment, and then pushed himself off the counter and walked toward her and took the glass. As he took the glass, their fingers met. The contact made his head swim, his vision darken for a moment, but he was careful not to flinch, not to show it on his face. He raised the drink to her and then drank the Scotch in several swallows. He didn't know much about Scotch, but it went down easily and tasted expensive. When he was done, he handed her back the glass, now just ice.

He wiped his mouth with the back of his hand. "I need to take a shower," he said.

"It's down the hall," she said. "Second door on the left. You'll find everything you need."

"My sanity?" he said.

She leaned forward as if to kiss him, but instead put her lips next to his ear, her cheek millimeters from his. The smell of her made him dizzy. Her breath was warm but sent a cold shiver down his spine.

"Long gone, darling," she whispered.

He had showered and changed into some clothes from the closet. A pair of tan corduroys and a blue button-down shirt. An undershirt. Underwear. Socks. They all fit perfectly. The pills had hit him in the shower, and the body aches and pain in his liver had subsided to be replaced by a white noise that felt soft and comfortingly familiar. It wasn't like it used to be. There was no more euphoria. But the pills dulled his sensations enough that he felt almost pleasant.

It was fully dark outside by the time he returned to the living room.

Gretchen had moved to the leather couch. The fire had died down a little, but still bathed the room in a warm orange glow. Archie sat down on the chair Gretchen had been in earlier. The laptop was gone.

"Do you want another drink?" she asked.

"Why not?" Archie said.

She got up and moved between the couch and the chair, brushing his arm with her fingertips as she did. He kept his eyes straight ahead, trying not to look at her. He could hear her behind him, putting the ice in the glass, pouring the Scotch. The liquid crackling on the ice. The ice clinking against the side of the glass. She returned and handed him the glass and then sat on the arm of the chair he was in. His body tensed. He couldn't disguise it; his hand tightened around the glass, his knees went rigid.

She laughed lightly and leaned against him, stretching an arm along the top of the back of the chair. He could feel the cashmere of her sweater lick the back of his neck. The glass stayed frozen in his hand.

"It will happen faster, the more you drink," she said.

He focused on the glass. It was heavy crystal with a silver lip. He took a sip of the Scotch, this time slowly, letting the alcohol sit on his tongue, savoring the taste.

"The liver failure," she continued. "That's why you're here, isn't it?"

He felt his body relax a notch, and lifted his glass at her and said, "To my health."

She picked up his free hand and turned it over in hers. His nail beds were white, his skin a shade too yellow. "It won't be long now," she said softly.

He needed enough time. Maybe days. "How long?" he asked.

"A few days, a few weeks," she said. She reached across him, her breasts against his chest, her pale neck at his chin, and lifted his glass from his other hand and then sat back. She smelled different than he remembered. Like some other flower. Roses. Maybe she had never smelled like lilacs. Maybe he had imagined it. He smiled at that, as she took a sip of the Scotch from his glass.

"You smell nice," he said.

She handed the glass back to him and he took it.

"It might be faster," she said. "It depends on how efficiently you poison yourself."

He looked at the exquisite glass in his hand. Not the kind of glass you'd find at a rental house. A vacation house then. She had rented it. Or killed the family. His stomach tightened. He couldn't think about that now.

The glass. If it all worked, his team would

find it later. Both sets of the fingerprints on the glass. Drinking buddies. "Were you really an ER nurse?" he asked.

Gretchen tilted her head and smiled and then unbuttoned the third button down on his shirt and reached under the fabric, her fingers tracing his undershirt, quickly finding the scar where she had sliced him open to remove his spleen. She raised an eyebrow. "You doubt my medical prowess?"

Archie could feel his breath quicken, his chest heave. He took another drink. "Practice makes perfect," he said.

She kept her hand in his shirt and lifted her right leg over his left, so their thighs were touching.

He searched for something to say, anything, and remembered the laptop. "What were you working on earlier?" he asked.

She didn't seem surprised by the question. He knew she'd been waiting for him to ask. "A present for you."

"Your autobiography?" he asked.

"Something like that. You'll have to wait and see." She reached up and moved a piece of his hair, smoothing it back behind his ear. "Do you still think about me?" she whispered.

Archie could barely speak. "Yes."

She put her face right in front of his, her eyes sparkling in the firelight. "Do you think Henry suspects?"

He drained the last of the Scotch and set the glass on the arm of the chair. "No," he said. It felt strange to talk about it. He'd kept the secret so long. Sat across from her in the prison, knowing what she knew, and wasn't saying. It ate away at him. "Henry thinks too highly of me to suspect anything."

"He never asked you about all those late nights?" she said, smiling. "How I had your cell phone number?" She raised an eyebrow. "He never asked why you really came to my house that night I took you?"

Archie shrugged weakly. "I wanted a psych consult about the latest body."

"And if one thing led to another . . . " she said, trailing off.

"I had never cheated on my wife," Archie said. "I loved my family." How many times had he told himself that over the past three years? And yet he still couldn't look them in the eye. He was sure his son knew. He didn't know how. No one else suspected. But Ben knew that Archie had betrayed them.

Gretchen's breath was feather-light on his cheek. "You were overworked, darling," she said. "You needed an outlet." She moved her mouth just over his ear, the words sending shivers down his neck, and took his earlobe in her mouth and bit it. The pain was nice, something he could feel. She suckled his earlobe for a moment and he could feel his heartbeat quicken.

"A lot of men have affairs," she said.

Archie tried to smile. "Mine just turned out to be with the person I was supposed to be hunting," he said.

Gretchen's voice was full of sympathy. "Sin is rarely without complication," she said.

She leaned in and kissed him. Their tongues met and he tasted the Scotch. In that moment she was all there was, the heat of her mouth, her warm hand still pressed against his rib cage. Surely she could feel his heart, his pulse, the erection pressing against her leg.

She lifted her lips from his and pulled away a few inches, so they were eye to eye. "Would you take it back?" she asked. "That first night you came to my house?"

It had been two A.M. He'd come from a crime scene. He could have gone home to his wife but instead he'd gone to Gretchen's house. He'd planned it. He'd thought about it on the drive there. And when Gretchen opened the door in her nightgown, he'd taken a step inside and then he'd kissed her.

It had been him. He'd started the affair.

He'd brought everything on himself.

And he had loved every minute of it. And later, when she tortured him, he couldn't help but think that he deserved it. That he had it coming, and at least he would be dead and Debbie would never know the truth.

"Why did you do it?" he asked Gretchen.

She smiled. "Out of love," she said.

He wasn't sure Gretchen even knew what he was asking about. The affair? The torture? The fact that she had turned herself in and saved his life? He looked for something in her pale blue eyes. "I would take it all back," he said. "I wish I'd never met you." He meant it, too. He meant it more than he had ever meant anything. "I would give anything for it not to have happened."

She tilted her head, her blond hair folding against her shoulder, and he thought he saw a flash of something authentic, a glimpse of who she really was, something sad and desperate.

Did she know why he was there, what he was planning?

"Do you want to fuck me now?" she asked.

He drew her face to his and kissed her. "Yes," he said.

CHAPTER
47

Susan sat in her car two blocks away from the task force offices. With the number of news vans already assembled around the old bank for the press conference, she'd been lucky to park that close. The windows were rolled up, but she still glanced around to be sure there weren't any other reporters lurking around before she opened up her phone and punched in a *Herald* number.

Derek Rogers picked up.

"It's me," she said. "I need you to call every gas station along Highway 22 through Santiam Pass."

"Uh, what?" Derek said.

"There aren't that many," Susan said quickly. The press conferance was going to start in fifteen minutes. She flipped down the visor and dug into her purse for some makeup. "I've driven that road. It's all timber towns. Gas every half hour." She paused to smear on some raspberry-colored lipstick. "But you'd need it. What does a Jag get? Twenty miles per gallon?" She blotted the lipstick with an old receipt she found in her purse. "She'd need gas."

Derek's voice was doubtful. "So you want me to call and ask all the gas stations along 22 if they've seen Gretchen Lowell?"

"No," Susan said. "Not Lowell. The car. That's what they'll remember. Ask them if they've seen a silver Jag."

"There's a fire up there," Derek said. "They're evacuating people. You think she's psycho enough to hide in the path of it?"

"Psycho like a fox," Susan said.

Derek wasn't convinced. "These calls will take hours," he said.

Susan pulled her pigtails out, dug her hairbrush out of her purse, and started brushing her hair. "I know," she said.

"Are you brushing your hair?" Derek asked.

"One more favor?" she asked. Something Archie had said before he'd walked away in the alley had been gnawing at her.

Derek sighed. "What?"

"Can you check the *Herald*'s database for any couples who might have gone missing about two years ago? They were in their twenties."

"What does this have to do with Sheridan

and Gretchen Lowell?" Derek asked.

"Nothing," Susan said.

"Do you realize the competition we have for this story? It's national." Derek lowered his voice. "Ian will shit if he finds out you're working on something else."

"I think it might have something to do with Parker," Susan said.

There was a short pause. "It will take a few minutes," Derek said. "I'll call you back."

Susan had opened the driver's window and was smoking a cigarette to get the taste of hazelnut-flavored coffee out of her mouth when Derek called back.

"There was a story," he said. "September 2005. Stuart Davis and his girlfriend, Annabelle Nixon. They lived together. Disappeared. They found their car parked on Twenty-third. No trace of them since. The story had some legs because he was a junior aide in Senator Castle's office."

"Zebra," Susan whispered.

"Huh?" Derek said.

The press conference was minutes away. Susan got out of the car and dropped the cigarette on the street. "E-mail me everything we have," she said.

It was all coming back to Senator Castle. Susan searched her mind for any clue from her investigation into the Molly Palmer story, anyone who acted suspiciously. She had interviewed a hundred people over the last few months. And frankly, they had all acted suspiciously. But there had been one kid in particular, a high school kid who knew one of Castle's sons. Maybe it was time to pay him another visit.

CHAPTER 48

Archie sat on the end of Gretchen's bed, his feet on the floor. The mattress was firm, the gray satin duvet slick beneath his hands. The master suite's vaulted ceilings made the room feel huge and off-kilter. The sideways perspective made Archie feel a swoon of vertigo.

Gretchen undressed. She did it uneventfully, as if this were something they did often together, as if they had always been lovers. Her clothes neatly folded on a chair by the closet, she turned back and faced him, naked.

Archie felt all the blood in his body rush south. She was bruised. Hematomas from her attack shadowed her ribs and stomach, her left clavicle was raw and swollen. And still she was lovely. Prison, if nothing else, created time for an excellent workout regimen, and Gretchen was toned and slim. But you didn't get that kind of face and body without the perfect mix of genetics. The DNA that had played a role in making her a monster had also made her a beauty. Without the mix that had granted her that perfect profile, who knows? She might have been another kind of person, a good person.

The ceiling fan rotated overhead, throwing shadows on the ceiling, her face, the carpet. Shapes shifted on the periphery of Archie's vision.

Gretchen padded over to where Archie sat, and took his face in her hands and lifted his chin so he was looking up at her. Their knees touched. He gripped the satin, slippery in his fingers.

She lowered her chin, and looked up flirtatiously. "Shall I hurt you?" she asked.

"No," Archie said.

She tilted her head and smiled. "Do you want to hurt me?"

Archie sighed. "No."

"What do you want?" she asked.

He lifted his hands from the bed and put one on each of her hips. The light in the room was low but he could see goose bumps rise on her flesh from his touch. "Redemption," he said. "Barring that, distraction."

"Distraction I might be able to help you with," Gretchen said. She leaned in and kissed him lightly on the cheek, his face still cupped in her hands. "You know," she said, "I am capable of human emotion."

He wanted to believe her. He wanted to believe that there was something real between them, some fucked-up twisted connection.

He pulled her to him and she moved her hands behind his neck and they kissed again. Her naked body in his arms was almost too much for Archie to bear.

He cleared his throat. "You taste sweet," he said.

"It's not me," she said. "It's you. Your system's not cleaning out toxins like it should."

"Undress me," he said.

He held up one wrist and she unbuttoned the cuff. Then he held up the other wrist and she unbuttoned that cuff. Then she went to work on the eight buttons that connected the front flaps. She did it by touch, never losing eye contact with him, just sliding her fingers down the vertical band of buttons until she found the next one. When the shirt was open, she slid it off his shoulders and held it for a moment before letting it drop to the carpet.

Her eyes still leveled at him, she reached toward his groin and freed the undershirt from under his waistband. He held up his arms and she lifted it off his torso and then dropped it on top of the dress shirt.

Her eyes immediately went to his chest. He could see them move over his scars, tracing the damage she had done to him. His flesh was a minefield. Even nurses had to steel themselves the first time they saw him. Not Gretchen. Her face shone with appreciation. She looked at it like it was a Picasso.

"Which is your favorite?" she asked, referring to the scars.

Archie thought she was kidding. "I'd be afraid I'd hurt one of their feelings if I said."

"I like the heart," said Gretchen. She touched the heart scar, running her fingers over its curves. "It's one of the best I've ever done. It's not easy to cut smoothly into chest muscle." She leaned her face in close to his clavicle. He thought that she was going in for a closer examination of her work, but instead she touched the scar with her tongue.

The sudden warm wet pressure on the tender tissue made him jump.

She pulled her head away and looked up at him and he threaded a hand behind her blond head and pushed her face back to his flesh and she put her tongue back on the scar. Her hair was soft and slick in his fist; he could feel the heat of her tongue ripple through his body. He leaned back on the bed and she straddled him, and then slowly, deliciously, traced the scar with her mouth.

Then she moved her tongue down the vertical scar from the spleenectomy over his tensed lower stomach to his belt, which she began to unbuckle.

His erection throbbed, wanting release. His head hurt. His body ached. But he wasn't as conflicted as he thought he would be. He'd felt guilty every time he'd fantasized about her, guiltier than he'd ever felt during their affair. He had paid emotionally for every imaginary fuck. But not this time.

"I want you on top," he said. "So I can see you."

She had the belt off and was pulling down his pants and underwear in a swift, practiced motion.

"I'll be the last woman you ever made love to," she said as she pushed him inside her. It took his breath away and he closed his eyes for a moment, lost in the sensation of her body, focusing on not coming instantly like a teenager. Then he let himself look up at her, hips rocked forward, head back slightly, her face relaxed with pleasure. She was the most beautiful woman he had ever seen. He put his hands on her slender hips and pulled her forward so he could push himself deeper into her.

"It's not love," he said.

CHAPTER
49

Susan fidgeted all through the press conference. It was a madhouse. They had set up a podium in the parking lot outside the bank. Both Henry and Claire spoke. Claire had powdered sugar on her chin the whole time. They'd gone over all they were doing to find Archie. Pleaded for citizen tips. They were treating it as a kidnapping. No one mentioned the fact that Archie had gotten into the car. Or that he had thrown his ammo and phone battery out the window. You could tell by the questions that half of the reporters there thought he was dead already. It was all a charade and everyone knew it. They couldn't find her. Not until she wanted them to.

Susan had been late so didn't get one of the metal folding chairs that had been set up in front of the podium. Instead she stood in the back, shifting her weight from one foot to the next, biding time.

When the press conference ended, Susan ran to catch up to Henry as he walked back toward the bank.

She caught up with him just as he reached the door. "I need you to come with me to Cleveland High School so we can convince the school to let us talk to a kid named Justin Johnson," she said.

"Who the fuck is Justin Johnson?" Henry asked.

"He came up as part of my investigation into Castle," Susan said. "He was a good friend of one of Castle's kids. He knows something about the senator's relationship with Molly. But someone got to him. He said that he'd been told not to talk to me. Maybe whoever shut him up had something to do with shutting Molly up."

Henry stopped and turned back toward her. "So you want me to use my badge to intimidate some teachers into letting you harass a minor without his parents' consent or legal representation?"

"Yes," she said.

"You know that school just got out?" he said.

"He's in summer school," she said.

Henry rubbed his bloodshot eyes with one hand. "What does this have to do with helping me find Archie?"

"It has to do with his case," Susan said. She tried to sound convincing. "With the park murders. He wanted me to finish it."

"I'm sort of busy right now, Susan. What with the whole 'escaped serial killer and kidnapped best friend' thing."

"You can wait for a call as well with me as you can here," Susan said. "Or you can help Archie." She leaned close to Henry to prevent anyone else from hearing. "He told me to. He has a plan. You said it. Then maybe this is part of it. Maybe if we follow up on the park case, it will help lead us to him."

Henry gave his head a defiant shake. "That is such bullshit."

"Before he left," Susan said in a hushed tone, "he told me that I would always remember my first corpse in the park. That's what he said. My first cigarette. First kiss. And my first corpse in the park. What?" Susan said. "You think he meant metaphorically? He wanted me to look into the park murders. And they all seem to be connected to Castle."

Henry stood with his hand on the door, working his jaw, staring at Susan.

She was pretty sure he didn't like her. But she needed his help and she had a weird feeling that Archie would want her to ask him for it.

"Why didn't you mention this before?" he asked.

"Because I don't know if I'm right," Susan said. "But there's nothing else, so what the fuck, right?"

Henry worked his jaw a little more. "I do get a kick out of strong-arming teenagers," he said finally.

Susan grinned, relieved. "It's fun, isn't it?"

Cleveland High was quiet, only a few cars in the parking lot. The marquee out front still said CONGRATULATIONS, GRADUATES.

Henry drove, parking in a visitor spot in the lot across the street from the big brick school, and they got out of the car.

"So you're going to tell them it's an emergency, right?" Susan said. She imagined bursting into the administration office, Henry throwing down his badge. "That we need to talk to him immediately. That it involves a case."

She looked up. About ten yards ahead, a handsome blond kid with a backpack was just getting out of his orange BMW. His shaggy surfer hair was tied in a tiny ponytail and his cargo shorts hung low on his hips. She stopped cold.

"That him?" Henry asked.

Susan nodded.

Henry walked right over to JJ. "The lady needs to talk to you. It's an emergency. It involves a case."

So much for bursting into the admin office. "Thanks," Susan said to Henry.

The kid glanced over at Susan, ducked his head, and cringed. "Oh, man," he said. "You don't take no for an answer, do you?"

Susan stepped forward. "Who told you not to talk to me?" she asked.

"Read the paper," JJ said. "Castle's dead." He heaved his backpack over one shoulder. "Let it go."

Henry's face flushed. He took a breath and set his shoulders back. "Listen, you privileged little son of a bitch," he said to JJ, blocking his way, "you don't want to even begin to fuck with me today. Answer the lady's question."

"Dude, that's harassment."

"You want me to search your pockets, Einstein?" Henry asked. "Because I smell weed. And when I smell weed I get to trample on a citizen's rights to determine its origin. You answer that question about have you ever been arrested for a felony yet on all those college applications? It would be a pain in the ass to have to go back and change them all."

JJ chewed on his lip for a minute and then shrugged. "My mom's ex-boyfriend," he said to Susan. "He thinks he's still a cop because he used to be chief of police."

Henry turned his head from JJ to Susan and back again. "The mayor?" Henry said.

"Yeah," JJ said with another shrug. He switched his backpack to the other shoulder. "Can I go now? I have to get through eight quarters' worth of biology this summer or they won't let me graduate."

He started to walk away but Susan stopped him.

"Did you know Stuart Davis and Annabelle Nixon?" she asked.

"Who?" JJ said.

"Davis worked for Castle," Susan said. "He disappeared almost two years ago. There were stories about it in the *Herald*."

JJ lifted the other strap of the backpack so it was secured on both shoulders and started toward the school. "I haven't seen Aidan Castle or his dad since Aidan got sent to Andover freshman year. And I don't read the *Herald*," he added. "We get the *New York Times*."

"Davis and Nixon?" Henry said, when JJ was out of earshot.

"The bodies in the park," Susan said. "The ME said they're a man and a woman. They match the ages of Davis and Nixon. Look to be about the right age."

Henry put his hands on his hips. "When were you planning on mentioning this?"

"I just found out," Susan said.

Henry started back for the car. "They'll have DNA in the missing person files. I'll have it run. If for no other reason than to close the damper on your journalistic fire."

"Why would the mayor tell JJ not to talk to me?" Susan asked, catching up.

"Maybe he was giving him good advice," Henry said. "Keep the family out of the story. Protect the kid from self-incrimination. If he knew about a crime and didn't report it, it might look bad."

Susan got in the car. The vinyl seat was already hot. "I don't like him," she said.

Henry started the car and pulled out of the parking lot. "Buddy? He's done a lot for Archie. Protected him over the past couple of years."

Susan rolled down her window. The air was warm and dry. It was going to be a hot day. "Yeah, he's done a great job at protecting Archie," she said. Then realizing the inappropriateness of her sarcasm, added, "Sorry."

CHAPTER
50

Henry took a moment to gather himself outside Debbie's door at the Arlington. His blood was still pumping from having to push through a dozen reporters to get through the club's front door. Their glee at the story's magnitude was palpable, the bloodsucking assholes. He had dropped Susan off at her car, just in time to get a phone call from Animal Control. Bill the poodle had taken a shit, and in it they had found a girl's class ring. Benson High class of 1997. He'd made a call and confirmed Susan's suspicions: Annabelle Nixon had graduated from Benson that year. He ran a hand over the stubble on the top of his head, and then let it settle for a moment and pinched the bridge of his nose. His eyes burned from lack of sleep. He needed more coffee. His stomach churned and his mouth was sour. It was shaping up to be one of the hottest days of the year. Ten A.M., and his T-shirt was already stained with sweat.

If he found Archie in time, he was going to slug him.

"Fuck," he said under his breath. Then he lowered his hand, opened and squeezed his eyes shut a few times, and tried to look awake and optimistic.

Henry knocked twice with the back of his hand. "It's me," he said. A patrol cop opened the door. Henry didn't see Bennett.

Buddy was sitting on the couch, where Henry had left him. An aide sat next to him and they were staring at a laptop on the coffee table. Buddy couldn't have gotten much sleep, but he somehow looked completely rested.

Buddy pointed to the two bedrooms. "They're finally all asleep," he said.

"Thanks for staying with them," Henry said, closing the door behind him.

"Any news?" Buddy asked.

Henry looked at the patrol cop and at the aide. "Can we talk alone for a minute?" he asked Buddy.

Buddy frowned. "I'm just preparing a statement for the press. Brian Williams is coming."

"It will just take a minute," Henry said.

Henry thought he saw a flicker of irritation in Buddy's eyes, but then it was gone and

Buddy shrugged and said, "Sure, pal." He smiled at his aide. "Give us a minute, huh?"

The aide stood and walked to the door with the patrol cop. "We'll just be in the hall, sir," the aide said.

"Thanks, Jack," Buddy said. "Love the press release. Really."

Jack almost blushed.

When they were gone, Henry walked to the window and looked out at the park. The AC was on, but he could feel the heat already pressing against the glass. He could see several news vans parked in a loading zone out front. He made a mental note to call and report them.

"You used to date Beverly Overlook," Henry said, glancing back at Buddy.

Buddy interlaced his fingers behind his head and leaned back on the couch. "God," he said. "Years ago."

"Did you tell her son not to talk to Susan Ward about the Molly Palmer thing?" Henry asked.

"I did. I didn't want them involved in a very messy story."

Henry had never been close to Buddy. Archie had known him better. But they had worked with him, of course, during those early years when Buddy had run the task force. And Buddy had always liked to talk about himself. "You used to work for Castle, didn't you?" Henry said. "Security?"

Buddy nodded. "When I was a cop, yeah. Before the task force. You're going back a long time, pal."

"You know those two kids who went missing? Stuart and Annabelle?"

Buddy made a dismissive motion with his hand. "That was after my time. I knew Stuart. Vaguely. Theory was he went off the deep end, killed his girlfriend, then himself. Cops never did find the bodies. I always thought he probably took her into the woods. You know, did her, did himself. Kid was always a little stressed out."

It might not be a bad theory, Henry thought. They parked on Twenty-third. Walked into the woods. Except that his body was the one fed into a wood chipper. So maybe she did it. Killed him, disposed of his body. Then couldn't face what she'd done; killed herself there in the bushes. Or maybe it wasn't even them. Maybe Stuart and Annabelle had just eloped and joined the Peace Corps. Maybe they were living in a hut in Malaysia.

"Did you know about Castle's relationship with his kids' babysitter?" Henry asked.

"I didn't have specific knowledge of it," Buddy said. He said it without hesitation, unblinking, his posture firm. "Sure, I heard rumors over the years. Like everyone," he added meaningfully. "But I swear to you, I thought she was older. An indiscretion. A lot of politicians fool around. It goes with the territory." He rolled down a sleeve and buttoned the cuff. "Shouldn't you be looking for Archie?" he asked.

Henry stood at the window. Another news van pulled forward and parked. "I think I am," he said.

He looked back at Buddy, who was working on the second sleeve. "When did you find out?" Henry asked. "Just out of curiosity."

"Senator Castle increased school spending by thirty percent, expanded health care to half a million kids, reinvented how we take care of the elderly in this state, and set aside more than a million acres' worth of wildlife refuge areas," Buddy said, buttoning his other cuff. He glanced up at Henry. "He was a great senator, and a great man. And that's how I'm going to remember him."

The two stared at each other for a moment. Castle had won two of his five terms by the smallest margin in the history of the state. But since he'd died, everyone Henry came across claimed to have always voted for him.

Henry looked back out the window. "I'll stay for a while," he said slowly. "You can go."

He heard Buddy close his laptop, then the sound of his expensive shoes slapping on the carpet as he exited the suite. Buddy was an operator and a political survivor and Henry had no doubt that he'd warned the kid not to talk to Susan. He also had no doubt that Buddy wasn't telling him the truth about what he knew and when he knew it. Henry just didn't know what old political gossip, even prosecutable gossip, had to do with locating Archie.

The door to Archie and Debbie's bedroom opened and Debbie walked in wearing a slip-dress nightgown, and pulling on a hotel robe over her freckled shoulders. Her short hair was flat against one side of her head; a pillow seam creased her cheek.

"Anything?" she asked.

"No," Henry said.

She walked over and laid her head on his shoulder and he put a hand on the back of her head. She didn't cry. Her shoulders didn't shake. Her breathing was even.

"I'm going to get someone else to come stay with you," Henry said. "Buddy had to go back to work." She lifted her head. This close he could see that her eyes were red.

"Can I brush my teeth?" he asked. "Borrow some deodorant?"

She nodded and gestured toward the bedroom. "In there."

The room was cool and dark, the bedding folded down. A dent in the pillows still marked where Debbie had been lying minutes before.

"You can lie down," Debbie said. "And rest if you want."

Henry moved quickly into the bathroom and picked up Archie's toothbrush and leaned over the sink. "I have to get back," he said. When he'd finished cleaning up he went back into the bedroom. The lights were on now, and Henry noticed several suitcases still lay on the floor half unpacked, and next to them, a cardboard box filled with reporters' notebooks and three-ring binders. Debbie had pulled on a pair of jeans and a T-shirt and was sitting on the bed.

"What's all that?" Henry asked, pointing at the box.

"Susan Ward's notes," Debbie said. "About Castle."

Henry looked at the box again. It was something. And at this point, anything might help. "Can I take them?" he asked.

"You can burn them if you like," Debbie said. "I don't care."

Henry went over next to Debbie and stooped down to pick up the boxes. He felt her hand on his shoulder and looked up.

"I want to help," she said. "If you want me to make a statement to the media. Anything. Just let me know. I could plead with him to come home."

"I don't think that would help," he said.

"He's on some sort of suicide mission," she said, finally voicing it.

Henry turned away, unable to look at her. If he'd taken better care of Archie, he could have stopped this. If he'd forced him into rehab. Stopped the visits with Gretchen. But they had all been too greedy. It had been so long. And there were so many victims still missing. "I know," he said.

CHAPTER
51

Archie smoothed Gretchen's hair with his hand. She was lying in the crook of his arm, her cheek on his chest. He felt great tenderness for her, her breaths, her breast moving against his rib cage, the curve of her hip. It was a postcoital illusion, he knew. His whole relationship with Gretchen was one long postcoital illusion. He lifted his hand from her hair. The hand was swollen again, and he made a fist a few times to get the blood flowing before settling it back on her head. Her breathing was steady and even and he wondered if she was asleep.

He could kill her now, he realized. He could take a pillow and cover her head and smother her.

She would fight it, but he could straddle her and use his weight as leverage, press the pillow hard into her face until she lost consciousness and then cover her mouth and her nose with his hand until he was sure she was dead.

"What are you thinking about?" she asked.

He cleared his throat. "We found three bodies in Forest Park," he said.

She turned over and looked at him. He was still startled by her beauty every time. He'd spent so long looking at her picture, imagining her in his mind, and still, he was never prepared for the fact of her.

"I think someone killed Senator Castle and they're trying to cover it up," he said.

She smiled sleepily. "Did I mention that liver failure often causes mental confusion?"

"He had an inappropriate relationship with a fourteen-year-old girl ten years ago. Susan Ward was about to make it public. The girl was killed a week ago. Her body dumped in the park." Archie wondered whether or not to add the last part. "Not far from where you left Heather Gerber."

The senator's secret didn't faze her. Neither did Heather's name. "Who stands to benefit from a cover-up?" she asked.

"Castle's publicist?" Archie said dryly.

Gretchen sat up and moved to the edge of the bed. She moved slowly. She was bruised and battered, but this was the first time she seemed actually sore. "His publicist would love it," Gretchen said. "They bill by the hour, you know."

"You didn't benefit from anyone you killed," Archie said.

Gretchen stood and walked to the dresser where Archie could see a bottle of prescription pills. "I find murder emotionally fulfilling," she said. She came back to bed and stretched out on her side next to him. "It's about power," she said. She opened the bottle and tapped five pills onto his chest. "Power feels good. It's the same reason people do drugs. You can pontificate all you want about social responsibility, but in the end people do drugs because they like it. It makes them feel good."

Gretchen arranged the pills on his chest into a neat little line that rose and fell with his breaths. "What about sex?" Archie asked.

"Sex has everything to do with power," she said. She picked up one of the pills between her teeth and held it out to him and he took it, kissing her for a moment, the Vicodin between their lips.

"Swallow it," she whispered.

He took the pill into his own mouth and swallowed. He wanted water, but he didn't want her to leave him.

"Did your father really abuse you?" Archie asked. She had told him that, in the basement, and Archie had wanted to believe that it was true. They didn't know anything about her, really. Her fingerprints weren't in the system. There were plenty of "Gretchen Lowells," but none that fit. She'd made up the name at some point. Her face was plastered on every newspaper in America and no one had ever come forward with information about her past. She had told them she was thirty-four. But for all Archie knew, she could have been lying about that, too.

Gretchen smiled. "No," she said. "But that's what you wanted, wasn't it?" She moved her fingertips from the pills on his chest, down his stomach to his groin, and cradled his balls in her hand. "To blame it on a man." She nuzzled against his neck. "Why do women kill?" she whispered. "It must be because of a boyfriend or a father or a husband. She can't possibly have gotten that way on her own."

"So you're a feminist homicidal psychopath," Archie said.

"The Betty Friedan of serial killers," she said. She moved her hand from his balls, hugging his cock with her thumb and forefinger, and with her free hand fed him another pill.

"Swallow it," she said.

He forced it down, the saliva in his mouth

barely enough to get the pill down into his throat.

"If he wants to stop the story," she said, lifting her hand to her mouth and wetting the palm with her tongue, "he'll go after Susan Ward next."

Archie felt his breathing change, the heat rising from his groin up to his neck. "How do you know it's a 'he'?" he asked, the pill still in his throat.

She slid her lubricated hand slowly up and down his cock. "Women aren't capable of murder, darling," she said. "You know that."

The time was almost right to put his plan into action. Gretchen didn't know it, but she wasn't going to leave that cabin a free woman. And if it all went the way he wanted it to, he wasn't going to leave that cabin at all. Not alive, anyway.

Henry would take care of Susan.

Gretchen fed him the remaining three pills one by one. Then moved her mouth down his body toward his groin, fluttering against his flesh, down his chest and across his belly, running the tip of her tongue up the shaft of his cock, around the rim of the head, until she finally took it into her mouth and began to slowly, teasingly slide his erection in and out of her throat. His breath was coming fast now, his heart racing. His face was hot, the sweat on his upper lip sweet and cold. He reached down to his groin and his hand found her head, the blond hair slick under his fingers.

He had nothing to lose. If he was going to be a sinner, he might as well enjoy the sin.

He knotted his fingers in her hair and moved her head up and down at his own rhythm. He watched her face the whole time, her eyes tearing, her cheeks flushed, saliva glistening at the corners of her mouth, as she took him again and again, and when her hair fell in the way, he moved it, so he could see her lips, so he could see himself fuck her. He hated her. He loved her. She started to lift her face when he came, but he held her head firm.

"Swallow it," he said.

CHAPTER
52

Susan brought in the mail: a copy of *The Nation,* a flyer from the co-op, two bills, and a packet of return address labels from the ACLU. She dropped them onto the table inside the door, along with her keys. Her mother's house was stifling. All the windows were closed. That's how they kept it during the day. It was the only way to combat the heat. You kept the windows and drapes closed until the sun went down and then you opened them all up and prayed for a light breeze. Susan didn't know how the Victorians had survived.

Susan's eyes burned with exhaustion. A few hours' sleep, and she would be ready to get back to work. She walked upstairs into her mother's room. She wasn't going to sleep in that hammock if she didn't have to. Her mother's room was painted red and she had what was probably the last water bed in the Portland metropolitan area. Susan turned on the oscillating fan on Bliss's dresser to get the air moving.

It had been years since she'd pulled an all-nighter and Susan had forgotten what it felt like. She actually felt sick to her stomach. She stretched out on Bliss's bed but the rollicking motion of the water under the plastic just made her queasier. She lay there for a while but every time she turned over a tidal surge would roll up and down the waterbed. She had a headache now. It felt like someone was squeezing a steel cap around her skull.

There was only one solution: a bath. She glanced at her watch. It was almost 11:00 A.M.

She got up, went into the bathroom off the upstairs hall, and turned on the faucet in the cast-iron tub, filling it with cool water and a healthy gob of eucalyptus foaming bath gel. There were dozens of candles along the perimeter of the tub, an assortment of different colors and scents that Bliss had carefully arranged to create the perfect bathing experience.

Susan flicked a lighter on and held it to one of the wicks. It caught fire for a moment, and then went out. She tried again. It went out. She tried another candle. It went out. Susan indulged in an indignant groan. That was just like her mother, to buy the cheapest candles at the import store. She stared at the lighter in her hand for a moment and then shrugged and set it back down next to one of the candles.

It felt good to shed the clothes she'd been wearing for twenty-four hours. She stuffed them into the Guatemalan basket her mother used as a bathroom laundry hamper. Her head really ached now. Even her eyes hurt. It wasn't just the lack of sleep, she realized, it was stress. Parker. Archie Sheridan. She needed to take it easier. Not push herself so hard. She wasn't going to be any good to anyone like this.

She stepped into the tub and sank slowly into the cool water, letting the pleasing menthol aroma of eucalyptus wash over her. She was noticing that her toenail polish was chipped when she heard the bee. It buzzed over her head and alit on the bathroom sink, which was strange because the house had been closed up for two days so a bee couldn't have gotten in. She was pondering this, her head resting against the back of the tub, when the bee did something else strange. It flew up into the air, buzzed around in a circle, and then stopped midair, and dropped to the floor.

Susan sat up in the tub and looked down.

Bliss had painted the bathroom's wooden floor light blue and there, on the blue floor, like a boat at sea, was the bee, legs in the air, dead.

Susan felt woozy. She couldn't remember, for a moment, what she was even doing there, why she was home. Archie Sheridan was missing. She had to get back to the task force offices. She had to find Henry.

Where was her mother?

She looked down at the bee. She'd done a story on a family of five in Lake Oswego that had narrowly escaped a carbon monoxide leak. Odorless. Tasteless. The pets had dropped dead. A hamster and a bird. The mother had been smart enough to get everyone out of the house. Another half hour, the cops had said, and the whole family would have been dead.

Susan pulled herself out of the tub, bath foam sliding off her naked body onto the floor, and immediately slipped and banged her face on the edge of the sink. The shock of pain cleared her head and she grabbed a towel, then wrapped it around her at the chest and started downstairs.

Get out of the house. She had to keep saying it in her head, over and over again. Because when she stopped, she started thinking about sleep. About how nice it would be to just close her eyes for a second, and then get out of the house when she woke up. But she wouldn't wake up.

Get out of the house.

She lost the towel. She didn't know when. She must have dropped it. But she was naked, stumbling down the stairs, tears running down her cheeks. No, it wasn't tears. It was blood. From hitting the sink. She was bleeding. The blood ran into her mouth, a sweet coppery tang.

She got to the front door and saw someone standing on the other side of the glass. It took her a minute to recognize him out of uniform. It was Officer Bennett, from the Arlington, their protector, their assigned security detail.

He'd come to save her.

She reached the door and turned the knob to open it, but it wouldn't turn. It was locked. She was locked in the house. She motioned with her hand to Bennett, pointing to the knob to indicate that it was stuck, to get her out.

He just stood there.

She turned the knob again, but it wouldn't budge. Something was wrong. The dead bolt was in the right position. The door should open. She pounded on the glass, her hands leaving wet prints on the window. "The bee's dead," she shouted.

Bennett just stood on the other side of the door staring at her, and then he held up her house keys. It was a brilliant sunny day, and behind him Susan could see the blue sky, not a cloud in it, and the bamboo that her mother had planted in a glazed pot on the front porch, and Susan's favorite rhododendron bush, emblazoned with scarlet flowers.

She was dizzy. It reminded her of a time in college when she'd had too many pot brownies and passed out on a friend's beanbag. She'd slept with her face on her hand and she'd woken up with an imprint of her watch on her cheek. She started to sink to the ground.

There was something she was supposed to do. Get out of the house.

She could call someone. But the phone was so far away.

There was a sound then, and she looked up to see Bennett's face flat against the glass, eyes closed. He stayed there for a moment, like a kid pressing his face against a window for laughs. And then he slid down the glass out of sight and Susan heard the sound of his body hitting the wooden porch.

The door opened and someone picked her up and began to drag her out of the house.

She felt the backs of her heels hit the door jamb, and then the steps down to the front yard and then she was on grass. The grass felt cool and soft and she was glad that she could finally sleep. She looked up and she saw her mother.

"Hi, Mom," Susan said sleepily.

"I hit him with the Buddha," she said.

Susan forced herself awake. Breathe, she told herself. Her chest heaved, filling with oxygen, her head clearing an iota with every breath. "Jesus, Mom," she managed. "You killed a cop." She closed her eyes. "Call nine-one-one. Call Henry. Don't go in the house. Carbon monoxide leak. Bennett. He locked me in."

"I don't have a phone," Bliss said.

Susan's mother was not good at problem solving. This was just the kind of insurmountable obstacle that could paralyze her for hours. They didn't have that kind of time. Susan lifted herself up and grabbed Bliss by the lapels of her polyester paisley pantsuit. "Use the fucking neighbors'," Susan said.

Then she folded back down in the grass and passed out.

Chapter 53

When Susan woke up she had an oxygen mask over her mouth and was being tended to by two paramedics. A wispy cloud drifted overhead. It looked like a jackrabbit. Susan turned her head and vomited on the grass.

"Sorry," she said to the paramedics.

A uniformed cop was walking by with the Buddha in a large plastic evidence bag. Bliss was following behind him. "I'll get that back, right?" Bliss asked.

Henry squatted beside Susan. She heard his knees crack as he settled onto his haunches. His black jeans rode up and she could see that his cowboy boots had tooled pictures of a Native American–style eagle on them. "You feeling better?" he asked.

Susan took off the oxygen mask. "Is he dead?" she asked.

"Unconscious," Henry said.

Susan felt a light-headed rush of relief. Her mother hadn't killed him. "Did Bliss tell you what happened?" she asked. One of the paramedics had put the mask back on and the words came out muffled through the plastic.

Henry rubbed the back of his neck. "She said she came home to check on the goat and found you naked and banging on the door and Bennett outside." He glanced over at Bliss, who stood arguing with the cop who held the Buddha, and he raised his eyebrow. "She perceived him as a threat and clocked him."

Behind Henry, Susan saw another cop walking into the house. She struggled to sit up. "I think there's a carbon monoxide leak in the house," she said.

"There was," Henry said. "The furnace in the basement was leaking. We shut it off."

Susan settled back down. She felt woozy from moving and she sat sucking in oxygen for another minute. It didn't make sense. None of it made sense. When she felt well enough, she moved the mask away again. "I came home to take a nap," she told Henry, "and I started to feel sick and when I tried to leave the house Bennett wouldn't let me." The wispy jackrabbit cloud had drifted into a shape that didn't look like anything at all. "He took my keys and locked me in."

"You must have really pissed him off,"

Henry deadpanned.

"This isn't funny," Susan said.

Henry looked around the yard at the ambulance, the patrol cars, the police. He seemed mystified. "Why would Bennett try to kill you?" he said.

"I don't know," Susan said. "But he did. I know he did."

Henry shook his head. "It could have been Gretchen," he said. He looked back at the house. "I want both you and your mother under protection full-time again. You always have a cop with you. Got it?"

Susan was suddenly aware of the fact that she was, except for a blanket, completely naked. "I need to get dressed," she said.

"You need to go to the hospital," Henry said.

No. He was not going to send her to the hospital. Put her under lock and key. Not with all this going on. "I've got to get back to work," she protested.

Henry lifted his finger and touched his nose. "Your nose is broken," he said.

Bliss appeared then. Susan couldn't help but notice her freshly applied red lipstick. When she looked at Susan, she winced, her top lip peeling back in disgust. Bliss had never liked the sight of blood.

The sink. Susan must have cracked her

nose on the sink when she fell.

"Fine," Susan said to Henry. "But I'm not going anywhere without my purse."

"I'll risk an officer's life immediately to retrieve it from your home," Henry said.

"Thanks," said Susan. She turned to the paramedics. "Take me to Emanuel," she said.

If she had to go to the hospital, she at least wanted to go to the one where Archie's doctor worked.

CHAPTER 54

"How old were you when you broke your nose?" Gretchen asked.

Gretchen ran her finger lightly from Archie's hairline over his forehead and then down to the bridge of his nose. He was lying on his back in the bed. She was on her side next to him. They had just had sex again and he felt strangely weakened by it. There was a new highness now. Different from the pills. The pills were soft, like a bright haze. This was darker, a blackness that skirted the edges of his vision.

"Seventeen," he said. He knew the question that came next. "I was in a car accident."

"Was anyone killed?" she asked.

He hadn't talked about it in so long that he was surprised when he told her the truth. But it didn't matter anymore, and the very fact that she had asked made him think that she must somehow know the answer. "My mother," Archie said.

"Aha," she said.

"Aha?"

"You were driving," Gretchen said.

"I haven't even told Henry this story," Archie said. Only Debbie. No one else. Not since he'd left home. It was his dirtiest little secret. Besides Gretchen.

"Was it your fault?" Gretchen asked.

"I didn't see a stop sign."

Gretchen touched his face, tenderly, he thought. Though it might have been something else. "Your father must have never forgiven you," she said.

Archie hadn't seen his father since he'd left home. "No," he said.

They were quiet for a time, and Archie watched the shadows that the ceiling fan threw.

"My mother died when I was fourteen," Gretchen said finally.

He wondered if it was even true. "Did you kill her?" Archie asked.

"No," she said. She lifted herself up on her elbows and looked at him. She looked worried, her brow furrowed a little at the center. "Does it scare you?"

He knew what she meant. "Dying?" he said. "Not right now."

"It's always all right, at the end," she said,

taking his hand. "They always look peaceful." She kissed his knuckles. "You did."

"That might have had something to do with the torture ending," Archie said. He withdrew his hand and sat up, putting his bare feet on the floor. "I'm getting up," he said. "I have to go to the bathroom. And then I need to eat something." It was a lie. But if his plan was going to work, he needed to get Gretchen into the living room.

CHAPTER
55

"You're going to what?" Susan asked. She was in an exam room at the Emanuel ER dressed in a snappy pair of borrowed green scrubs. She took her oxygen mask off and said it again. "You're going to do what?"

"I'm going to realign your nose," the doctor said. Susan was pretty sure he was eighty years old. When he'd first come in, she'd thought he was one of those old people hospitals used to staff the gift store.

"With your hands?" she asked, horrified.

"Yes." He reached up, and before she could defend herself, he took hold of her nose with both hands. There was a flash of pain and she made a garbled noise and he lowered his hands and smiled.

"There," he said. "That wasn't so bad, was it?"

Susan lifted her hands to her face. "Ow," she cried.

"The nurse will splint and bandage you

and you'll be ready to go."

"Don't I get pain meds?" Susan asked.

The doctor patted her on the hand. "Ice and Advil. You'll be right as rain." He turned to Henry, who had insisted on coming and was sitting in a chair next to the examining table. "This your husband?"

"No," Henry and Susan both said quickly.

The doctor walked out of the examining room. "No one gets married anymore," he said on his way into the hall.

The nurse smiled. She was tall with dark hair pulled back in barrettes and features that were all scrunched together at the center of her face. "He's old-school," she said. "He doesn't even use anesthesia."

Susan touched her nose. The slightest brush of her fingers made it throb. Her mother had been taken back to the Arlington by two patrol cops. Bliss didn't have the stomach for emergency rooms anyway. Susan wasn't sure if the patrol cops were supposed to protect Bliss or keep her in custody.

The nurse started dressing her nose with white gauze and tape.

Henry stood up. "I'm going to check on Bennett," he said. "Don't go anywhere."

"Is Dr. Fergus working today?" Susan asked the nurse as soon as Henry was gone.

"Yes," the nurse said. "Do you know him?"

Susan smiled sweetly. It made her whole face ache. "I'm a family friend," she said. "Can you ask him to stop by and see me?"

Susan was sitting cross-legged on the exam table wearing the oxygen mask and reading *People* magazine when Fergus came in. He looked the same as the last time she'd seen him, when she'd interviewed him for her profile on Archie Sheridan. Same white bristle cut. Same hulking figure. Same superior attitude. He'd agreed to participate reluctantly, and then only after Archie had signed a HIPAA waiver.

He squinted at her for a moment, not recognizing her with the turquoise hair and bandaged nose. Then he blanched, his upper lip lifting. "Oh, it's you," he said.

Susan didn't give him time to leave. She knew Archie took a lot of pills. And she'd started thinking that he might need a refill. If he did, it might be a way to find him. She let the oxygen mask drop to her lap. "Archie's medication," she said. "Does he have enough, or would he need more?"

Fergus sighed and put his hands in the pockets of his white medical coat. "I can't talk about my patient with you."

"He's in trouble," Susan said.

371

"Detective Sobol has been in touch," Fergus said. "If anyone tries to refill any of Archie's meds, Sobol will be notified."

"Oh," Susan said. She probably should have known that Henry had already thought of it.

Fergus turned to leave.

"He's sick, isn't he?" Susan called out.

Fergus stopped. His shoulders lifted and fell. She thought he was going to tell her something. It was the way he set his shoulders back, like he wanted to get something off his chest. She leaned forward, ready to hear it.

"You'll want to keep ice on that," he said.

Henry found Claire in the ER waiting room. She'd found time at some point that day to go home and change and was wearing a T-shirt with a picture of a grizzly bear on it and jeans and red cowboy boots. He felt grimy and tired and his scalp itched. A simple explanation. That's all he wanted. An accidental carbon monoxide leak. A misunderstanding. Bennett to get a few stitches and laugh it off. Anything that would allow Henry to go to bed for a few hours.

Claire was on her cell phone next to a big sign that read NO CELL PHONES. She got off the call when she saw him.

"What's the word?" he asked her.

"He's in surgery," she said. "She drove a fragment of his skull into his brain." She smirked. "That Buddha packed quite a wallop."

So much for the nap. "He going to live?" Henry asked.

"Possibly," Claire said. She put her hands on her hips and shook her head slowly. "He did it."

Henry raised his eyebrows.

"Heil just called," Claire said. "We got Bennett's prints on the furnace. He loosened the thingy."

"The thingy?" Henry said.

"There might have been a fancier word for it," Claire said. "Anyway, house closed up like that, it filled right up with poison. A few hours later, she would have been dead three minutes after she came in the front door."

No. It couldn't be simple. Not with Susan Ward involved. Henry tried to sort this information out. Why would Bennett try to kill Susan? He rubbed his head. The lack of sleep had settled in his brain like a fog. "He was the first responder to the Molly Palmer crime scene," Henry theorized. "Maybe he didn't fall."

"You think he was trying to destroy

evidence?" Claire asked.

"Let's say he killed Molly Palmer and tried to cover it up. That might give him a reason to go after Susan."

"Why Susan?"

"She's working on a story tying Molly Palmer to Castle."

Claire's eyes widened. "She was the kid you told me about, the kid he fucked?"

"I think I used a fancier word for it," Henry said.

He had to protect Susan. He could do that. Archie would want him to. Henry would keep her safe.

If he could keep himself from killing her.

"Let me know if he wakes up," he said. "We searching his house?"

"Just filed for warrants," Claire said. Her phone rang and she checked the caller ID. "It's Flannigan," she said, lifting it to her ear. Flannigan was back at the task force offices, running the search for Archie. "Let me get this." She reached up and touched Henry lightly on the shoulder. "It could be good news."

CHAPTER
56

"You'll like this," Gretchen said. "Draw a star."

They were sitting on the sofa in the living room. Gretchen had put on a white silk blouse and a pair of slacks. Archie was dressed again in the blue shirt and corduroys. He had built a fire while she had made him a sandwich, and now he sat with the sandwich on a plate on his lap. Gretchen had found a pen and notebook in her purse and now handed Archie both.

He put the pen to the pad and tried to draw a star. It came out wrong, one side trailing off. It looked like a triangle. He tried again. The same thing happened.

"I can't," he said, examining the pen.

"You can track your neurological decline," Gretchen said. She got up, leaving Archie to ponder the lopsided lumpy drawing. "It will get worse," she said as she walked to the bar.

"I tried to make love to Debbie yesterday,

and couldn't get hard," Archie said, putting the notebook on the floor with the sandwich. He couldn't eat, and his urine was tinged with blood.

Gretchen was pouring them two drinks at the bar. She walked back to the couch and handed him a glass and stretched out on her back, putting her feet in his lap. "Did you try thinking of me?" she asked.

Archie examined the whiskey for a moment and then took a drink. "Yes."

Gretchen smiled. "Did she know?" she asked.

"Yes," Archie said.

"Good," said Gretchen. She moved her foot, pressing it against his groin. "Maybe I'll have our love child," she said.

"You had your tubes tied," Archie said. "I saw the prison medical reports."

Something flashed in her eyes. Then it was gone. "Yes. Even at the tender age of seventeen I knew I shouldn't reproduce."

It was maybe the most responsible thing she'd ever done. And still, it was sad, Archie thought. To make that decision so young. "And you found a doctor who'd do the operation?" he asked.

"The same one who did the abortion a month earlier," Gretchen said. She rolled on her side and faced the fire, the orange light reflecting off her smooth skin. "That was the first person I killed," she said.

"The baby?" Archie asked.

"The doctor," Gretchen said.

CHAPTER
57

Susan's phone rang. It wasn't supposed to be on and she scrambled to find it in her purse before the nurse came back and busted her. The *Herald*. She picked it up.

"Are you okay?" Derek asked. "It came through on the scanner." He sounded breathless. "Your mom shot a cop?"

"I'm fine," Susan said.

"Is something wrong with your nose?"

Susan could feel her face blush. Great. She sounded nasal. Perfect. "It's sort of broken," she said.

Derek paused. "Dude," he said slowly.

The nurse would be back any minute. "So I'm supposed to keep this oxygen mask on," Susan said, trying to get off the phone.

"There's a Texaco in a town called Mills Crossing on 22," Derek said. "It's about an hour and a half off of 5. Sixty-five people. Guy I talked to said he pumped gas into a Jag last night at about eleven P.M. Didn't remember the driver, but said the car had some sort of special wheels. Let me find it in my notes."

Susan's mouth went dry. "Sabre?" she said softly.

"Yeah," Derek said. "What are those anyway?"

"I have no idea," Susan said. "Listen, I've got to run."

"Okay. Ian's sending someone over. You know, to interview you and your mom."

"Tell Ian to go fuck himself," Susan said. She got her hairbrush out of her purse and started brushing her hair. The oxygen mask lay humming uselessly on the exam table.

"I'll find a way to rephrase it," Derek said. "Are you brushing your hair again?"

Henry walked in scratching his neck.

"I've got to go," Susan said, hanging up.

"What's going on?" Henry asked.

Susan started opening drawers in the exam room's cabinets. "There's a Texaco on 22 — an attendant saw a silver Jag with Sabre wheels last night at eleven. Fits the time frame."

"Mills Crossing?" Henry said.

Susan stopped, surprised. "Yeah."

"We do police work, too. Flannigan just called Claire. We've had cops calling gas stations all over the state. A car like that?

Sometimes people notice it."

Susan opened another drawer and found what she was looking for — a cold pack. "What are you going to do?" Susan asked. She squeezed the pack until it cracked and started turning cold.

"Send a local cop over with a picture of Gretchen." Susan zipped her purse up and slipped it over her shoulder. "Where are you going?" Henry asked.

Susan held the ice pack against her face. "I need to get some gas," she said.

"You need to rest and take in oxygen," Henry said. "There's a fire up there. Mills Crossing will probably have been evacuated by the time you get there."

Susan turned to Henry. Her face hurt. She felt like she was going to throw up. It was starting to affect her cheery disposition. "Bennett was trying to stop me from writing the Molly Palmer story," she said.

Henry worked a finger along his upper lip. "Maybe."

"He didn't have to," Susan said. "The *Herald* killed it. I'm going to find Archie. I'm going up the mountain, fire or not. You can stay here." She walked through the doorway and turned back. "Or you can come."

"Susan," Henry said.

"Yeah," she said, turning.

Henry smiled. "Did you want to stop by the Arlington and change?"

Susan looked down at the green scrubs she was wearing. "Right," she said.

CHAPTER
58

"Let's go back into the bedroom," Archie said. He stood up and held his jaundiced, swollen hand out to her. She looked vulnerable, lying there on the sofa, no makeup, her bruised clavicle visible at the neckline of the blouse. Maybe something or someone had turned her into a monster. Or maybe it was just who she was. Archie didn't care anymore. It didn't matter. The blackness was closing in. He had to act fast.

She took his hand and stood and he led her around the sofa.

"I try to be good," Gretchen said. "You know that, right?"

"Yes," Archie said gently.

They were near the banister now and Archie paused to tie his shoe. As he knelt, he retrieved the handcuffs he'd hidden in the bathroom and then stuffed in his sock. He'd counted on her hubris, believing she wouldn't search him. It was her fatal flaw —

she thought her control over him was absolute. But it wasn't. Not quite.

In a swift motion he snapped one end of the cuffs on Gretchen's slender right wrist, and snapped the other cuff around the wrought-iron banister. She reacted immediately, whipping her trapped arm in the air, pulling at the cuffs like someone staked to the bottom of the ocean, drowning. It was instinct. All animal. Archie took the moment to step away from her, out of reach. She snapped her head up at him. Her lips were wet, her eyes blazed. She swung at him, her fingertips almost brushing against his shirt. Her eyes darted back and forth, her mind working, looking for a way out. The red spots on her cheeks only made her look more beautiful.

She gathered herself, smoothing her hair with her free hand, lifting an eyebrow. "Darling," she said slowly. "This. Is. A. Very. Bad. Idea."

He didn't say anything. It took all of his focus to concentrate on what he had to do. He left her and walked to the bathroom down the hall. It was a small bathroom, a toilet, vanity, and fiberglass shower all in close quarters. A watercolor print of a deer standing in snow hung over the toilet. The mirror above the vanity was surrounded with large round lights. He took a minute, hands gripping the counter, to steady himself through a wave of dizziness. His heart felt like it was beating too slowly. The pain in his side throbbed. He wiped the sweat from his forehead, knelt down, and opened the vanity drawer under the sink. Then he reached behind the extra rolls of toilet paper and found the small cell phone and folded piece of paper that he had hidden there that first night along with the cuffs.

He carried the phone and the folded piece of typing paper back into the living room, where Gretchen had twisted her body in an effort to get out of the handcuffs.

"They're police issue," he said. "They're not going to give."

She stopped moving and looked at him, her chest heaving.

He held up the phone so she could see it, and hit the ON button. The phone came to life with a series of chimes. Then he walked over to the bar and set it on the counter. They'd trace the signal. But it might take hours or days. He could have called Henry, but he didn't want them to find him too soon, before the pills had had a chance to do their work.

He reached into his pants pocket and put the key to the cuffs next to the phone, where Henry could find it.

Then he poured the contents of one Vicodin bottle out onto the bar. The pills made a satisfying sound as they skidded across the granite and then stopped at his open hand. So here it was, finally. He'd thought about this so much over the past few years that it seemed almost anticlimactic. It felt familiar, natural. He'd been killing himself slowly ever since he'd been released from the hospital. Now he was just going to speed things up a little. The trick was to pace himself so that he kept enough of them down to kill him. He put one pill in his mouth and let it sit on his tongue, sucking on it until the bitterness filled his sinuses. He wanted to taste it. Eyes wide open. He wanted to experience every part of it. If he was going to die, he might as well know it. Gretchen had taught him that.

He scooped another couple of pills into his hand and put them in his mouth, licking the bitter chalky powder off his fingers.

"Archie," he heard her say. "Don't. There's a forest fire. Can't you smell it?"

He sniffed the air and smelled it then, like a campfire burning. He laughed. They were in the path of the forest fire. Fucking perfect.

"You can't leave me here," she said.

"They'll find you," he said. "And if they don't, then we'll both be dead."

CHAPTER 59

"You're not going to vomit, are you?" Henry asked Susan.

She had her window down and was leaning her head against the car door. They had wound an hour up Highway 22, through the woods and occasional one-gas-station towns, and Susan felt carsick. The air was dry and hot, and the wind blowing through the open window blew hair in her eyes and chapped her lips. Every bump in the road reminded her of her broken nose.

"I'm fine," she said in a nasal voice, swallowing some warm saliva that had pooled at the back of her throat. She didn't know if it was Henry's driving or the carbon monoxide poisoning, but her money was on Henry's driving.

They had made good time. There was a caravan of cars coming down the mountain, but with the exception of Forest Service vehicles and fire trucks, very little traffic headed up. She'd seen no evidence of the fire yet.

Susan saw a green highway sign that read MILLS CROSSING, POPULATION 52, PLEASE DRIVE CAREFULLY, and sat up. "This is it," she said. Mills Crossing appeared to be a gas station, roadhouse, a few old houses, and an "antiques shop" consisting of old dishes and paperbacks laid out on sheets in the roadhouse parking lot.

Henry flipped on his turn signal to pull across the highway to get to the gas station, but the line of cars coming down the mountain continued at a solid pace. Finally he put the siren on the hood, hit a button on the dash, and the siren whooped once. The cars immediately parted to let him through.

"Must be nice," Susan said.

"It is," said Henry.

He pulled up and parked next to the gas station. Susan counted eight cars waiting to get gas. A single attendant was manning the station's two pumps. Oregon hadn't had self-serve gas since the state had passed a statute against it in the 1940s. Back then the state was afraid people would blow themselves up. Now the statute was supposed to protect the environment, jobs, and old people who might succumb to fumes.

This guy looked like he would have been

fine letting the customers risk it.

Henry and Susan got out of the car and moved between the bumpers of two SUVs to get to the gas pump. The attendant was Susan's height, and didn't weigh much more. His skin was tan and tough. He wore a T-shirt that read SPOTTED OWL TASTES LIKE CHICKEN.

"You Big Charlie?" Henry asked.

"Yep," the little man said. He had a toothpick in his mouth and it rotated from one corner of his mouth to the other while he talked. "Cash only," he said to a man in a VW bus. "Visa machine's down." The man in the bus handed Big Charlie a crumpled ten and Big Charlie inserted the nozzle into the bus's gas tank and hit a lever on the pump. The pump's dial meter began to rotate slowly. A woman in a Honda Element waiting for gas on the other side of the pump honked her horn. Big Charlie ignored her.

The traffic coming down Highway 22 was a caravan of Monteros, Subaru wagons, and Jeep Wagoneers, punctuated by the odd log truck. Some of the SUVs were hauling speedboats. Some had three or four bikes on the grille. But Susan noticed other cars, too, that were packed for more than a recreational holiday, with Hefty bags and boxes roped to the tops of their roofs.

Susan surveyed the line of cars, shielding her eyes from the sun with her hand.

Big Charlie took off his baseball cap, dabbed at his forehead with a rag, and put the cap back on. "They're evacuating," he said. His gray eyes flicked down to Susan's burning American Spirit. "Some jackass tossed a cigarette," he said. "Happens every summer."

Susan glanced down at her cigarette and rotated it behind her thigh. "What?" she said, looking between Big Charlie and Henry. "It wasn't me."

The gas attendant jammed his thumb toward a NO SMOKING sign affixed to the gas pump.

"Sorry," Susan said. She took one more quick drag and ground the cigarette out in a steel trash can filled with empty soda bottles, urine-soaked diapers, and other crap people stored up in the back of their cars on road trips.

Henry flipped open his badge and showed it to Big Charlie. "You saw a silver Jaguar?" he asked.

"Yeah," Big Charlie said. The bus's tank was full and he pulled the nozzle out, hung it back on the pump, and gave the bus a friendly pat on the windshield as it pulled away. "Nice car. Came through last night. I filled the tank with plus."

"You remember who was driving?" Henry asked.

"A woman. I told the fellow on the phone, I mostly remember the car."

"Can I show you a photograph?" Henry asked, holding Gretchen's mug shot out.

Big Charlie tipped his head up so he could see the picture under the bill of his cap. "Might have been her." He glanced up at Susan. "Might have been you. What'd she do?"

"She's Gretchen Lowell," Susan said.

Big Charlie greeted this with a blank stare.

"The Beauty Killer," Susan said.

The woman in the Honda Element honked her horn again. Big Charlie didn't flinch. And didn't rush. "I'm more of a John Wayne Gacy man myself," he said. He squinted at Susan. "You should put some ice on that."

CHAPTER
60

It was easier than he thought it would be. Maybe it was because his body was used to it. Maybe it was because his mind was ready to let go. He'd taken two bottles of pills now. He'd done it methodically. Three pills at a time. Washing each mouthful down with three swallows of Scotch. You got into a rhythm after a while. And he'd grown to like the taste of the Scotch. The heat of it filled him like bathwater. He wished he'd appreciated it more while he was alive. The thought made him smile. He probably couldn't have afforded Scotch this good on his salary anyway.

"Please," Gretchen said. "Stop."

The remaining pills were on the counter. Archie arranged them into a little wagon train. Then lifted them, one by one. When he'd taken all the pills, he turned back to Gretchen.

She stood frozen, staring at him, her lips

parted, her head slightly tilted. Her eyes were large, the whites pink from crying. She looked distraught, like a child who didn't understand why she was being punished. Her desperation almost made him feel sorry for her.

"Sorry," he said. "Commitment issues."

"Uncuff me," she said.

He shook his head.

Her entire face was red now, tears streaming down both cheeks. "I'll tell them everything."

"No you won't," Archie said. "I don't know why." He rubbed his eyes, which were feeling heavier by the minute. "But you won't."

"I'll tell them everything," Gretchen said, louder. "It will ruin your career, your marriage, your family, your legacy. Free me."

"You can't be free," Archie said simply. "You'll hurt people."

"I won't. I have control over it. I do."

Archie walked over to Gretchen. She straightened hopefully, pushing her hair behind her ears and wiping the smeared makeup from under her eyes. He pulled the folded piece of paper from his pocket, unfolded it, and held it out to her along with a pen.

Her eyebrows furrowed.

"It's a confession stating that you killed Heather Gerber," Archie said. "Sign it."

She took the paper and pen, sat back down, and, using the floor as a writing pad, signed the paper and held it up for him. He took it and the pen and walked back toward the bar.

"The key," she said, rattling the handcuffs. "The fire," she reminded him.

"No," Archie said.

"This isn't what's supposed to happen."

Archie fumbled around behind the bar until he found another bottle of Scotch, then came around and sank to the floor, his back against the bar. He opened the bottle and lifted it to his mouth. Not much longer.

His heart was beating too slowly again. He unbuttoned his shirt and placed his hand on his chest to see if he could feel the rhythm under his skin.

"You'll have to make a new deal. Give them something more. Or they'll make sure you get the needle . . ."

"Bring me my purse," she said.

A pleasant darkness surrounded him. The air felt inky. Under the scar she had carved on him, his heart fought to pump. "I feel strange," he said. It slurred a little in his mouth.

Fifteen feet away from him Gretchen

slumped to the floor, her arm dangling above her, cuffed to the banister. He could feel it, even here, even like this. That's how strong his desire for her was.

He tried to stand up and slumped to his knees, overcome by a wave of vertigo. She reached her free arm toward him, stretching her fingers in the air. And he crawled to her, first on his hands and knees, then, as his skin got cold and his muscles failed, he dragged himself to her on his elbows.

He collapsed when he reached her and she took his head in her lap.

"You fucking moron," she said.

"I know," said Archie.

CHAPTER
61

Gretchen Lowell crosses her legs and leans forward on the striped chair.

"So, how do we do this?" Archie asks. He feels out of place in Gretchen's house. He agreed to the individual sessions she offered mostly to be polite. He didn't expect them to be in her home. It feels vaguely inappropriate.

Her blue eyes widen. "You've never been in therapy before?" she says.

He has only known Gretchen Lowell a few weeks, since she appeared at the task force offices to offer her help in catching the Beauty Killer. She makes him feel self-conscious. He'd sat in his car outside for ten minutes working up the nerve to come in. "Just the group session you led," he says.

She smiles. She is wearing a skirt and she threads her fingers and hooks them around one knee, and the skirt exposes an inch of her thigh. "Well, it's easy," she says. "You tell me what's on your mind. And we talk about it."

Archie shifts uncomfortably in his chair, his gun pressing into his hip. He does have something on his mind. Something he hasn't even told Henry about. "I'm thinking about asking for a transfer," he says. "I'd like to spend more time with my family." It feels good to finally say it. It gives it power. Like he might actually do it this time. He looks up at Gretchen. She's a woman. He expects her to encourage him to choose his kids over his work. It's one of the reasons he's come.

But she doesn't.

"Is it hard on your marriage?" she asks. "Working so much?"

Archie considers this. He knows the answer. He's just not sure how much he wants to disclose. "My wife would like to see me in a different job," he says.

Gretchen leans forward a little more, and her skirt inches up another notch. "But you're so good at what you do," she says.

Archie laughs. "I have one job. To catch the Beauty Killer. Which I haven't done."

"I think you're close," she says. She reaches out and puts a hand on the armrest of Archie's chair. She doesn't touch him. Just the chair. "Don't give up now," she says. "You need to stay focused on the case."

Archie shakes his head. "I need to be home more," he says. "I don't want to end up being one of those people who miss their kids' birthdays." He'd already missed too much of their growing up. It was easy to justify working late when you could convince yourself that lives depended on it.

"How long have you and your wife been together?" Gretchen asks.

"Since college," he says.

"How many women have you slept with?" Gretchen asks.

Archie feels his face flush. He looks out the window, at a stand of cherry trees planted in the yard. "Just her," he says.

"Really?"

He clears his throat. "I had a girlfriend in high school who wanted to wait until she was married. I respected that. Then I met Debbie in college. And that was it."

"And you never cheated on her?" Gretchen asks.

"No."

"That's unusual," Gretchen says.

"Is it?" Archie asks.

"To have been with only one person your whole life?"

Archie shrugs. "I love her."

"Is the sex good?" Gretchen asks.

Archie feels hot. He reaches up and rubs

the back of his neck. The only sound in the room is the ticking of Gretchen's grandfather clock. "I feel really strange talking about this with you," he says.

Gretchen nods sympathetically. "In order for this to work," she says, "you have to be honest with me."

"Yes," Archie says, looking away. "The sex is good."

"How do you know?" Gretchen asks.

Archie smiles. Touché. "I know," he says.

Gretchen touches the chair again. "It's okay to fantasize about other people," she says. "It's not cheating." Gretchen's hand rests on the arm of Archie's chair. Her fingers are slender, alabaster, boneless. Her nails are manicured. "You are attracted to other women," she says.

Archie splays his fingers out helplessly. "I'm male," he says.

"Are you attracted to me?" she asks. She pauses, just long enough for him to sputter awkwardly, then sits back and smiles at him. "It's an academic question. It's useful to know from a therapeutic point of view."

Archie searches for something he can say, something true, but not too true. His mouth is suddenly very dry. The clock continues to tick. He settles on "I think you're very beautiful."

Her face lights up and she laughs. It's a pleasant laugh, a shared joke. "I've made you uncomfortable," she says.

"Yes," he says.

"I only ask about your sex life because sex is an excellent stress reliever. And I know you've been under significant stress."

"I don't like having sex with Debbie after a crime scene," Archie says. "I can't get the images out of my mind. It feels wrong."

"The images stay with you?" Gretchen asks.

Archie lifts a hand to his forehead, as if he might be able to wipe the images away manually. "Yeah."

He feels the full weight of her attention. "Any one more than the others?" she asks.

"Heather Gerber," he says. "The first victim we found. In the park. She wasn't the worst, in terms of the torture. But her face. Her eyes were open. And she looked at me. That sounds crazy, doesn't it?"

"Do the images keep you up at night?"

His phone vibrates in his pocket. He pulls it out and flips it open. It's a text from Henry. Another tip. "Fuck," he says before he can catch himself. He looks up at Gretchen, suddenly self-conscious about his language. "Excuse me," he says. "It's Henry. I have to go."

He stands up, adjusting the gun on his hip. She stands, too, and walks over and puts her hand on his arm, just above his elbow.

"I want to see you again," she says. "I think I can help."

She smells like lilacs.

Archie doesn't move. He doesn't want to surrender the pressure of her touch. He feels a strange connection to the place, to her. It's ridiculous. He barely knows her. She's beautiful and she's paying attention to him and he's responding like a seventeen-year-old.

He decides not to set up another appointment right away. He'll wait a few days. So he doesn't seem too desperate.

The ticking stops. He looks up at the grandfather clock. It's silent, the hands frozen at 3:30.

He clears his throat. "Your clock just stopped," he tells her.

She drops her hand from his arm and looks back at the clock. "That's funny," she says.

He takes a step to leave and she turns after him, her form backlit from the light coming in the window, a vision of loveliness. There was nothing wrong in noticing that, Archie tells himself. It was just an observation.

"If you're having trouble sleeping," she

says, "I can give you a sample of something that might help."

He smiles. Maybe he won't wait a few days to make that next appointment. Maybe he'll call back later today. Just to hear her voice. "Thanks," he says. "But I don't like to take pills."

CHAPTER
62

Henry ran the siren for a while, but it didn't help — there was nowhere to pull over. They were stuck in traffic. The highway carved down the mountain, hundred-foot-tall Doug firs a hedge on either side. You could barely see the sky sometimes. The passing lanes were only occasional, and then only for the briefest interludes. Henry would flip on the siren again and gun it past thirteen cars. But they were still inching down the mountain at a glacial pace. The upside was that they were going so slow that Susan wasn't carsick anymore. Big Charlie had given her some ice from the ice machine for her face, and she was feeling pretty good.

"Take your feet off the dashboard," Henry said.

"Sorry," Susan said, tucking her bare feet under her. She hoped Henry couldn't see the toe prints she'd left on his windshield. "I still don't know why I can't look for her."

"I've put a bulletin out for Highway 20, Highway 22, and for eastern Oregon. You heard the guy. It might have been her. It might not have."

"How can a police car not have air-conditioning?" she asked. She'd bought a bottle of water at the gas station and had slowly been peeling off the label ever since. Now she tore another minuscule shred and rolled it between her fingers.

"It's broken," Henry said.

Susan turned to look in the backseat to see if there was a magazine she could fan herself with or something. Her backseat was filled with magazines. But Henry's was empty. Except for a cardboard box. She recognized the handwriting on the side.

"Those are my Castle notes," Susan said.

"Yeah," Henry said. "I kind of borrowed them."

"I lent them to Archie," Susan said. She twisted around so she could open the box. "You better not have gotten them out of order."

"I haven't touched them," Henry said.

Susan pulled the top notebook out with one hand, using the other to keep the plastic bag of ice on her face. "Did you write on this?" she asked. The notebook was flipped open and a name was circled. John Bannon.

"I haven't even opened the box," Henry said.

That meant that Archie had done it. "Does the name John Bannon mean anything to you?" Susan asked Henry.

Henry moved the car forward another few feet. "He was Buddy Anderson's old partner," he said. "Back when Buddy ran the task force."

"Molly said he was her contact," Susan said. "He was the guy she called when she needed more money. He was Castle's lackey."

"Bannon's been dead ten years," Henry said. The guy in the car behind them started blasting ZZ Top. He had a good sound system and the Crown Vic pulsed with the bass beat.

Another dead end.

The ZZ Top fan turned up his stereo.

"For fuck's sake," said Henry, lifting his thumb and forefinger to the bridge of his nose.

"Heather Gerber," Susan said suddenly.

Henry lowered his hand. "What?"

"This is all about Heather Gerber," Susan said. "Archie said that you never forget your first one. Your first cigarette. Your first corpse in the woods. I thought he was talking about the two bodies we found that night in Forest

Park." Susan cringed at her narcissism. "*My* first corpse in the woods. But he was talking about *his* first corpse. His first big case — Heather Gerber."

"Okay," Henry said.

"So maybe we should be looking for her," Susan said. She tore another shred off the label and dropped it onto the floor. "If you were looking for someone, what's the first thing you'd do?"

"Pick that up," Henry said.

Susan leaned down and picked up the piece of label off the floor. "Sorry," she said.

"Trace their cell phone," Henry said. "That's the first thing I'd do."

"You can do that, right?" Susan asked. "Triangulate a general position using pings off cell towers?" The ice was starting to melt, and cold water was trickling down her arm.

Henry slid her a surprised look. "Listen to you," he said.

"I did a story on those hikers they found lost in the woods last year," Susan said. The weather had been bad and the search had been called off. They'd found their bodies the next morning.

"We can do better than that. Newer phones have built-in GPS signals. We can get a location within fifty to a hundred meters."

"It would be a new account," Susan said.

"He would have set it up in her name in the past few days."

"You think Archie has a phone in Heather Gerber's name? If he has another cell phone, why doesn't he just call us on it?"

"I don't know."

Henry flipped open his cell phone and hit a speed-dial button.

"I want to see if we can find a cell phone registered to Heather Anne Gerber," he said into the phone. There was a pause. "Archie's carrier is Verizon," Henry said. "Start there."

CHAPTER
63

Henry drummed his fingers against the hot steering wheel. Susan had her feet up on the dashboard again, but Henry was letting it slide. They had moved only a car length when Henry's cell phone rang again. He picked it up.

Above them, a few hundred feet straight up to the right, a cliff side was being held together with chicken wire. A yellow sign warned ROCKS.

"Found it," Claire's voice said. "Heather Anne Gerber. Archie added the phone to his family plan. He said she was his daughter."

"Give me the number," Henry said, tearing a Post-it off the pad affixed to the dash. "Then get a trace on it and call me back."

Claire read him the ten digits and Henry wrote them down.

"Well?" Susan asked when he hung up. With the leaking ice pack against her face,

Henry could barely make out anything she said.

He didn't answer. Instead he punched in the number of the phone Archie had registered to a dead girl.

The phone went right to voice mail.

"It's me," Archie's recorded voice said. "Hurry." The voice mail beeped.

"God fucking dammit," Henry said into the phone. "You better have a fucking epic excuse for all this." His voice thickened and he swallowed hard, turning his head to hide his emotion from Susan. "I'm on my way."

He hung up and turned to Susan.

"It's him," he said.

His phone rang and he snapped it to his ear before it could get to the second ring. "There's a timber road at mile post 92 off Highway 20 near the Metolius River. We're getting a hit two miles up that road. Flannigan checked and there's only one house up there."

They had just passed mile post 38. Susan had been right. It had been Gretchen. And Henry had headed in exactly the opposite direction. No time to kick himself now. "Okay," he said. "I'm going up there. Get everyone you can to that house."

"You know there's a fire, right?" Claire asked.

Henry flipped on the siren, pulled into the oncoming lane, and executed a U-turn. Up ahead a plume of flesh-colored smoke rose ominously from the horizon. "Yep," he said.

Henry hadn't said ten words since he'd gotten off the phone with Claire. He was white-knuckling the steering wheel, taking the curves fast, his aviator sunglasses reflecting the road. There was no traffic to impede them now. They passed Big Charlie's gas station and continued farther up, snaking through the Doug firs, siren wailing.

The trees were getting taller, the sky a skinny river above their heads. Dark shadows dappled the road. The ice had melted.

They cleared a curve and saw a Forest Service roadblock up ahead. It was Susan's first glimpse of the fire. An orange wall of flame formed a squiggle along the back of one of the tree-thick ridges ahead of them. Beige smoke blocked out the whole eastern sky.

"Jesus," she said.

Henry pulled up to the roadblock. The westbound lane was still open to let through the stragglers fleeing the fire, but the eastbound lane was blocked with sawhorses. A big sign read ROAD CLOSED DUE TO FIRE.

A park ranger with a ponytail walked up to

the car. He wore a standard-issue brimmed ranger hat and a wet bandana tied around his nose and mouth. "You have to turn back," he said to Henry, motioning back down the mountain.

Henry pointed to the siren on the hood. "Portland PD," he said.

"Have you come to arrest the fire?" the ranger asked.

"I need to get to a timber road near the Metolius," Henry said.

The ranger shook his head. "Fire's too close to the road. It's closed. You can go around."

"Can't," Henry said. "I need to get through now. I think Gretchen Lowell's up there. With Archie Sheridan."

The ranger lifted his chin and surveyed the fiery hillside. For a second Susan wondered if Henry might just drive through the roadblock.

But he didn't have to. "If the fire overtakes your car," the ranger said, "stay in your vehicle. Lie on the floor and cover your head and face. Breathe shallow breaths through your nose. If you have to get out of the car don't run uphill from the fire."

Susan leaned forward so she could speak across Henry. "Why?" she asked.

The ranger took his handkerchief off and

wiped the back of his neck with it. "Because heat rises," he said, "and the fire will outrun you."

He motioned to one of the other rangers to move the sawhorses so the Crown Vic could pass.

"Now go," he said. "If the fire jumps the road get the hell out of there."

Henry looked at Susan. She knew what he was thinking. "No," she said, crossing her arms and facing straight ahead. "I'm staying with you."

There were wildflowers along the highway; great fields of pink and purple carpeted the north shoulder where the hillside rose at a one-hundred-twenty-degree angle of rocky outcroppings. Susan had put her boots on and had her feet on the floor so she could lean forward and watch the smoke, a plume so huge it looked like a mountain. The road was eerily quiet. They had gone several miles and passed only a few yellow Forest Service trucks. Henry had the light and siren on and no one in the trucks had given them a second look. They had other things on their minds. The Doug firs were giving way to ponderosa pines. Just beyond the next hill, Susan could see two planes dropping red fire retardant. The red retardant looked like blood hemorrhaging from the planes' split bellies.

A doe lay dead on the side of the road.

A bullet-riddled sign marked a SNO-PARK.

The smoke was thick enough now that Henry snapped on the headlights.

Susan glanced down at her cell phone. She'd been on roam for the last few miles. Now she didn't have any signal at all. "I've lost service," she said.

"Me, too," Henry said.

Susan felt a cramping in her stomach that seemed a lot like fear.

It started to rain. Henry turned on the windshield wipers and the raindrops smeared gray along the glass. It wasn't rain.

"What is it?" asked Susan.

"Did I ever tell you the story of how I ended up married to a Lummi Indian princess?" Henry asked.

"It's not rain," she said.

Henry accelerated. "It's ash," he said.

Susan rolled up her window. She did it quickly, putting her whole arm into it. The ash fell from the sky like snow, covering the car and the road with a fine gray dust.

The highway curved and opened up as they cleared the hump of the pass. The road began its descent into forest as far as the eye could see, half of it on fire, the sky orange with it, a weird psychedelic sunset.

"How much farther?" Susan asked. Her eyes burned from the smoke. It was getting thicker, so Henry had to slow down to stay on the road.

"Five miles," Henry said.

The fire had burned the woods to the south of the highway. The ground was black, the ponderosas white stalks, their branches curled and naked. The woods to the north, where the fire hadn't jumped the highway, were pristine, tall pines and alders, prairie grass an unbelievable yellow-green. And then, every so often, a single tree would be burning like a torch.

"It's jumping the highway," Susan said. It was getting hard to breathe and Susan closed the vents on the dash, though it didn't do any good.

"I know," said Henry.

Susan coughed and lifted a hand to her mouth, trying to filter out the ash with her fingers. "The ranger said that if it jumped the highway, we should turn back," she said. Breathe through your nose, the ranger had also said. But her nose was packed with cotton.

"It's too late," Henry said. He jammed a finger behind them and Susan turned to see that both sides of the road were on fire now.

There was an explosion and Susan braced herself, hands on the dash, thinking that a tire might have blown. But the car stayed on the road. She was disoriented for a moment and turned to Henry for an explanation, but he was leaning over the steering wheel, trying to see through the smoke. Then she realized: It was the trees. The trees were exploding.

Susan heard Henry say "Shit," and looked up just in time to see an elk, standing stock-still in the center of the lane.

Henry slammed on the brakes and the car spun.

Susan squeezed her eyes shut as the inertia of the car pressed her against the passenger-side door. She heard the tangled metal sound of the car hitting the guardrail and opened her eyes long enough to see orange sparks fly as the car ruptured it. The car lunged down the hill and then flipped, and she was upside down, hands pressed against the roof of the car. She closed her eyes again. The sound of the metal roof of the car sliding down the hillside smashing into the charcoaled skeletons of trees was loud, like an animal baying, and she thought of Parker in that moment, going off the bridge. How time slows down during car accidents, so he must have had time to think, to know what was happening, just like she did now.

And then it was quiet.

She was still alive.

She did a mental inventory of her body parts. Feet. Legs. Arms. Hands. She was still whole. She opened her eyes. Dust swirled inside the car and stung her eyes and made her cough.

"You okay?" Henry asked.

"I think so," Susan said. "Did we hit it?" She didn't know why she was so concerned about the elk.

"Can you get out?" Henry asked.

She struggled to get out of the car, unclipping her seat belt and falling on her shoulders and then to a fetal position on her side. The car was full of glass and dirt and her shoulder hurt from the impact but she made herself keep moving. The windshield was broken and she slithered out onto the blackened soil. It was still warm, the charcoal like burned toast in her mouth.

She scrambled away from the car, trying to get out of the dust storm of soot that the crash had stirred up. The car had come to rest against a blackened tree. It had spun entirely around and was facing the road, the trunk against the tree, the hood up the incline. The wheels were still spinning. Susan shook the twigs and beads of auto glass from her hair and stood up, but a wave of light-headedness forced her back to her haunches, coughing.

Her nose. She touched her face. The bandage was still on. Her face hurt. But not more than normal.

She looked up. They were thirty feet from the road, overlooking the lake. She blinked against the blinding smoke. Beyond the lake the surrounding hillsides were devastated, charred relics of trees; it looked like the end of the world.

She heard Henry get loose with a thud, and in a minute he pulled himself through the windshield. "Radio's busted," he said.

He moved around to the back of the car. "Fuck," he said. "Trunk's jammed."

Susan half slid down the embankment to join him. The trunk of the Crown Vic was wrapped around the tree.

"You think?" she said.

"Emergency kit's in there," Henry muttered. "Flair gun, flashlight, everything." He rubbed his forehead for a minute. "Okay," he said. "We'll have to walk out." He started up the darkened hillside.

"Come on," he said, turning back.

Susan didn't budge. "The ranger said to stay in the car."

"The car is upside down," Henry said.

Susan crossed her arms. "I'm staying here."

"I'm not leaving you," Henry said, holding out a hand.

"No, really," Susan said. "It's okay. Leave me."

"Come on, Susan. It's going to be dark soon. We'll have a better chance on the road."

Susan stared at him for another minute and then turned back to the car, got down on her hands and knees, and crawled halfway through the passenger window.

"Susan," Henry groaned.

She saw what she was looking for in the backseat and grabbed it. "I'm getting my purse," she said. She backed out of the car and stood up, pausing to brush the glass off the knees of her jeans.

Henry held out his hand again and she took it. "I'm never coming to the woods again," she said, as he pulled her up the hillside.

The elk was gone. "We must not have hit it," Susan said.

"I don't give a shit about the elk," Henry said.

"Why did you swerve then?" Susan asked.

"I wanted to protect the car," Henry said.

Susan raised an eyebrow and looked down the hillside at the crunched Crown Vic. "Oh," she said.

Something caught her eye across the road and she ran over to it and picked it up. "Hey, look," she said happily. "My water bottle."

"Excellent," Henry said.

"We'll see how sarcastic you are when you're dying of thirst," Susan said, brushing the dirt and crud off the plastic bottle. She dug two Advil out of her pocket and washed them back with a swig from the bottle.

"We're not going to die of thirst," Henry said. He pointed up ahead where a mile post sign read: 90. "We're almost there. We just need to walk four miles."

"On foot?" Susan said, looking down at her Frye boots. Her throat hurt, and the choking pink haze wasn't getting any thinner.

"By the time we get there the entire cavalry will have arrived. If they're not there already."

"So, tell me the story," Susan said.

"What story?" Henry asked.

"About how you ended up married to the Lummi Indian princess."

CHAPTER
64

They had walked out of the fire zone into the green forest of ponderosa pines. A scorch mark on the road marked the dividing line. On one side, burned ruin, on the other, pine needles and pinecones, purple flowers and prairie grasses. The air was still heavy with smoke and the only sound was the occasional engine of a Forest Service plane or helicopter flying overhead. No police cars. No sirens.

Susan noticed that Henry's skin, hair, and clothes were coated with ash. She wiped her own face and her hand came down smeared with dirt.

Darkness fell fast in the mountains. The setting sun looked like a streetlight obscured by orange fog. Half the sky was bejeweled with stars, half the sky was blank, the stars hidden by soot and particulate matter. They didn't have much time. On foot, without a flashlight, they would be blind in another hour.

Susan's eyes felt raw from the smoke and she rubbed at them, which only seemed to make them more irritated. She looked at her hands. They were covered with ash. She rubbed them on her jeans.

"This must be it," Henry said, stopping near mile post 92, where a gravel road snaked up into the wooded hillside.

Henry flipped open his cell phone, a pale blue glow in the violet dusk. "Still no service," he said. "Tower must be down."

Susan peered up the road. The smoke made everything look soft and oddly still. "Where's the cavalry?" she asked.

Henry drew his weapon from his shoulder holster and looked up and down the highway, and then up the gravel road. "They're not here yet."

"Why?" asked Susan. They'd called Claire an hour ago. Something was wrong. They should be here by now.

"The fire," Henry said. "The Sisters cops are probably evacuating the town. Airport's maybe closed so the others can't get in. I don't know. You should wait here. A fire crew will come by."

Susan shook her head. "No, one won't. We'd have seen them by now. They're fighting the fire somewhere else. You're not leaving me."

"The fire's headed north," Henry said.

Susan looked up at the sky. "What if the wind changes?"

Henry turned his head in both directions down the abandoned highway, then turned and started up the gravel road, his gun at his thigh. "Fine."

Susan got in step behind him. "Okay," she said.

It took a half hour to get to the house. It wasn't hard to find if you were looking for it. It was the only place up the long, dark road. They saw the mailbox first. Then the lights through the trees.

The house wasn't that old. It was Northwest lodge style, with cabin logs and a stone façade around a big front double door. The silver Jag was parked out front.

"Stay here," Henry said, lifting his gun and starting toward the house.

Susan scrambled to stay behind him, pine-cones and twigs crunching under her feet.

"Oh, for fuck's sake," he said, turning around.

"I'm not staying out here alone," Susan said. The glow of the western sky had faded to purple.

Henry took her by each shoulder. "I need you to stay here, so that if Archie's in there, and something happens to me, you can go get help." She didn't know how she was going to do that. Walk to Sisters? Flag down a helicopter? But the seriousness in Henry's expression made her nod her consent.

Henry lifted his gun again and moved toward the house, ducking as he made his way by the front windows. He reached the porch and moved toward the door.

"Do you need a warrant?" Susan called in a whisper.

Henry didn't seem to hear her. He opened the door and moved inside the house. Susan was alone.

A few minutes passed. A squirrel scrambled up the tree Susan was standing next to. It reached the top in four clawed hops, then froze.

The front door to the house stayed open.

Susan felt around on the ground and picked up the sharpest stick she could find. In one hand she had the stick, in the other the water bottle. She could stay outside alone or she could go inside and see what was going on. Either choice was dangerous. But if she went in, at least she wouldn't be alone. Parker would go in. Parker wouldn't even hesitate.

Fuck it. She put down the water bottle and followed Henry into the house.

There was music inside. Susan could barely hear it over the rush of her own pulse. A faint classical concerto drifted from the main room up ahead at the end of the hallway.

For a second Susan let herself believe that maybe this was the wrong house. Maybe Archie wasn't here.

She slid along the wall a few feet at a time, the stick held in front of her like a sword. It was dirty and crooked and she gripped it so tightly she worried it might snap in her hands.

Henry was standing at the end of the hallway completely motionless.

"What have you done to him?" she heard Henry ask.

Susan continued along the wall, drawn forward by a compulsion beyond her control. She wasn't even aware of moving forward until she found herself at the mouth of the hallway.

A huge fireplace loomed up ahead, the embers of a dying fire flickering within it. Then Susan realized that it wasn't the dying embers flickering, it was the forest fire. On either side of the floor-to-ceiling stone mantel were picture windows and Susan could see the ridge of red flame growing closer in the darkness, a vision of sinister splendor. It was a mile away, at the most.

Susan couldn't breathe.

Next to her Henry stood with his gun leveled at Gretchen Lowell. Susan couldn't get enough oxygen, couldn't concentrate. Gretchen was wearing slacks and a white silk blouse and her hair was half undone from a bun, blond strands falling against her cheeks. Archie was dead, his head in her lap. Susan tried to get air, but her gauze-packed nose made her feel like someone had a hand over her face. Gretchen's white blouse was splattered with Archie's blood.

Susan wheezed, a wet rattle of a noise, like something dying.

"Susan, get out of here," she heard Henry say. Henry's eyes were still fixed on Gretchen. "Back away from him," he barked.

Susan saw Gretchen hold an arm up, revealing a pair of steel handcuffs that bound her wrist to the banister. "I can't," Gretchen said. There was a little irritation in her voice, as if she shouldn't be bothered with something so obvious.

Henry started inching forward toward Gretchen, gun raised. Susan felt a hard nut of panic in her chest. A thousand possibilities streamed through her head. What she would do if something happened to Henry, if she were left alone with

Gretchen, with Archie there on the floor. She looked at the stick in her hands and then glanced around for some better kind of weapon, a knife, a hammer, anything. She noticed the white purse on the bar, the key, the piece of paper, the empty prescription bottles, but no blunt objects. Then she saw a paring knife, on the bar. She dropped the stick on the floor, grabbed the knife, and tucked it into her hand. Henry had reached Archie and was kneeling beside him, gun leveled at Gretchen's head as he reached a hand to Archie's neck to feel for a pulse.

"What have you done to him?" Henry demanded.

"Guess again," Gretchen said.

Susan got her phone out and looked at it. There still wasn't any service. If she lived through this, she was definitely changing carriers. She looked around for a landline and didn't see one.

"Both your hands where I can see them," Henry said to Gretchen. He said it through gritted teeth, so it came out hard and fast.

Gretchen raised her other hand. "He's in liver failure. I've got naloxone. I can save him. There's a key on the bar. Uncuff me."

Susan glanced over at the small key on the bar. Then back at Gretchen. Then the realization knocked her back on her heels: It wasn't Archie's blood all over Gretchen's blouse. It was Gretchen's. She'd split the flesh of her own wrist open struggling against the cuff.

He might still be alive.

"Fuck you," Henry said to Gretchen.

"He'll die," Gretchen said. She said it calmly, with complete conviction. "Uncuff me. And I'll save him."

Susan looked back and forth between Gretchen and Henry. Somebody do something.

"You're going to help him," Henry said with just as much conviction. "Or I'll shoot you in the head."

Archie was still alive. Susan felt light-headed. Her nose was running through the gauze and she wiped it. The snot was black with particulate matter from the fire and blood. Archie was dying.

Gretchen looked at Susan. "Uncuff me," she said. Susan glanced back at the key. Gretchen's authority was so absolute that Susan hesitated.

"Susan, stay where you are," Henry said.

"Tick, tock," Gretchen said.

Archie was going to die. Like Parker. Like her father. He was dying right in front of them.

At that moment Archie's back arched and

he started to seize. Susan couldn't see well, didn't know what was happening, but she could see his legs move, and his chest horribly buckled in the air. Susan had watched her father have seizures just like it. "Help him," she pleaded. She was crying. She couldn't help herself. She didn't belong there. She couldn't stop shaking. She couldn't think straight. Everything was falling apart.

"Susan — my purse," Gretchen said.

Susan wasn't going to let Archie die. Nothing else mattered. Gretchen seemed so confident. She had been a nurse. She knew what to do. She could save him. She had done it before. Susan looked over and saw the white purse on the bar, grabbed it, and hurled it toward Gretchen.

She regretted it as soon as it left her hands. But there was no taking it back.

The purse flew through the air and landed near Gretchen's knee.

The motion distracted Henry and he took his eye off Gretchen for a moment and shouted, "No!"

In a flash, Gretchen had the purse open and had a gun to Henry's head. They faced each other on their knees. The barrels of their guns were only inches from each other's skulls. Gretchen grinned, her eyes bright, saliva glistening in the corners of her mouth. Archie's prone body lay between them, the seizure over. He was probably dead, Susan realized. She lifted her fingers to her throat, horrified by what she had done.

Gretchen smiled. "Shouldn't work with amateurs, Henry."

CHAPTER
65

"Susan," Henry said softly. "Get out of here."

It was too late. Susan couldn't move. Not because she was frozen with fear, but because she was so fucking pissed off with herself she couldn't think straight.

"Don't even think about it, pigeon. You want to save Archie's life, don't you? The hypo's in my purse. Come here."

Susan couldn't respond. She was paralyzed.

"You can save Archie's life, if you get your ass over here in the next few minutes."

Susan wiped some more bloody snot from her lip and then forced herself to find the will to move. She slipped the paring knife in the back pocket of her jeans and took a halting step toward Gretchen.

"Get out of here," Henry said. "Go to the road, try to get to town."

But Susan kept walking. She could feel the

sharp little knife pressing through the denim against her flesh and it was the only thing driving her to move. She went through a mental catalog of targets: Gretchen's perfect blue eye, her elegant jugular. Stab and twist. It was a little knife, sure. But it would be all Henry would need to wrestle Gretchen's gun away. Or shoot her between the eyes.

As Susan got closer she could see Archie better. His eyes were white slits and his skin was tinged with blue. She fought back hot, angry tears. Henry still had one hand on Archie's pulse. That was a good sign, Susan told herself. It meant there was a pulse to feel.

Susan stopped walking and sank to her knees in front of Gretchen. The jugular was best, she decided. More room for error.

"Good girl," Gretchen said. "Now reach into the outside pocket of my purse. There's a hypodermic with a plunger on the needle and a rubber tourniquet. Get them now."

Susan retrieved the hypo and tourniquet. "I don't know how to use these," she said.

"You'll learn," Gretchen said. "And if you fuck it up, Archie will die. And then I'll kill Henry. And you. Now, tie the tourniquet around his arm and find a vein," Gretchen said. "Do you see one?"

Susan rolled up Archie's sleeve, tied the

rubber tourniquet around Archie's bicep, and picked up Archie's arm. The skin was bluish and cool. But she could see a vein bulging out on the inside of his elbow. "I think so," she said.

Gretchen's voice was completely controlled. "Position the needle bevel side up. Push it in. You'll feel a little pop as you enter the vein."

Susan positioned the hypo, bevel side up, and pushed it into Archie's arm. She felt the pop. "I think I'm in," she said.

"Good," Gretchen said. "Is there any blood in the syringe?"

Susan looked at the hypo. There wasn't any blood. "No," she said.

"That's okay," Gretchen said. "Pull back on the plunger a little."

Susan pulled back on the plunger. A tiny squirt of red entered the syringe. "I see blood," she said.

"Good," Gretchen said. "That means you're in a vein. Now make sure the bevel is still up and push the plunger in."

Susan checked the bevel and then pushed the plunger in. She'd done it. She'd given him the drug. She wanted to laugh and cry and dance around the room. Then she caught sight of Henry's grave face, his gun still leveled at Gretchen's head. Susan pulled the hypo out of Archie's arm. She didn't have anything to stop the bleeding at the needle site so she bent his elbow and held it.

Archie's color immediately started to improve.

"Now, give me the key to the handcuffs," Gretchen said.

Susan got up and got the key and came back. She told herself that she had to do what Gretchen said. Gretchen still had the gun trained on Henry. Susan put the little key into the lock on the cuffs and turned it. The cuff sprang open and Gretchen was free and in that moment Susan reached into her back pocket and with a movement faster than she thought possible she plunged the knife into Gretchen's torso, below her rib cage. It was easier than she thought it would be. The knife slid in past the gristle with a series of knotty pops, bouncing off bone, then sliding below her ribs like it was going into hard cheese. When Susan withdrew her shaking hand, the knife was still there, driven into Gretchen's silk blouse to the hilt, a ring of dark red around it.

She hadn't even come close to the jugular.

But it was enough. Gretchen's eyes widened and her mouth formed an "oh," where a tiny sigh escaped as the knife penetrated her. Henry seized the opportunity and lurched forward, connecting his forearm with Gretchen's elbow. Susan lost sight of the gun behind Henry's frame as he dove for it, wrestling it from Gretchen's hand and then sending it skidding across the carpet.

As Henry scrambled to recover the weapon, Susan watched as Gretchen slid her hand down her side, her fingers folding around the knife Susan had plunged into her.

"The knife," Susan managed to say, as Gretchen pulled it out with a pop of her elbow. The silver blade was slick with blood. Gretchen held Archie's head up by a fistful of hair, and pressed the knife to his throat.

"I like knives better anyway," Gretchen said.

There was smoke in the house. It was just enough to soften the focus of the room. Susan wasn't even sure that Gretchen or Henry had noticed it.

The wind had changed direction.

Gretchen slid backward on the floor in a modified crab walk, one arm now around Archie's chest, the other holding the knife to his neck, pushing herself along on her elbows and haunches, dragging Archie with her like an animal with prey toward the open glass door to the deck.

"No," Henry said. He was lying on the carpet on his side, his arms extended, gun raised, pointed at Gretchen.

"Have you ever killed a chicken, Henry?" Gretchen asked sweetly, pressing the knife against Archie's flesh. "Some people use a chopping block. But you can also use a metal cone." She smiled. "You tie the bird's feet and stretch the neck through the hole at the bottom of the cone. Then you cut its neck." She moved the knife along Archie's neck, the blade turned on its side so it didn't cut his throat. "The key is to sever the jugular, so it bleeds out. But you want to avoid the windpipe." She winked. "They say it's stressful for the birds."

"Not another inch," Henry said. "You don't escape from this."

"His body's been through a lot," Gretchen said. "How much blood do you think he could stand to lose?"

Henry sat up, the gun still level at Gretchen's head. And then, slowly, he stood. "You won't do it. He's too important to you."

Susan thought she saw Gretchen falter. Her eyebrows flickered and she held Archie closer, pressing her knees on either side of his torso.

Henry was right, Susan thought, gaining

confidence. She wouldn't kill Archie. She'd just saved him. Again. She needed him alive. Henry took a step toward her, gun raised.

Gretchen cut Archie's throat. The knife pressed into the flesh, and it opened gently like the skin of an eggplant. Blood seeped from the wound, darkening Archie's neck and chest.

Susan felt woozy from adrenaline and shock and fear. She wished she'd kept hold of the stick so she could have jammed it into Gretchen's eye. It might not have killed her. But it would probably have gotten infected. And at the periphery of her consciousness she thought she heard the faint sound of sirens.

Gretchen's eyes blazed at Henry. "Don't ever think you can know what I'll do," she said. The knife and her hand were covered in blood, her hand like a red glove. Gretchen licked the blade and grinned. "I like a man with a damaged liver," she said. "The blood is so sweet."

Every vein in Henry's head bulged. Susan thought she could see his pulse, racing, threatening to burst through his skin. His hands gripped the gun like it was Gretchen's neck.

"Not yet," Gretchen warned him.

Archie was still alive. He was bleeding. But

there wasn't any splatter; she hadn't hit an artery. His color was pale, but he was still sweating. Dead people didn't sweat, did they?

"Keep pressure on the wound," she said to Susan. "Tell them he was in liver toxicity. He took about forty pills about three hours ago." Her lips were smeared with the blood from the knife.

She whispered something in Archie's ear, kissed him on the cheek, leaving a bloody lip print, and then laid his head gently on the floor and was gone out the door to the deck. Henry fired a shot in Gretchen's direction and then launched himself after her. Susan heard him fire three more shots into the woods.

Susan ran back to the bar, grabbed a plaid dishtowel, then ran back to Archie and held it against the wound in his neck. "Don't die," she said to him. She used the sleeve of her shirt to gently rub the bloody kiss off his cheek. "You better not die."

Outside, the sound of sirens got louder.

CHAPTER
66

"You're still alive," Henry said. "And she got away."

There was a sprinkler head directly above Archie's hospital bed. This was the first thing he saw. The second thing he saw was Henry, standing over him. Then Debbie, sitting in a chair on the other side of the bed, a magazine open in her lap.

Oh, God. Debbie.

"She fled into the fire," Henry said. "There was a lot of smoke." He ran his hand over his head. "We're still searching the area. She might have gotten caught in the fire. But I won't believe it until we have remains."

Archie closed his eyes again and curled onto his side. His skin burned with sweat and his whole body hurt. He shifted on the bed, trying to find a tolerable position. The movement made his gut cramp. His hands shook so violently he clamped them between his knees. He opened his eyes. Even the light hurt. "What's wrong with me?" he asked weakly.

"Withdrawal," Henry said. "You're on an antinarcotic called naloxone. You OD'd. The naloxone blocks your opiate receptors. So it's cold turkey, friend."

Archie searched his memory for any clue as to what had happened and came up with nothing. The bedsheets were cold and wet with his sweat. His last memory was of Gretchen, holding him. A wall of pain shuddered through his body like electricity, and Archie curled further into a fetal position. They had found him too soon. But he didn't understand how she had gotten away. Then he felt the deep ache in his throat and reached up a trembling hand and let his fingers trace the rough bandages around his neck. He didn't know how that had happened. But he knew this: She'd escaped. It was all for nothing.

He started to laugh.

"She used you as a hostage," Henry said. "She used the naloxone to save your life. Then she cut your throat."

"I slept with her," Archie said. It was half the truth.

The magazine slid from Debbie's lap and slapped onto the linoleum floor.

Henry leaned down over Archie and put a

439

hand on his shoulder. "Don't ever say that out loud again," he said.

"I just thought you both should know," Archie said. He swallowed hard, causing his neck to throb. "I don't suppose I could get some pain meds for my throat," he said.

Debbie's hands were fists, the knuckles white, like it was all she could do not to throttle him with her bare hands. He didn't blame her. He wished she would try. He wished she would put a pillow over his head and suffocate him. It would be the humane thing to do.

"It's not real," she said. "Whatever you think you have with her."

He had to concentrate to talk. Every muscle in his body felt starved for oxygen, cramping in pain. Over the past few years, he had thought about what withdrawal might be like.

This was worse.

"I thought I could catch her," he said helplessly.

A nurse appeared in peach-colored scrubs. She adjusted the drip on Archie's IV. "This will help you sleep," she said.

Archie nodded gratefully.

Henry pinched the bridge of his nose. "Maybe let us in on the plan next time."

They both knew Henry could have stopped him.

"You let me go," Archie said. "You let me go to the bathroom by myself. That wasn't like you."

Debbie turned and looked at Henry.

Henry glanced at Debbie, then back at Archie. "I would never let you use yourself as bait," he told Archie. "You're lucky to be alive."

Lucky to be alive. For what? What had it all been for?

"You found the confession?" Archie asked.

"Yeah," Henry said.

There was that at least. He'd accomplished that.

"You can close it," Henry said with a grunt. "You can close that one case. Fourteen years old. A runaway without any family. And you closed it. Was it worth it?"

Archie closed his eyes and smiled. He could feel the sleep drugs hit his system. It was a small measure of relief. "Yes," he said.

He must have drifted off because when Archie came to again Henry was standing over him on the other side of the bed. Debbie was gone.

Archie leaned over and gagged. Henry got a rose-colored plastic bedpan in front of him and he vomited into it, his body shaking. When he was done, he lay back in the bed, chest heaving.

Henry disappeared into the bathroom with the bedpan. Archie heard a toilet flush and the faucet go on and then Henry returned with the empty bedpan and set it on the tray next to the bed.

"You about done?" Henry asked.

Archie didn't know what Henry was talking about.

"You've been vomiting for the last hour," Henry said. "You don't remember?"

Archie curled on his side. "No," he said.

"Rosenberg came to see you," Henry said. "And Fergus was here," he said. "Remember that?"

Archie shook his head. He was covered with blankets, and he was still cold. He pulled the blankets up to his shoulders. His arms and legs were shaking. It felt like his bones hurt.

"He said you make it twelve hours on the naloxone, they can give you more pain meds. Taper you down."

"How much longer is that?" Archie asked.

Henry looked at his watch and raised his eyebrows. "Seven hours," he said.

Archie felt more acid rise in his throat and he turned over on his side and lifted his knees to his chest. "Keep talking to me."

Henry sat down. "Susan was with me," Henry said. "When we found you."

Archie winced. He hadn't meant for Susan to be put in danger. But he had known, when he gave the clue about Heather Gerber, that if she figured it out, she'd see it through. There was no way she was going to let Henry follow the lead by himself. If he'd gotten her killed, he wouldn't be able to live with himself. "She okay?" he asked.

"She'll want to talk to you," Henry said. "I told her she could write about all of it. If she keeps some details out."

Henry proceeded to tell Archie about Susan's escape from carbon monoxide poisoning and Bennett, who was still in a coma one floor up, and then about Susan identifying the other park bodies.

Archie thought of John Bannon and Buddy Anderson. "I need to talk to her," he said. "But first," he said, his gut cramping, "I'm going to need that bedpan again."

The doctors and nurses came and went. He had thirty-five stitches in his neck. She'd missed the windpipe and the jugular. They continued to pump him full of naloxone.

Debbie was back. She hadn't brought the kids and he hadn't asked. It was better that they not see him like this. They had seen too much already.

"Did you get it out of your system?" she asked.

He closed his eyes. "No," he said.

"What do you want, Archie?"

What did he want? He wanted to die. That had been the plan.

He turned his head away from her. "To sleep," he said.

Archie saw a form in the doorway. It took him a moment to realize it was a kid. At first he thought it might be Ben. He smiled and tried to sit up. He wanted it to be Ben.

But it wasn't Ben. It was the kid from the park. He motioned for the kid to come in, and he did. He was wearing the same clothes he'd been wearing in the woods, a Ducks T-shirt and cargo shorts.

"Hi," the kid said, raising a hand awkwardly.

"You remember me?" Archie asked. "From the woods?"

The kid looked for something to do with his skinny arms, crossing them and then putting his hands into his pockets. "Can I get my nest back?" he asked.

"It's evidence," Archie explained.

"Oh," the kid said.

The colossal coincidence of the kid being there was dawning on Archie through his haze. Had he come to see Archie? "What are you doing here?" Archie asked.

The kid shrugged. "My mom works here," he said.

Archie thought about that. It seemed plausible. "I want my partner to meet you," he said.

The kid backed away. "I'm sorry," he said. "I've got to go." He lowered his voice. "You should go, too. My mom says that hospitals are dangerous." He looked around the hospital room. "You can get secondary infections."

"Hey," Susan said. Archie had been dreaming. He glanced up at the clock on the wall. He had drifted in and out of consciousness all night and morning. Fergus had finally come at noon, and given him morphine. He had injected it into the IV, like Gretchen had done those last few days of his captivity.

"You awake?" Susan asked.

Archie looked around groggily for the boy from the park. "Where's the kid?" he asked.

Susan glanced around the room and then raised an eyebrow. "There's no kid," she said.

Archie rubbed his face and looked at Susan. Henry had said that she had broken her nose, but Archie wasn't prepared for the fact of it. She had a bandage and two black eyes that had probably come in overnight. "Are you okay?" he asked her.

"I need to talk to you," she said. "About Davis and Nixon. About Molly Palmer."

"Who are Davis and Nixon again?" Archie asked.

"The bodies in the park," Susan said impatiently. "Henry said he told you."

"Right," Archie said.

"Anyway," Susan continued, "we'll get to that." She pulled her legs up under her in the chair. "But there's something you should know first. They made an announcement this morning. They've appointed a new senator to serve out Castle's term." The color in her cheeks rose. "It's the mayor. It's Bud Anderson."

"Buddy?" Archie said.

"I went and talked to him," Susan continued. "I told him the *Herald* was finally going to run the Castle story and that I was going to reveal that he lied in his public statements about not knowing about the statutory rape. That's obstruction of justice. I told him that Henry was reopening the Nixon/Davis case, and that it was all going to come unraveled."

Archie's brain was foggy. He tried to follow. "The *Herald*'s running the Castle story?"

Susan shook her head. "No, I lied."

"Why are you telling me this?" Archie asked.

"Because Buddy said he'd go on record," Susan said. "Spill everything. What he knew and when." She paused dramatically. "After he talked to you."

CHAPTER
67

Buddy was standing in Archie's room, his fingers spreading open the blinds so he could see out the window. He'd been standing there for what seemed like five minutes.

"Senator," Archie said.

Buddy chuckled. "Not yet," he said.

Archie had known Buddy for almost fifteen years, attended his last two weddings. Buddy had visited Debbie in the hospital after both the children were born, held them as infants in his arms. He'd been to the house for dinner. Had had Archie's family to his house. He and Archie had worked twelve-hour days on the Beauty Killer case. Buddy was one of the few people who understood what it had been like, those long nights, the obsession, the violence, and grief. After Archie's kidnapping, it had been Buddy who'd arranged the disability, who'd signed off on the victim identification project. Archie owed him more than he could repay.

And now he was going to accuse him of murder.

"You were Molly Palmer's contact, when she needed more money from Castle," Archie said. "You used John Bannon's name. But it was you."

Buddy scratched the side of his face and nodded absentmindedly. "I moonlighted on Castle's security detail my first few years out of the academy," he said. "You never knew that, did you?" He looked into the middle distance with a slight smile. "I was always a great admirer of his. He did a lot for law enforcement."

"Did you kill Nixon and Davis?"

Buddy came and sat down in the chair next to the bed and picked up a paper cup of coffee from the commissary that was sitting on the floor and peeled off the thin white plastic top. He took a sip of the coffee and then tucked it between his knees. "I had it cleaned up," Buddy said. "It was murder-suicide. The kid left a note." Buddy lifted his fingers in air quotes. "He'd been betrayed by politics. He mentioned the Molly Palmer thing specifically." He shook his head. "Didn't know shit about it. He'd heard rumors. But the kid was sensitive." He took another small sip of coffee and then returned the cup to his knees. "Shot her in the head, then himself. Right in the grass in Lower Macleay Park." He looked down at his coffee and then up at Archie. "I'm sorry," he said. "Did you want some coffee?"

"I'm not sure I'm allowed," Archie said.

"You'll tell me if you change your mind? It's no problem," Buddy said.

"Okay," said Archie.

"The kid called the senator first," Buddy continued. "Told him goodbye and fuck you. I got down there and cleaned up the site. I took Bennett with me. He worked for Castle for two years after college, before I encouraged him to join the force. It was just the two of us, so we couldn't move the bodies far. I remembered Heather Gerber." He smiled and shook his head. "Isn't it funny how that stuff comes back to you? We dragged the bodies up there. There was a house up the hill. They were having some work done. There was ivy everywhere and they had hired a crew to come in and clean it up and they had a wood chipper. Dog barked like a bitch in heat but his owner must be deaf, because no one came out of the house. I fed the boy into the chipper but it jammed. So I just left the girl in a shallow grave. I destroyed the note. Hosed the wood chipper down. Moved the kid's car a mile away. And left."

"And Molly Palmer?" Archie asked.

"She got in touch with me. Wanted ten grand to disappear forever. I met her there in the park. Gave her some money and some heroin and let nature take its course."

"The heroin was bad."

"I didn't put the needle in her arm, Archie. She did that all by herself. Once a junkie, always a junkie. She was bad news when she was fourteen. And she died bad news."

"Where's the money?" Archie asked.

"Bennett recovered it," Buddy said. "When he responded to the call."

So Bennett hadn't slipped. He'd gotten there first, taken the money, and then fallen on purpose. He'd wanted to pollute the crime scene. "It must have been frustrating when Castle died and it was all for nothing," Archie said.

Buddy rubbed his temples with one hand, as if he had the vaguest beginnings of a headache. "I knew Susan Ward wouldn't let the story go. Even with Molly gone. Castle wanted to go public." He looked up at Archie, and shrugged. "I had to kill him. He was weak. He had arranged to confess everything to Parker. I had Bennett do it. I'm not sure I could have gone through with it. Bennett followed Castle and Parker over the bridge and then fired an air pistol at the front tire. The tire got shredded going through the fence, so they never saw the bullet hole. Maybe if Parker had been sober, he could have avoided going off the bridge, might have at least hit the brakes. I hated doing it, but someone had to protect his legacy. Castle was the best senator this state's ever had."

"You killed him to protect him," Archie said.

"He would have been publicly humiliated," Buddy said. "I couldn't let that happen. You understand that, right? When you work your whole life in public service, you don't want to end it in disgrace." He took a sip of his coffee and gazed off into the middle distance again. "I protected you, you know. I saw you once." He smiled and turned back to Archie. "With her."

Archie's mouth went dry. Buddy knew about Archie's affair with Gretchen? And he'd never said anything. He'd let Archie see her in prison, week after week, for two years. Why?

"Don't worry," Buddy said with a wink. "I won't tell anyone." He leaned over and carefully placed his coffee on the floor. Then he reached to his hip, pulled out a semiautomatic, and shot himself under the jaw. The gunshot echoed through the room and Buddy's body slammed back and then slumped in the chair. One of Buddy's feet jerked, knocking the coffee cup. It teetered for a moment before it tipped and splattered coffee onto the linoleum.

Susan stepped out of the bathroom. She had one hand over her mouth. And in the other hand she held a digital recorder. "Jesus fucking Christ," she said.

CHAPTER
68

They had moved Archie to another room while the crime scene guys scraped the mayor's brains off the walls.

Henry had gotten six hours' sleep. He had shaved his head. He was wearing clean clothes. Archie was alive. The park murders had been solved. Bennett looked like he might come to and learn how to feed himself in jail.

Things were looking up.

Fergus was in with Archie, so Henry was standing out in the hall. He saw Debbie get out of the elevator and walk toward him. Her face was stricken. "I heard what happened," she said. "Christ, Henry."

"Archie's okay," Henry said. "We can go in in a minute."

Debbie's eyes filled with tears. "I'm not going in," she said. "I can't see him anymore. You know that, right? I love him. I do. But I can't do this. He doesn't want me to. I'm done."

"He needs you," Henry said.

She smiled and touched Henry's face, her eyes still wet. "He needs you," she said.

He watched as she walked down the hallway and stepped onto the elevator. She waved once as the doors closed.

Fergus exited Archie's room with his hands in his pockets and his eyes on the ground. And walked right into Henry.

"Sorry," Fergus said.

"How is he?" Henry asked.

"Not out of the woods," Fergus said. He pulled at a fat, fuzzy earlobe. "You need to get him clean and you need to keep him clean."

"He's ready," Henry said.

Fergus put a hand on Henry's shoulder. It was an awkward gesture. "You can't make someone stay alive if they don't want to," he said.

Henry watched Archie sleep.

He had sat like this before, after Archie's first run-in with Gretchen. That time Archie had spent three weeks in a medically induced coma. They'd thought they'd freed him. But Henry realized now that Archie had always been her prisoner.

"Are you going to get the phone?" Archie asked without opening his eyes.

Henry got his ringing cell phone out of his pocket, looked at it, and then put it back. "It's an unknown caller," he said.

Archie opened his eyes. "Pick it up," he said.

Henry hit TALK and lifted the phone to his ear. "Hello?" he said.

"Hello, dear," Gretchen said.

Henry thought about hanging up. Just hang up the phone. Wrong number. Stop it now. Tell Archie something, anything, to explain it away. But he couldn't. Because as much as Archie wanted to catch Gretchen, Henry wanted to catch her more. "How did you get this number?" he asked.

Archie sat up on his elbows in bed.

"Put him on," Gretchen said.

Henry hated her. He hated himself for not shooting her when he'd had the chance. He hated Archie for giving in to her. He hated the system for not jamming a needle into her arm. "Fuck you, bitch," Henry said.

"He'll kill himself, Henry," Gretchen said. Her voice was reasoned and calm. "He'll do it slowly with pills. Or he'll put a gun in his mouth. I'm the only one who can stop him. You know I'm right."

He did know she was right. He looked at

Archie. He was holding out his hand for the phone. His color looked good. He was alert. He looked the best he'd had since he'd been admitted. He looked like he might live.

Henry handed him the phone.

CHAPTER
69

"Sorry about the neck, darling," Gretchen said.

Archie touched the bandage on his throat. "What's one more scar?" he said.

She paused. "I'm worried about you."

"Yes," Archie said, "you've always shown such concern for my well-being."

"Has Debbie left you?" Gretchen asked.

"Yes," Archie said.

"I don't want you to die."

Archie rubbed his face and sighed. "That might not be something you can control." The plan was to taper him off the painkillers. Then they'd see if his health improved. If it didn't, he'd need a liver transplant.

"If I hear that you've died I'm going to kill the first person I see. The first person I see who reminds me of you. And then the first children I see who remind me of your children."

She knew exactly how to manipulate him,

exactly what to say. He marveled at that. She knew him better than anyone. "You have an interesting response to grief," he said.

"I'm serious, Archie."

The thing was, he knew her, too. "It works both ways, sweetheart," he said. "If I hear about a murder anywhere with anything close to your signature, deal's off. I'll use a gun next time."

"Abstinence then?" she asked.

"Abstinence," he said.

Henry was leaning close to him, trying to catch every word.

"I like to think of you not being able to end your suffering," she said.

"I like to think of you not being able to satisfy your bloodlust," he said.

She laughed. He liked the sound of her laugh. It reminded him of 1940s movie stars. "I enjoyed our romantic getaway," she said flirtatiously.

Archie glanced at Henry. Henry raised his thick eyebrows.

"If you turn yourself in," Archie said to Gretchen, "I'll come and see you every day."

"Tempting," Gretchen said. "But it's too high a price. See you later, darling."

"See you later," Archie said.

Archie hit END CALL and held the phone out to Henry.

"Gretchen says hi," Archie said.

They had moved one of the interns to Parker's old desk. Parker's wife had come and packed up all his stuff in a box and taken it away. The flowers were gone. Susan had stolen his Hooters' mug and it now sat on her desk, filled with pens. She'd finally gotten her mother moved back home from the Arlington. Bliss announced she was pursuing membership, but Susan wasn't sure how her mother would go over with the Arlington membership committee.

She still hadn't gotten the Buddha back.

Derek appeared and sat on the edge of Susan's desk. They were both up for Parker's job, crime-beat reporter. "I hear they're running the Molly Palmer story," he said.

Susan grinned. "The mayor's confession kind of changed the climate," she said.

Derek held out his hand. "Parker would be proud," he said.

Susan took his hand and shook it. "Thanks."

Derek paused, staring at the ground. "Did you ever wonder why Parker was with Castle that morning?"

"I'm guessing that Castle wanted his side of the story told," Susan said. "That he offered Parker an exclusive."

"He was going to scoop you," Derek said.

Susan reached out and adjusted the Hooters' mug, so that the owl faced forward. "I know," she said.

"Doesn't it piss you off?"

Susan shrugged. "He was a reporter."

Derek looked at his watch. "Do you want to get a drink?" he asked.

"No," Susan said.

"Coffee?" Derek asked.

"No," Susan said.

"Bottled water?" Derek asked.

"No," Susan said. She tilted her head at Derek. She'd seen herself in the mirror that morning. The bandage, the black eyes. It wasn't pretty. "I'll have sex with you," Susan said. "But I don't want to get emotionally involved."

"Okay," Derek said.

Susan smiled. "Do you have a bed?" she asked, thinking of the hammock.

"Yes," he said. "And air-conditioning."

"Wow," she said.

Forest Park was pretty in the summer. A light breeze tickled the leaves. The creek hummed and churned, birds chirped.

Archie sat on the ground near where they had found Heather Gerber's corpse. He'd worked tirelessly on that case. His efforts

461

had led to identifying the Beauty Killer's signature, to the formation of the BK Task Force. Henry had thought it was because Heather was Archie's first homicide. But it wasn't that. It wasn't even because Heather was a prostitute and a runaway and there was no one to care but Archie.

It was her ring. It had been embedded in the swollen flesh of her broken hand. A silver Irish Claddagh ring, worn on her right hand with the heart facing outward, away from the body, indicating that she was still looking for love.

He got up, brushed the dirt off his pants, and headed for the car. Henry was waiting in the driver's seat, listening to the radio.

"You ready?" Henry asked.

Archie strapped on his seat belt as Henry pulled out of the park's parking lot. He still had pain from his swollen liver, and he was exhausted all the time. But Fergus had him down to five pills a day. "Yep," he said.

"So," Henry said. "Have you punished yourself enough for your sins?"

Archie looked at Henry. Henry raised his eyebrows. "How much do you know?" Archie said slowly.

"I let you go," Henry said. "That night at the Arlington. I figured you'd try some crazy-ass shit plan to catch her, and I let you go because I thought it was our best chance." He waited. Archie didn't say anything. "Is there anything you want to tell me?" Henry said.

Archie shrugged. "No," he said.

"Seriously?" Henry said.

"I don't believe you," Archie said. "You'd never let me use myself as bait."

"Yes I would," Henry said.

"No you wouldn't."

"This from a guy who shtooped a serial killer."

"I thought we weren't going to talk about that."

Henry snorted. "So, twenty-eight days," he said, changing the subject. "Long time."

"Will you come and visit me?" Archie asked.

"Yeah," Henry said. "And Debbie said she'd bring the kids."

Archie searched for the words to express what he wanted to say. "You know, you can ask Debbie out. If you want to."

Henry drew back his head and looked at Archie like he was insane. "Why would I do that?" he asked.

Archie shrugged. "You two would be good together," he said.

"I've been seeing Claire for the past few months," Henry said. "We wanted to tell you. But it's against policy and we weren't sure what you'd think about it."

"I thought Claire was gay."

"Because she has short hair?"

"I guess," Archie said.

"Progressive."

"I'm happy for you guys." Archie thought about Henry's five marriages. "You're not going to marry her, are you?"

"I don't think my last divorce was ever legalized."

"Nice." Archie leaned forward and tried the AC. It blasted to life. "You got the AC fixed," he said.

Henry cleared his throat. "Different car."

They didn't mention Gretchen. Archie turned and looked out the window. They were going over the Fremont Bridge. Archie could see Mount Hood and Mount St. Helens, huge on the horizon. The city looked green and beautiful.

Gretchen was smart. She was far away by now.

But Archie wasn't worried.

He touched his pants pocket where his new cell phone was. It had the same number.

And he knew it was just a matter of time before she called.

ACKNOWLEDGMENTS

Thanks to my husband, Marc Mohan, and our daughter, Eliza Fantastic Mohan; you are my two guys. Thanks also to my super-hero agent, Joy Harris, and her left brain, Adam Reed, at the Joy Harris Literary Agency; Nick Harris at the Rabineau Wachter Sanford & Harris Literary Agency; my editor, Kelley Ragland, and her assistant, Matt Martz; Andrew Martin, George Witte, Sally Richardson, Matt Baldacci, Matthew Shear, Steve Troha, and the talented marketing team and sales force at SMP; my foreign publishers and editors, especially Maria Rejt and Katie James at Pan Macmillan; also Freddy and Pilar DeMann at DeMann Entertainment; Karen Munday at the Portland Audubon Society; Patricia Cain and Philip Miller for their medical expertise; Chuck Palahniuk, Suzy Vitello, and Diana Jordan for helping me unpack my depravity; Lisa Freeman for teaching me how to use a hypodermic (that's going to come in handy someday, I know it); Barry Johnson and my other friends at *The Oregonian;* my elementary school librarian and Nancy Drew supplier, the late great Beti McCormick; our contractors, Amy Frye and Eli Lewis, because, after eight months, they are finished, and I miss them; and to every reader who's ever e-mailed or wrote, especially the ones I never responded to (I meant to, I swear, you have no idea). Special thanks to my friends, who put up with me even though I don't return calls, don't e-mail, and almost never leave the house. I am going to name corpses after all of you.

ABOUT THE AUTHOR

Chelsea Cain lived the first few years of her life on an Iowa commune, then grew up in Bellingham, WA, where the infamous Green River killer was "the boogieman" of her youth. The true story of the Green River killer's capture was the inspiration for the story of Gretchen and Archie. She started writing *Heartsick* to kill time while she was pregnant. Also the author of *Confessions of a Teen Sleuth,* a parody based on the life of Nancy Drew, several nonfiction titles, and a weekly column in *The Oregonian,* Cain lives in Portland with her husband and daughter.

We hope you have enjoyed this Large Print book. Other Thorndike, Wheeler, and Chivers Press Large Print books are available at your library or directly from the publishers.

For information about current and upcoming titles, please call or write, without obligation, to:

Publisher
Thorndike Press
295 Kennedy Memorial Drive
Waterville, ME 04901
Tel. (800) 223-1244

or visit our Web site at:

http://gale.cengage.com/thorndike

OR

Chivers Large Print
published by BBC Audiobooks Ltd
St. James House, The Square
Lower Bristol Road
Bath BA2 3SB
England
Tel. +44(0) 800 136919
email: bbcaudiobooksbbc.co.uk
www.bbcaudiobooks.co.uk

All our Large Print titles are designed for easy reading, and all our books are made to last.